SCHOLARSHIP IN WOMEN'S HISTORY: REDISCOVERED AND NEW

Editor

GERDA LERNER

A CARLSON PUBLISHING SERIES

For a complete listing of the titles in this series,
please see the back of this book.

Liberty, Equality, Sorority

THE ORIGINS AND INTERPRETATION
OF AMERICAN FEMINIST THOUGHT:
FRANCES WRIGHT, SARAH GRIMKE,
AND MARGARET FULLER

Elizabeth Ann Bartlett

CARLSON
Publishing Inc

BROOKLYN, NEW YORK, 1994

Please see the end of this volume for a listing of all the titles in the Carlson Publishing Series *Scholarship in Women's History: Rediscovered and New*, edited by Gerda Lerner, of which this is Volume 1.

Copyright © 1994 by Elizabeth Ann Bartlett

Library of Congress Cataloging-in-Publication Data

Bartlett, Elizabeth Ann
    Liberty, equality, sorority : the origins and interpretation of American feminist thought : Frances Wright, Sarah Grimké, and Margaret Fuller / by Elizabeth Ann Bartlett.
        p. cm. — (Scholarship in women's history: rediscovered and new ; 1)
    Includes bibliographical references and index
    ISBN 0-926019-62-7
    1. Feminism—United States—History—19th century. 2. Feminist theory—United States—History—19th century. 3. Wright, Frances, 1795-1852. 4. Grimké, Sarah Moore, 1792-1873. 5. Fuller, Margaret, 1810-1850. I. Title. II. Series: Scholarship in women's history ; 1.
    HQ1418.B37 1994
    305.42'0973—dc20.   94-17649

Typographic design: Julian Waters

Typeface: Bitstream ITC Galliard

Jacket and Case design: Alison Lew

Index prepared by Scholars Editorial Services, Inc., Madison, Wisconsin.

Printed on acid-free, 250-year-life paper.

Manufactured in the United States of America.

Contents

Editor's Introduction to the Series ix

Acknowledgments xix

I.   Introduction 1

II: Intellectual Traditions 9

III: Frances Wright 25

IV: Sarah Grimké 57

V: Margaret Fuller 89

VI: Conclusion 119

Notes 137
Bibliography 163
Index 173

For my sister, Jeannie.

Editor's Introduction to the Series

An important aspect of the development of modern scholarship in Women's History has been the recovery of lost, forgotten or neglected sources. In the 1960s, when the practitioners of Women's History were so few as to be virtually invisible to the general profession, one of the commonly heard answers to the question, why is there nothing about women in your text? was that, unfortunately, women until the most recent past, had to be counted among the illiterate and had therefore not left many sources. It was common then to refer to women as among the "anonymous"—a group that included members of minority racial and ethnic groups of both sexes, most working-class people, colonials, Native Americans and women. In short, most of the populations of the past. These ignorant and erroneous answers satisfied only those who wished to stifle discussion, but they did make the issue of "sources" an urgent concern to practitioners of Women's History.

To historians who had done work in primary sources regarding women, it was obvious that the alleged dearth of sources did not exist, but it was true that the sources were not readily available. In archives and finding guides, women disappeared under the names of male family members. The voluminous records of their organizational work were disorganized, uncatalogued, and not infrequently rotting in file boxes in basement storage rooms. Since few if any researchers were interested in them, there seemed to be little purpose in making them accessible or even maintaining them. There were no archival projects to preserve the primary sources of American women comparable to the well-supported archival projects concerning Presidents and male political leaders. There were only a few and quite partial bibliographies of American women, while the encyclopedic reference works, such as the *DAB* (*Dictionary of American Biography*) or similar sources traditionally neglected to include all but a small number of women notables.

When the three-volume *Notable American Women: 1607—1950: A Biographical Dictionary* appeared in 1971, (to be followed by a fourth volume in 1980), it marked an important contribution to sources on women.[1] This comprehensive scholarly work consisted of 1,801 entries, with a biographical essay and a bibliography of works by and about each woman under discussion. It readily became obvious to even the casual user of these volumes how few modern biographies of these notable women existed, despite the availability of sources.

The real breakthrough regarding "sources" was made by a "grand manuscript search," begun in 1971, which aimed to survey historical archives in every state and identify their holdings pertaining to women. This project was started by a small committee—Clarke Chambers, Carl Degler, Janet James, Anne Firor Scott and myself. After a mail questionnaire survey of 11,000 repositories in every state, to which more than 7,000 repositories responded, it was clear that the sources on women were far wider and deeper than anyone had suspected. Ultimately, the survey resulted in a two-volume reference tool, Andrea Hinding, ed., *Women's History Sources: A Guide to Archives and Manuscript Collections in the United States*.[2]

The project proved that there were unused and neglected sources of Women's History to be found literally in every archive in the country. Participation in the survey convinced many archivists to reorganize and reclassify their holdings, so that materials about women could be more readily identified.

The arguments about "illiterate women" and absence of sources are no longer heard, but the problem of having accessible sources for Women's History continued. Even after archives and libraries reorganized and reclassified their source holding on the subject, most of the pertinent materials were not available in print. Many of the early developers of Women's History worked on source collections, reprint edition projects and, of course, bibliographies. The rapid and quite spectacular expansion of the field brought with it such great demand for sources that publishers at last responded. The past twenty years have seen a virtual flood of publications in Women's History, so that the previous dearth of material seems almost inconceivable to today's students.

For myself, having put a good many years of my professional life into the development of "source books" and bibliographies, it did not seem particularly urgent to continue the effort under the present conditions. But I was awakened to the fact that there might still be a problem of neglected and forgotten sources in Women's History as a result of a conference, which Kathryn Sklar and I organized in 1988. The Wingspread Conference "Graduate Training in U.S. Women's History" brought together 63 representatives of 57 institutions of higher education who each represented a graduate program in Women's History. As part of our preparation for the conference, we asked each person invited to list all the dissertations in Women's History she had directed or was then directing. The result was staggering: it appeared that there were 99 completed dissertations and 236 then underway. This was by no means the entire national output, since we surveyed only the 63 participants at the conference and did not survey the many faculty persons not represented, who had directed such dissertations. The questions arose—What happened to all these dissertations? Why did so many of them not get published?

When Ralph Carlson approached me at about that time with the idea of publishing "lost sources" in Women's History, I was more ready than I would have been without benefit of the Wingspread survey to believe that, indeed, there still were some such neglected sources out there, and to undertake such a project.

We used the dissertation list from the Wingspread Conference as a starting point. A researcher then went through all the reference works listing dissertations in history and other fields in the English language from 1870 to the present. Among these she identified 1,235 titles in what we now call Women's History. We then cross-checked these titles against the electronic catalog of the Library of Congress, which represents every book owned by the LC (or to define it differently, every book copyrighted and published in the U.S.). This cross-check revealed that of the 1,235 dissertations, 314 had been published, which is more than 25 percent. That represents an unusually high publication ratio, which may be a reflection of the growth and quality of the field.

A further selection based on abstracts of the 921 unpublished dissertations narrowed the field to 101. Of these we could not locate 33 authors or the authors were not interested in publication. Out of the 68 remaining dissertations we selected the eleven we considered best in both scholarship and writing. These are first-rate books that should have been published earlier and that for one reason or another fell between the cracks.

Why did they not get published earlier? In the case of the Boatwright manuscript, an unusually brilliant Master's thesis done in 1939, undoubtedly the neglect of Women's History at that time made the topic seem unsuitable for publication. Similar considerations may have worked against publication of several other earlier dissertations. In other cases, lack of mentorship and inexperience discouraged the writers from pursuing publication in the face of one or two rejections of their manuscripts. Several of the most valuable books in the series required considerable rewriting under editorial supervision, which, apparently, had not earlier been available to the authors. There are also several authors who became members of what we call "the lost generation," historians getting their degrees in the 1980s when there were few jobs available. This group of historians, which disproportionately consisted of women, retooled and went into different fields. Three of the books in this series are the work of these historians, who needed considerable persuasion to do the necessary revisions and editing. We are pleased to have found their works and to have persisted in the effort of making them available to a wider readership, since they have a distinct contribution to make.

The books in this series cover a wide range of topics. Two of them are detailed studies in the status of women, one in Georgia, 1783-1860, the other in Russia in the early 1900s. Two are valuable additions to the literature on the anti-woman's suffrage campaigns in the U.S. Of the four books dealing with the history of women's organizations, three are detailed regional studies and one is a comparative history of the British and American Women's Trade Union League. Finally, the three biographical studies of eighteenth- and nineteenth-century women offer either new information or new interpretations of their subjects.

Eleanor Miot Boatwright, *Status of Women in Georgia, 1783—1860*, was discovered by Professor Anne Firor Scott in the Duke University archives and represents, in her words "a buried treasure." An M.A. thesis written by a high school teacher in Augusta, Georgia, its level of scholarship and the depth of its research are of the quality expected of a dissertation. The author has drawn on a vast range of primary sources, including legal sources that were then commonly used for social history, to document and analyze the social customs, class differences, work and religion of white women in Georgia. While her treatment of race relations reflects the limitations of scholarship on that subject in the 1930s, she gives careful attention to the impact of race relations on white women. Her analysis of the linkage made by Southern male apologists for slavery between the subordination ("protection") of women and the subordination of slaves (also rationalized as their "protection") is particularly insightful. The work has much information to offer the contemporary scholar and can be compared in its scholarship and its general approach to the work of Julia Spruill and Elizabeth Massey. When it is evaluated in comparison with other social histories of its period, its research methodology and interpretative focus on women are truly remarkable.

Anne Bobroff-Hajal's, *Working Women in Russia Under the Hunger Tsar: Political Activism and Daily Life*, is a fascinating, excellently researched study of a topic on which there is virtually no material available in the English language. Focusing on women industrial workers in Russia's Central Industrial Region, most of them employed in textile production, Bobroff studied their daily lives and family patterns, their gender socialization, their working and living conditions and their political activism during the Revolution: in political organizations, in food riots and in street fighting. The fact that these women and their families lived mostly in factory barracks will be of added interest to labor historians, who may wish to compare their lives and activities with other similarly situated groups in the U.S. and England. Drawing on a rich mixture of folkloric sources, local newspapers, oral histories, workers' memoirs and ethnographic material, Bobroff presents a convincing and intimate picture of working-class life before the Russian Revolution. Bobroff finds that the particularly strong mother-child bonding of Russian women workers, to which they were indoctrinated from childhood on, undermined their ability to form coherent political groups capable of maintaining their identity over a long period of time. Her thesis, excellently supported and well argued, may undermine some commonly held beliefs on this subject. It should prove of interest to all scholars working on gender socialization and to others working on labor culture, working-class activism, and class consciousness.

Rosemary Keller, *Patriotism and the Female Sex: Abigail Adams and the American Revolution*, is a sophisticated, well-documented interpretation of Abigail Adams's intellectual and political development, set firmly within the historical context. Compared with other Abigail Adams biographies, this work is outstanding in treating her seriously as an agent in history and as an independent intellectual. Abigail Adams emerges from this study as a woman going as far as it was possible to go within the limits of the gender conventions of her time and struggling valiantly, through influencing her husband, to extend these gender conventions. This is an accomplishment quite sufficient for one woman's life time. Professor Keller's sensitive biography makes a real contribution to colonial and women's history.

Elizabeth Ann Bartlett, *Liberty, Equality, Sorority: The Origins and Integrity of Feminist Thought: Frances Wright, Sarah Grimké and Margaret Fuller*, is another work of intellectual history. It attempts to define a common "feminism" emerging from the thought of these important nineteenth-century thinkers and concludes that feminism, in order to sustain itself, must balance the tensions between the concepts of liberty, equality, and sorority. The lucid, well-researched discussions of each woman's life and work should appeal to the general reader and make this book a valuable addition to courses in intellectual history and women's history and literature.

Mary Grant, *Private Woman, Public Person: An Account of the Life of Julia Ward Howe from 1819 to 1868*, is a sensitive, feminist study of Howe's life and thought up to the turning point in 1868, when she decided to dedicate her life to public activism in behalf of women. By carefully analyzing Howe's private letters and journals, the author uncovers a freer, more powerful and creative writer beneath the formal *persona* of the author of "The Battle Hymn of the Republic" than we have hitherto known. She also discusses in detail Howe's fascinating, never published, unfinished novel, "Eva and Raphael," which features a number of then taboo subjects, such as rape, madness and an androgynous character. This well-written biography reveals new aspects and dimensions of Julia Ward Howe's life and work.

Jane Jerome Camhi, *Women Against Women: American Anti-Suffragism, 1880-1920*, and Thomas J. Jablonsky, *The Home, Heaven, and Mother Party: Female Anti-Suffragists in America, 1868-1920*, are complementary studies that should be indispensable for any serious student or scholar of woman suffrage. They are, in fact, the only extant book-length studies of anti-suffragism. This important movement has until now been accessible to modern readers only through the somewhat biased lens of contemporary suffragists' observations. They consistently underestimated its scope and significance and did not engage with its basic paradox, that it was a movement by women against women.

Jane Camhi's comprehensive study of nationwide anti-woman's suffrage movements makes this paradox a central theme. Camhi analyses the "antis' " ideas and ideology and offers some thought-provoking theories about the competing and contradictory positions women took in regard to formal political power. Her insightful profile of a noted anti-suffragist, Ida Tarbell, is an additional contribution this fine book makes to the historical literature.

Thomas Jablonsky's study is focused more narrowly on the organizational history of the rise and fall of the movement. The book is based on extensive research in the organizational records of the anti-suffragists on a state and national level, the records of Congressional hearings, biographical works and the manuscripts of leaders. Jablonsky takes the "antis" seriously and disproves the suffragists' argument that they were merely pawns of male interest groups. He offers a sympathetic, but critical evaluation of their ideas. His detailed attention to organizational efforts in states other than the major battlegrounds—Massachusetts, New York and Illinois—make this book a valuable resource for scholars in history, political science and Women's History.

The four remaining books in the series all focus on aspects of women's organizational activities. Taken together, they reveal the amazing energy, creativity, and persistence of women's institution building on the community and local level. They sustain and highlight the thesis that women built the infrastructures of community life, while men held the positions of visible power. Based on research in four distinctly different regions, these studies should prove useful not only for the intrinsic worth of each, but for comparative purposes.

Darlene Roth, *Matronage: Patterns in Women's Organizations, Atlanta, Georgia, 1890-1940*, is a thoroughly researched, gracefully written study of the networks of women's organizations in that city. The author's focus on conservative women's organizations, such as the Daughters of the American Revolution, the Colonial Dames, and the African-American Chatauqua Circle, adds to the significance of the book. The author defines "matronage" as the functions and institutionalization of the networks of social association among women. By focusing on a Southern city in the Progressive era, Roth provides rich comparative material for the study of women's voluntarism. She challenges notions of the lack of organizational involvement by Southern women. She traces the development of women's activities from communal service orientation—the building of war memorials—to advocacy of the claims of women and children and, finally, to advocacy of women's rights. Her comparative approach, based on the study of the records of white and African-American women's organizations and leadership—she studied 508 white and 150 black women—is illuminating and offers new insights. The book should be of interest to readers in Urban and Community History, Southern History, and Women's History.

Robin Miller Jacoby, *The British and American Women's Trade Union Leagues, 1890-1925: A Case Study of Feminism and Class*, is a comparative study of working-class women in Britain and America in the Progressive period. Although parts of this work have appeared as articles in scholarly journals, the work has never before been accessible in its entirety. Jacoby traces the development of Women's Trade Union Leagues in Britain and America, exploring their different trajectories and settings. By focusing on the interaction of women's and labor movements, the author provides rich empirical material. Her analysis of the tensions and overlapping interests of feminism and class consciousness is important to feminist theory. Her discussion of protective labor legislation, as it was debated and acted upon in two different contexts, makes an important contribution to the existing literature. It also addressees issues still topical and hotly debated in the present day. The book will be of interest to labor historians, Women's History specialists, and the general public.

Janice Steinschneider, *An Improved Woman: The Wisconsin Federation of Women's Clubs, 1895-1920*, is a richly documented study based on a multitude of primary sources, which reveals the amazing range of women's activities as community builders and agents of change. Wisconsin clubwomen founded libraries, fostered changes in school curricula and worked to start kindergartens and playgrounds. They helped preserve historic and natural landmarks and organized to improve public health services. They built a sound political base—long before they had the right of suffrage—from which they trained women leaders for whom they then helped to secure public appointments. They worked to gain access for women to university education and employment and, in addition to many other good causes, they worked for world peace. Steinschneider's description and analysis of "women's public sphere" is highly sophisticated. Hers is one of the best studies on the subject and should prove indispensable to all concerned with understanding women's political activities, their construction of a public sphere for women, and their efforts and successes as builders of large coalitions.

Margit Misangyi Watts, *High Tea at Halekulani: Feminist Theory and American Clubwomen*, is a more narrowly focused study of clubwomen's work than are the other three, yet its significance ranges far above that of its subject matter. Watts tells the story of the Outdoor Circle, an upper-class white women's club in Hawaii, from its founding in 1911 on. Its main activities were to make Hawaii beautiful: to plant trees, clean up eyesores, preserve nature and rid the islands of billboards. To achieve these modest goals, the women had to become consummate politicians and lobbyists and learn how to run grassroots boycotts and publicity and educational campaigns, and how to form long-lasting coalitions. Above all, as Watts's fine theoretical analysis shows, they insisted that their female vision, their woman-centered view, become an accepted part of the public discourse. This case study is rich in theoretical implications. Together with the other three studies of women's club activities it offers not only a wealth of practical examples of women's work for social change, but it also shows that such work both resists patriarchal views and practices and redefines them in the interests of women.

Gerda Lerner
Madison, Wisconsin

Acknowledgments

This book was conceived and written as my doctoral dissertation more than a decade ago. Many people helped me in the original research and writing of this work. I would like to thank Gayle Graham Yates, L. Earl Shaw, W. Philips Shively, and Donald Geesaman for their careful reading and advice.

The Graduate School of the University of Minnesota provided a research grant that helped pay my travel expenses to the various libraries housing manuscript collections important for my research. The University of Minnesota later provided a single-quarter leave for revision of the book.

The archivists at Houghton, Schlesinger, Boston Public, and Clements libraries and the Library of Congress were all very helpful in finding and retrieving materials for me. The Cincinnati Historical Society was especially helpful in providing any and all materials I needed through the mail.

Bonnie Drummond and Helen Prekker helped me with many technical details.

I wish to extend my deepest appreciation to my adviser and dear friend, Mulford Sibley, who suggested the topic for this book. He inspired me with his insights, challenged me with his questions, supported me with his warmth and concern, and always helped me to grow.

My parents were a constant source of support and encouragement.

My sister, Jeannie, through countless long-distance phone calls, kept my spirits high. She is my inspiration for the concept of sorority, because she has given such a special meaning to having and being a sister.

My women's studies students have taught me a lot about feminism and have given me perspectives and insights that greatly enriched this book.

Three years ago, Ralph Carlson of Carlson Publishing, contacted me, at the suggestion of Gerda Lerner, requesting that I publish my thesis as a book. I wish to thank both Gerda Lerner and Ralph Carlson for their belief in and support of this work.

I would also like to thank the editor at Carlson Publishing for her excellent job of editing.

Finally, my thanks to my husband, David, for his support and care, and to my three-year-old son, Paul, who, sitting beside me with his paper and pens, "worked like Mommy" and provided me with much companionship and good cheer.

Liberty, Equality, Sorority

ONE

Introduction

I began this study, to paraphrase Alice Walker, in search of our foremothers' gardens. I was aware of the fruits borne in contemporary feminism, but I wanted to know more about the early plantings—the roots and the soil in which feminism had been cultivated. I particularly wanted to know about the intellectual roots of early nineteenth-century feminists, who were writing at a time (1830s to 1840s) when feminism as a social movement and as a political philosophy really came into its own in the United States. What were these women reading? What were they thinking? With whom were they discussing their ideas? How did all of this influence the growth of feminist thought?

This search led me to three sets of questions. First, what were the intellectual roots of nineteenth-century feminism in the United States? What philosophical writings and assumptions did these women bring to their work? Second, what impact did these intellectual roots have on the feminist theories they nourished? How were these theories inspired, shaped, and constrained by intellectual traditions that had largely excluded women's voices and experiences? Finally, in what ways is nineteenth-century feminist thought original?

Several studies have provided significant research into the social origins of nineteenth-century feminism.[1] However, with only a few notable exceptions,[2] major texts of United States political thought devote only a few pages or paragraphs to the topic; others disregard it.[3] Of the analyses that do exist, most attribute the origins of nineteenth-century feminist thought to the Enlightenment.[4] Feminist theorists, analysts claim, took the Enlightenment theories of individualism and of natural rights to liberty and equality and popular sovereignty, and extended these to include women. These claims are for the most part not documented and appear to be based primarily on a comparison of the time frames in which feminists were writing and the terms they employed to those of Enlightenment theorists. A major purpose of my study is to provide an accurate assessment of the intellectual roots of nineteenth-century feminism in the U.S., from which a more valid and valuable interpretation can be developed.

Just as one can better understand the thought of political philosophers (or of anyone, for that matter) when one has some knowledge of their personal history and background, our interpretation of the texts change when we come to them with an understanding of the intellectual influences and underpinnings.[5] In examining its roots, my study seeks to deepen and clarify our understandings of early U.S. feminist thought.

Having discovered these roots, I examine how Western male intellectual traditions have influenced them. I seek to discover how they inspired feminist thought, which ideas and concepts feminists adopted, and how and why they modified them. Perhaps more significantly, I examine how these early feminists were constrained in their thinking by the intellectual traditions in which they matured. I pursue the question of how these traditions acted as perceptual/conceptual blinders. I want to know what questions—what visions—were disallowed by intellectual traditions that had developed without female voices and experiences.

Finally, I explore those ideas and approaches which are original to nineteenth-century U.S. feminism. Both historical and recent analyses of feminism have tended to regard feminist theorists as some type of female appendage to their respective male counterparts. Typical is Judith Sabrosky's analysis of nineteenth- and early twentieth-century feminist thought, which concludes: "When male radicals criticized society and proposed changes, unusually well-educated women in each radical circle of men applied these critiques and changes to woman's societal condition in particular."[6] In other words, men have created the ideas; women have followed. The Coopers agree, arguing that feminist theory is jerry-built from numerous male ideologies. They argue that feminist theorists have relied entirely on male ideologies without contributing substantially to their development.[7]

Henry Steele Commager's evaluation is revealing: "And what would it [reform movement] have been without their disciples, without Bronson Alcott and Margaret Fuller who *looked to* Emerson; and Dorothea Dix and Wendell Phillips who *depended* on Channing; and S. G. Howe and Horace Mann who drew strength from Parker; without the evangelical fervor of a Theodore Weld [why not a Sarah Grimké?] and the piety of the Tappan brothers [why not the Grimké sisters?], and the moral fervor of the *daughter* of the Reverend Calvin Stowe! [Does not Harriet Beecher Stowe have a name of her own?]"[8]

I argue that feminism is not more jerry-built than any other philosophical belief system. All bring together wisdom and insight and perspective from those who came before. One could just as easily argue that Marxism is jerry-built from Hobbes, Locke, Rousseau, Smith, Hegel, and Hebraic thought. But this discounts the fact that something unique has been brought to these others, something that redefines them and defines a separate body of thought.

Beyond these original approaches to a male intellectual tradition, I investigate what ideas central to feminism grew from seeds that had no roots in a male tradition, that is, those which grew from the soil of female experience and women's ways of knowing.[9]

Many have provided careful and thoughtful analyses of the divisions in feminist thought. Comparing feminist theories with respect to such characteristics as ordering principles, goals, and strategies, Gayle Graham Yates formulates three basic categories of feminist thought: 1) feminist, which seeks the integration of women into the existing male-defined system, i.e., women-equal-to-men; 2) women's liberationist, which regards men as the enemy and thus seeks a woman-defined reality separate and apart from men, i.e., women-over-against-men; and 3) androgynous, which seeks a redefinition of male and female roles by women and men together, i.e., women and men equal to each other.[10]

Alison Jaggar and Paula S. Rothenberg have developed a framework that separates the spectrum of feminist thought according to underlying political ideologies—liberal feminism, Marxist feminism, socialist feminism, radical feminism, and the feminism of women of color.[11]

Within the feminist academic community, one current discussion of feminist difference focuses on the minimalist/maximalist debate. Minimalists argue that women and men are essentially alike and what differences do exist are structurally imposed and should be minimized. Maximalists argue that significant inherent differences exist and they should be recognized, appreciated, and developed to their maximum potential. Maggie McFadden helpfully divides feminist thought into minimalist and maximalist categories and then subdivides these categories along a linear spectrum of change (status quo to radical transformation). However, she expresses dissatisfaction with the dichotomy and the linear structure of her classification scheme and suggests the double helix as a model that more adequately expresses the fluidity of the categories and the links between the maximalist and minimalist positions. She charges the feminist community to discover and create connections between the two positions.[12]

It is these connections among the varieties of feminism that I set out to discover. What enables them all to claim the label of *feminism*? Is it merely that they all take as a primary focus the question of gender? Or does feminism offer an original conceptual base that makes it a separate body of thought, distinct from other political theories? In looking for its origins, I hoped to get a sense of the integrity of feminist thought.

I limit my examination of the intellectual roots of nineteenth-century feminism in the United States to three of the major theorists—Frances Wright, Margaret Fuller, and Sarah Grimké. Some analyses of this era have attempted a broad analysis of feminism.[13] They have successfully given us a general overview of feminist thought, but they have failed to provide a deeper understanding of the intellectual origins and substance of nineteenth-century feminism. Most analyses are limited to a surface appraisal of many theorists' most famous works. I focus on only three women so that I can examine the whole body of their works.

Such a study suffers from the limitations of race and class bias. I do not include the writings of women of color or working-class women (though I think Wright would have claimed solidarity with the working class). This bias is not deliberate; rather, it is a consequence of narrowing my analysis to the works of well-educated women, a rarity even among the privileged classes. I by no means purport to provide a comprehensive examination of all of nineteenth-century feminist thought. This is instead an initial examination of one aspect, its intellectual roots.

I focus on Wright, Fuller, and Grimké for two reasons. All three were major theorists and were regarded as spokeswomen for feminism by their contemporaries, and are still so regarded. Yet their intellectual backgrounds and philosophical approaches are quite different from one another.

These women were major theorists in their own right. Each was the author of an important feminist work. Frances Wright wrote several articles and tracts on "the woman question," addressing women's roles in education, labor, the economy, and religion. Sarah Grimké is most noted for her *Letters on the Equality of the Sexes*, in which she responded to the New England clergy's indictment of her and her sister Angelina's public speaking as "unwomanly." She developed her response to address a number of issues involved in the equality of women. Margaret Fuller is best known for *Woman in the Nineteenth Century*, which examines women's nature, capacities, and role.

Wright's contemporaries honored her by placing her picture on the frontispiece of the first volume of *History of Woman Suffrage*.[14] She was recognized in her own day as a pioneer of women's causes. Analysts today still regard her as the first radical leader in the women's movement, and her effect endures.[15] As Eleanor Flexner has stated, "No woman in the first half of the nineteenth century who challenged tradition escaped the effect of Frances Wright's leavening thought."[16]

Like Wright and Fuller, Grimké was included among the eighteen women to whom the *History of Woman Suffrage* was dedicated. The impact of her *Letters* on Grimké's contemporaries was significant. Lucy Stone traced her involvement in the women's movement to the Pastoral Letter and Sarah's response to it.[17] Lucretia Mott described the *Letters* as "the most important work since Mary Wollstonecraft's *Rights of Women* [sic]."[18] Apparently, when Elizabeth Cady Stanton and Lucretia Mott visited England in 1840, they found the *Letters* well known there. Though recognized in her own day, the true significance of her contribution to feminist theory is only now being recognized. Her *Letters on the Equality of the Sexes*, written before Fuller's *Woman in the Nineteenth Century*, was the first cogent philosophical treatise addressed specifically to "the woman question" in the United States. As Sabrosky has said, *Letters* "far surpassed in analytical sophistication any previous feminist analysis,"[19] and is still today one of the better-articulated and more compelling arguments in feminist theory.

Partly because of the importance of *Woman in the Nineteenth Century*, and partly because of her early death at the age of forty, Margaret Fuller was heralded in her own time as the visionary of the women's movement. After her death, there were great outpourings of affection and loss. Stanton praised her as the most influential woman in America, and Paulina Wright Davis acknowledged that she had hoped Fuller would take over the leadership of the women's movement.[20] *Woman in the Nineteenth Century* is no less significant today. Barbara Welter calls it "one of the most important statements of feminist method and theory in history."[21]

Wright, Grimké, and Fuller represent three distinct philosophical backgrounds. Wright's theoretical assumptions are based primarily in moral sense, utopian socialist, and utilitarian philosophies. Though it is difficult to place Grimké in any particular intellectual tradition, she seems to be representative of the Anglo-American radical sectarian tradition. Fuller's thought grows primarily from the Romantic tradition of Idealism and Transcendentalism.

I examine the intellectual background of Wright's, Grimké's, and Fuller's feminist thought separately from a discussion of the precepts of their thought.

In examining their intellectual backgrounds, I look to those philosophical traditions and persons who were in fact influential in the development of each theorist's thought. This helps to clarify the true intellectual origins of nineteenth-century feminism, as well as provides insight into the impact of various philosophical traditions on feminist thought.

Second, I examine in-depth Wright's, Grimké's, and Fuller's feminist thought. For purposes both of unity and comparison, I focused on three concepts that occur significantly in each of their works—liberty, equality, and a concept that I term *sorority*.[22] I use this last term to encompass the related ideas of sisterhood, gender role, female identity, and self-identity—all ways of looking at the experience and the meaning of being a woman. As these themes are interwoven in the women's writings, I address them in a unified manner in the cluster concept of sorority.

Let me give a brief definitional framework for liberty, equality, and sorority.

Liberty, in general, is being allowed to think or act or express oneself autonomously, that is, without coercion or constraint. It is the ability to make and to act on reflective, authentic choices. It is both freedom from obstacles of oppression and constraint and freedom to pursue and achieve one's goals.[23] The meanings are varied within the context of feminism. Yet, whether the claim for liberty is that of Frances Wright for free inquiry, or of Sarah Grimké for political liberties and reproductive freedom, or Margaret Fuller's quest for self-definition and authenticity, most feminists recognize that liberty is the ability of women to overcome oppression and to pursue and achieve mental, moral, physical, spiritual, sexual, economic, political, and social autonomy.

Equality entails the recognition of the equivalent worth of two or more distinct entities. It does not claim that the entities are the same, but rather that separate and different entities are of equal value. The implication is that their differences are not appropriate bases on which to determine their value. Thus, in the context of feminist theory, equality is the recognition of the fact that although biologically different, females and males have the same inherent worth and deserve equal opportunity and treatment in education, employment, the political sphere, and everywhere else. It also implies that traditional "female" roles and qualities—nurturing, caring, intuitive knowledge, etc.—are to be valued in society equally with male roles and qualities. The idea of equality manifests itself, for example, in Wright's and Grimké's demands for the equal education of women and men; in Grimké's claim that women and men fell from innocence, but not from equality; and in Fuller's equal valuing of the feminine and masculine. While there are differences in the specific application of the concept of equality, the central theme is that women and men, "femaleness" and "maleness," should be awarded the same respect, value, and treatment by society.

Sorority encompasses both the idea and experience of female bonding in sisterhood and the self-affirmation and identity discovered in a woman-centered vision and definition of womanhood. The specific meaning of sorority varies within the broad context of feminist thought, being incorporated in such diverse theories as Margaret Fuller's celebration of the feminine, the maternalists' affirmation of the unique qualities and contributions of female experience,[24] and the visions of woman-centered separatists.[25] Certainly it appears in Sarah Grimké's notions of sisterhood and Margaret Fuller's advocacy of a time apart in which women can discover their own identity.

The point could be made that liberty, equality, and sorority, claimed separately and independently of one another, could and have been advocated by nonfeminists, indeed by antifeminists. A prime example is the antifeminist philosophy of Jean Jacques Rousseau. Rousseau championed the political liberty and equality of all men, as well as the unique nature and sphere of women (though not sisterhood). The same man who wrote that in forming the social contract, *men* gain civil liberty and "a moral and legal equality which compensates for all those physical inequalities from which men suffer," also made detailed plans for the unequal education of men and women based on their differences and natures, men being far superior with regard to intellect and morals.[26]

Granted, Rousseau's notion of a distinct female nature does not amount to what I intend by sorority. However, others, such as Catharine Beecher,[27] who think highly of women's distinct nature, who indeed have argued for women's superior moral natures, and who feel a strong sisterhood with other women, have used these arguments to maintain the status quo rather than to advance the cause of feminism.

Thus it is in the interweaving and counterbalancing of these concepts of liberty, equality, and sorority that specifically feminist thought is most likely to emerge.[28]

Each of these concepts is explored in terms of its specific meanings in the feminisms of Wright, Grimké, and Fuller, in addition to the examination of their intellectual origins. To help the reader understand the implications of the various intellectual traditions that undergird nineteenth-century feminist thought, Chapter 2 specifically outlines the basic beliefs of these traditions. In the final chapter, I explore some of the questions and answers that arise from the analysis of Wright's, Grimké's, and Fuller's writings, with respect not only to their intellectual origins, but also to those factors which define feminism. Specifically, I examine how the concepts of liberty, equality, and sorority contradict one another yet coexist. I argue that the juxtaposition of the three concepts of liberty, equality, and sorority provides a core and integrity to feminist thought.

This study is primarily an examination of the intellectual heritage and the uniqueness of nineteenth-century feminist thought in the United States. It is an examination of its true intellectual origins and the parameters and influences of those origins on its assumptions and interpretations, and an evaluation of its originality. However, it is also an interpretation of feminist thought as a whole. An analysis of the writings of Wright, Grimké, and Fuller reveals the conceptual core and the integrity that characterize contemporary feminism. These foremothers do indeed provide us with insights into the conceptual definition and the originality of feminism.

TWO

Intellectual Traditions

Most analyses of nineteenth-century United States feminism place its heritage in the Enlightenment. This is ambiguous and unhelpful because the Enlightenment has different expressions in the French, German, Scottish, and American enlightenments and spawns three political theories—natural law, utilitarian liberalism, and moral sense. To say that feminist theory was influenced by this or any other philosophical tradition, without providing a definition and framework of the tradition, only increases the confusion.

This chapter provides just such a framework of the predominant philosophical traditions from which the thought of Wright, Fuller, and Grimké grew. These traditions include the Enlightenment and the three political theories it spawned: Romanticism, utopian socialism, and Anglo-American radical sectarianism. I do not offer a definitive and in-depth conceptual analysis of these philosophical traditions or a detailed explanation of how each of them defines American feminism. Rather, this chapter outlines briefly the fundamental elements of each tradition to provide a common definitional framework.

Enlightenment

Putting a precise definition on the Enlightenment has been elusive. It was an era in which ideas were constantly developing and contained within it the germ of both individualism and organicism, mechanism and harmony, empiricism and rationalism.[1]

Nevertheless, some common elements to Enlightenment thought exist. The philosophes shared their appeal to antiquity, their tension with Christianity, and their pursuit of modernity, in other words, their classicism, impiety, and science. And they were united in a program, which Enlightenment scholar Peter Gay summarizes as a "vastly ambitious program, a program of secularism, humanity, cosmopolitanism, and freedom, above all, freedom in its many forms—freedom from arbitrary power, freedom of speech, freedom of trade, freedom to realize one's talents, freedom of aesthetic response, freedom, in a word, of moral man to make his own way in the world."[2]

If nothing else, the Enlightenment had a common epistemology. The Enlightenment has been called the Age of Reason, interweaving two distinct aspects of reason: the reason of induction and the scientific method; and deductive reasoning, with its reliance on a priori and eternal truths held in common by human and divine minds.[3] Gay has argued that the Enlightenment was a revolt against the rationalism of the seventeenth century and the reign of eighteenth-century empiricism that meant the demise of Descartes and the deification of Newton.[4] However, though the Enlightenment saw the reign of fact, the belief that all knowledge is based on experience, it continued to invoke rationalist premises, particularly in its political values. This intermingling of rationalism and empiricism is evident in Enlightenment feminist thought, especially that of Wright. Still, the predominant theme was that the scientific method was the key to understanding and to the progress of knowledge.

A corollary to their epistemology was the philosophes' "faith" that the world was indeed understandable. They believed that the world was orderly and subject to universal laws of nature. The truth of nature lies not in God's word, as medieval scholars had asserted, but rather in God's work. The laws of nature can be found by following nature's own course, through observation and experience.[5]

Thus, the fundamental beliefs of the Enlightenment were in direct opposition to the predominant religious beliefs of the day. Most Enlightenment philosophers viewed the world as divided between those who denied life and played on the superstitious fears of the masses and those who affirmed life and knowledge—between the priests and the philosophers,[6] a very important theme in Wright's feminism. According to the philosophes, religion epitomized the calamity of superstition and impeded the progress of knowledge.

Religion was the primary target of the Enlightenment's critical attitude, but it was not the sole target. Government, history, and language were also subject to criticism.[7] Recognizing no single set of convictions and no single culture as providing absolute standards, the Enlightenment opened up an era of critical inquiry, clearing the way for feminism's critique of the position of woman in society.

Despite their relativism, the philosophes were passionate advocates for humanity and had definite political ideas. They called for a secular, humane, reasonable, and liberal political order.[8] They insisted on the individual's essential autonomy. The individual is responsible only to himself, to his self-development, and to the welfare of his fellow beings—not to God and not to the State. He is a product of his environment, entering society as a tabula rasa, and thus capable of being educated. Because of this malleability, he can hope for improvement through his own efforts, especially through education. (The philosophes defined the individual as male, so I use the masculine pronoun to discuss Enlightenment thought.)

Enlightenment politics was the politics of modern liberalism. It emphasized secular government, popular sovereignty, rule of law, free speech, and tolerance. It denounced war and slavery, and crusaded for criminal justice. Though it retained the womanly ideal as pious, thrifty, orderly, gentle, and submissive, it did criticize the legal disabilities of woman as violating the natural equality of all humans and recognized that much of women's supposed inferiority was the consequence of male domination. It was, as Gay has called it, "politics of decency."[9]

Beyond these general beliefs and goals, Enlightenment thinkers were divided on political theory. Gay distinguishes the natural law politics of the first half of the Enlightenment from the utilitarian politics of the second half. To this I add the unique political thought of the Scottish Enlightenment—moral sense.

Natural Law

The roots of natural law reach back, as does so much of Enlightenment thought, to Greece and Rome. Though the philosophes accepted many of the ancient natural law principles, they tended to abandon the assumption of the inherent social and political nature of human beings in favor of a much more individualistic and atomistic assumption. This modern interpretation of natural law was expressed by John Locke: "The state of nature has a law of nature to govern it, which obliges every one, and reason, which is that law teaches all mankind, who will but consult it, that being equal and independent, no one ought to harm another in his life, health, liberty, or possessions."[10] Here Locke defined the major elements of the natural law conception of political philosophy. To begin with, an objective, transcendent natural law, which is discoverable through reason, exists. Unlike divine law, which has its basis in God and is made known through divine revelation,[11] and unlike positive law, which is simply the sum total of governmental enactments, natural law springs from the pure idea of government and proves itself by its own nature and reason.[12]

A second idea expressed in the quotation is that of individualism, of being "equal and independent." Individualism is central to natural law politics and contains within it several other important natural law notions, in particular, the individual's priority to society, equality, and freedom, defined as independence, autonomy, and self-sovereignty.

A basic principle of much Enlightenment natural law theory is the priority of the individual to the group.[13] The individual, not the group, is the basic unit of human existence. Society, if you can call it that, is made up of discrete individuals rather than forming any type of organic whole. Natural law theory draws the picture of isolated persons leading separate, self-centered lives, independent of one another. To draw an analogy to physics, we are each individual atoms, occasionally colliding, occasionally linking up to form molecules of one type or another, but never merging with other atoms and never splitting apart (at least not in the eighteenth century).

Within this atomistic definition of society is found a fundamental equality. Each of us is, after all, simply an atom. No one type is better than another. No hierarchy of power or social status exists. All are subject only to natural law, never to one another. All are alike. Judged only on our essential elements as human beings, all are equal.

Each is sovereign unto himself. Because we exist as equals, no one else can dictate our actions or beliefs. Each individual thinks and acts freely and is responsible only to himself—not to a god, not to a king, and not to other persons. Each is autonomous and self-sufficient.

If the individual is sovereign over his own actions, then how do we explain civil society and its multitudinous sovereigns? What is the basis of the authority of civil government? The answer given by many natural law theorists is the social contract. According to contract theory, the basis of civil society is a legal transaction, by which previously free and equal individuals consent to live in a society and alienate their right of self-sovereignty in favor of the group.[14] This does not, however, negate the role of natural law, for all positive law should be based on natural law principles. Nor does this negate the role of the individual, for the individual still remains the source of authority for civil society, and the government can rule only with the consent of the governed.

Finally, Locke expressed the idea of natural rights, that "no one ought to harm another in his life, liberty, or possessions." According to this doctrine, natural rights, the most basic of which are liberty and property, existed before any social or political organization. Certain of these original rights of the individual are inalienable and not transferrable. Thus, they cannot be surrendered, even by contract. Distinct from acquired rights, which are subject to a system of positive law, these inherent rights are based on natural law and cannot be removed or transformed by legislative action.[15]

In sum, we exist as free, equal, independent beings who live according to the dictate of a natural law, which is discoverable through the use of reason. This natural law is the basis of all our relations with others, especially with government, and is the foundation of positive law and the guarantor of natural rights.

One of the critical issues for feminism in natural law theory is the notion of individualism. All the basic principles that would be applicable to feminism—equality, freedom, autonomy, rights—stem from the natural law idea of the individual. Yet, as Susan Okin has argued, it is not the individual so much as the family that forms the basic unit of political society in natural law.[16] Equality, freedom, autonomy, and rights exist among the male heads of those families, but not within the family. If feminist thought is to incorporate natural law theory, it must affirm the individuality of woman as well as man and apart from a family relation.

Utilitarianism

Utilitarian theorists rejected natural law, natural rights, and the idea of contract. They regarded these as fictions, pulled out of thin air. The premises of natural law could not stand up to the rigorous tests of empiricism. Despite the loftiness of its ideals and its insistence on a transcendent structure of law, natural law—and all other moral theories—must fail if not based on a more tangible measure of conduct. That measure was utility.

Jeremy Bentham, the major exponent of utilitarianism, summed up the notion of utility:

> By utility is meant that property in any object, whereby it tends to produce benefit, advantage, pleasure, good, or happiness, (all this in the present case comes to the same thing) or (what comes again to the same thing) to prevent the happening of mischief, pain, evil, or unhappiness to the party whose interest is considered: if that party be the community in general, then the happiness of the community: if a particular individual, then the happiness of that individual.[17]

Thus the utility of an action is determined by a pleasure/pain calculus. Whatever produces pleasure or prevents pain is useful, and therefore right, and whatever produces pain or prevents pleasure is not useful, and therefore wrong. (It also follows from this that whatever produces the greater pleasure is more right.) Morality is a "simple" matter of gauging one's own sensations of pleasure and pain, happiness and sadness, or, in utilitarian terms, one's interest. For the utilitarian, moral and political judgments can be made only on the basis of the consequences of an action. A value is determined by its effect on one's interest, on whether it increases pleasure and pain, happiness and sadness.

To act morally, then, an individual should, and usually without even thinking does, act in his or her own interest. It is left to each of us to discover what our own best interest is. So we find in utilitarianism an even more radical concept of autonomy than we did in natural law. In the utilitarian scheme of things, the individual acts autonomously, free not only from the laws of God and the state, but also from natural law. Individuals create their own moral standards according to their own best interests.

But what if the party whose interest is involved is the community? How is the community interest defined? It is, simply, "the sum of the interests of the several members who compose it"?[18] From this statement we can derive two political principles: equality and the "greatest happiness principle" of government.

The community's interest is the sum of all interests. This does not say that some or one individual's interests are more important, or better, than another's. Nor does it imply that some persons should be represented and others not. All interests are to be taken into consideration and all interests are to be counted equally in order to arrive at the sum. It assumes a fundamental equality of human beings.

The second principle is the utilitarian maxim for good government—the greatest good for the greatest number, or, as both Bentham and Mill have called it, the greatest happiness principle. Generally speaking, the utilitarian justification for any political principle or action was the amount of happiness and improvement it brought to the community. Whether it be free speech, or justice, or rights of the accused, the policy had to meet this practical test of its consequences.[19]

Feminist thought picked up on this utilitarian standard and used it to justify the free and equal status of women. J. S. Mill's application of this utilitarian justification to "the woman question" in his *The Subjection of Women* is the best known.[20] However, many United States feminists, Wright foremost among them, justified the improvement of woman's status by the benefits, in terms of increased civility, intelligence, and happiness, it would reap for men specifically and for society in general.

Utilitarianism rests on the pleasure/pain calculus of the utility principle. This principle established the corollary principles of individual interest, autonomy, and equality, and provided a standard for political justification and action often adopted by feminists—the greatest happiness for the greatest number.

Moral Sense

Though today dismissed as a minor philosophy of morals, in the mid-eighteenth century moral sense was the predominant philosophy of ethics in Europe and became central to the British-American philosophical endeavor.[21] Moral sense philosophers rejected the utilitarian calculus of the pleasure of the typical five senses, but incorporated in moral theory the judgments of a sixth sense, a moral sense.

The moral sense was defined as a faculty, more akin to the five senses than to rational inquiry, by which we distinguish moral right and wrong. David Hume defined it: "The approbation of moral qualities most certainly is not deriv'd from reason, or any comparison of ideas; but proceeds entirely from a moral taste, and from certain sentiments of pleasure and disgust, which arise upon the contemplation and view of particular qualities or characters."[22]

Through the moral sense we are able to apprehend the virtue of actions and affections, much as we can apprehend the blue of the sky or the tartness of an apple. It has no relation to innate ideas or the ability to recognize something as innately good, though there are some strong similarities. Nor is it derived from custom or education. Rather, it is a power of perception that determines our approval of actions, characters, and affections.

One of the most striking qualities of moral sense, especially in contrast with utilitarianism, and the aspect that most appealed to Wright, is the disinterestedness of the spectator. According to moral sense theory, some actions have immediate goodness to humankind. By moral sense we approve actions of others and ourselves without any view of gain or advantage from them. There is no consideration of obtaining pleasure or reward.

Frances Hutcheson argued that if all we cared about were interest, then our affections toward a fruitful field would be the same as toward a generous friend, since both are advantageous to us. If we determined approbation only with regard to self-interest, we would always favor the winning side, without regard to virtue. Self-interest will recommend actions only according to the good they do ourselves, and not give us high ideas of the public good. But we do have higher ideas of virtue and the public good, and these must come from somewhere—from the moral sense.[23]

Moral sense has this in common with other senses: however our *desire* of virtue may be counterbalanced by interest, our *perception* of its beauty cannot. If advantage were the only measure of judgment, then we would regard anything we pursued in our interest as good and everything else as evil. However, we do pursue things in our interest *despite* our acknowledgment that they are evil.

Virtue is lovely from its raising love in the spectator, not from the agent's perception of it as advantageous. The true spring of virtuous action is a sense, an instinct antecedent to all reason from interest, which influences us to love others. Real love arises when we expect nothing in return. This general principle of love and goodwill toward others is the foundation of moral excellence. It is the foundation of political society. People seek to join together in society not for the advantages that will accrue from it, but from a basic sociability and benevolence.

It is also the foundation of political excellence. Through moral sense we judge our governments, rights, obligations, and laws. That we do not obtain our ideas of moral good from the laws is apparent from our inquiry into the justice of the laws themselves. We are obligated by the laws to approve or perform certain actions when they are in conformity with our moral sense; we are constrained by the laws when they are opposed to our moral sense.[24] This is particularly important for Wright's feminism, which judges the political principles of justice, liberty, equality, and rights on the basis of their conformity with moral sense—and not with the law, which denied these to women.

These axioms and principles are drawn from common sense—not in the sense of "ordinary," but rather in the sense of "communal." Common sense is the shared wisdom of the community, the whole community. Common sense is the great leveler, for it is apparent to everyone, perhaps even more to the fool than to the philosopher.[25]

Herein lies the fundamental egalitarianism of moral sense. All persons are equal in their capacity of not just any faculty, but the highest faculty, the moral sense. Garry Wills expressed this well: "To say that men are equal in their exercise of this faculty is to define them as *essentially* equal, for the moral sense is what makes man accountable to himself and others, self-governing and consenting to social obligation. This separate faculty, equal in all, makes differences in other capacities comparatively minor, unable to reach the rights of self-regulation."[26] For moral sense philosophers, our equality lies in our equal ability to judge and act morally in society.

In sum, moral sense philosophy provides a unique standard for moral and political principles—not reason and natural law, not the calculus of pleasure and pain, but a faculty of the mind, a superior sense that perceives virtue. Moral and political action are taken out of the realm of self-interest into that of benevolence, and on this are based our notions of law, rights, and civil government. Most important, this moral sense is open to all. In our relations with others in society, we are all equal.

Romanticism

Romanticism, like the Enlightenment, was a major era, encompassing not only a philosophy, but also art, literature, music, history, political movements. It also included many separate schools of thought: German idealism, British poets, American Transcendentalism. Margaret Fuller is often associated with American Transcendentalism, but she wove many of these interpretations in her thought. The following is a very general summary, emphasizing the common themes of all Romantic thought. Certainly, on specific areas, there are many varieties of interpretation within Romanticism.

Romanticism, which has been identified by some as being feminism in and of itself,[27] burgeoned forth in the late eighteenth and early nineteenth centuries as a response to the Enlightenment. It surveyed the wonders of the scientific method, analytical reason, atomistic individualism, and the social contract—and rejected them all. To science it counterposed imagination and poetry; to individualism, the organic society; and tied them all together with the idea of the universal living whole.

To comprehend Romanticism, one must first grasp the concept of this universal whole, or all-encompassing unit, or simply, the All. All other Romantic concepts—organic society, nature, spirit, aesthetics, freedom—are bound up in the notion of the universal whole.

The whole pervades all of life. It is not intellect, nor is it sense. It is independent of limitations and knows no time or space. It is energy; the unity of humankind in one soul; total understanding; the consummation of the good, the true, and the beautiful. It perceives and reveals truth, if we will but listen. It expresses itself through every individual; we are each a part of the universal whole.

An important component of and avenue to the universal All is nature. To the Enlightenment philosophers, nature was at worst an external impediment to overcome, at best a mysterious mechanism to analyze and control. To philosophers of Romanticism, it was a living, self-determining process, linked to the human spirit through the universal spirit. All products of nature, including human beings, are built on the same principles, are held together by the same spirit, and are aspects of the whole.

Just as Romantics rejected the Enlightenment philosophy of nature, so did they reject its philosophy of knowledge. The Romantics did not believe that all knowledge is derived from sensory experience. People were capable of nonsensuous insights. They saw reason as a crude tool that needed to be supplemented by the imagination. By imagination they did not mean whims or figments. For the Romantics, there was no such thing as *"just* your imagination." Imagination was an avenue to knowledge, an intellectual insight. Shelley in particular praised what he called the poetical faculty and ascribed to it two functions: it creates new materials of knowledge, power, and pleasure; and it engenders in the mind the desire to reproduce and arrange materials according to the rhythm and order of the beautiful and the good.[28] Among those materials to be ordered according to the rhythms of beauty is the polity. The most important political principles to be derived from this Romantic vision of the political world are the organic conceptions of society, equality, and freedom.

Society, according to the Romantics, is more than the sum of its parts. It is an organic unit. Individuals as conceptualized in Hobbes's or Locke's state of nature could not exist, for individuals are always linked through society and through the universal whole. The political implications of this organic conception range from Shelley's anarchism (in which the social bonds between people are so strong that government is unnecessary) to Hegel's omnipotent

State (in which the State becomes the ultimate realization of the universal will). However, the main point is that the individuals exist in a society that is an organic entity in and of itself. Individuals are linked through something greater than the sum of their parts, through society and the universal whole. For feminism, especially that of Fuller, this implies an interweaving of male and female, masculine and feminine, in divine harmony. It also provides a framework for the reconciliation of the tension between equality and freedom.

Through this universality individuals find a true equality. As Emerson said, to the One, "every part and particle is *equally* related."[29] The universal whole recognizes no privilege. None is excluded; none has "better connections." The concept of the universal soul, of which every soul is an expression, is a marvelous equalizer. A soul knows no distinction of race or sex, of intellect or strength, of wealth or status. A soul is more fundamental than these. Despite differences in individual characteristics, ultimately everyone's soul is equal, for each expresses the same thing—the universal soul.

Finally, the most important political and moral goal in Romanticism, and the feminism that draws on it, is freedom. Though this may include the types of political freedoms discussed by the liberal political philosophers of the Enlightenment, its fundamental concern is for a more personal freedom, freedom for the individual to become himself or herself, to be self-determining. In essence, this means facilitating the individual's quest for self-knowledge and knowledge of the whole. It is being at one with oneself, in harmony with the spirit of the universe.[30]

Romanticism encompassed a wide variety of thought and expression, but it shared a common body of beliefs. Central to it was the rejection of the rationalism and empiricism of the Enlightenment and the reliance instead on a faculty that transcends calculating logic. It was an era in which intuition, spirituality, sensibility, imagination, and the infinite were exalted and found political expression in the equality and freedom of the soul.

Utopian Socialism

The utopian socialists Robert Owen, Henri de Saint-Simon, and Charles Fourier were especially important influences on the feminist thought covered here. The utopian socialists brought a unique interpretation to elements of both Enlightenment and Romantic thought.[31] They were a wide-ranging group who, though different in many ways, shared a common commitment to humanity. All were socialists to the extent that they criticized the existing social and economic order and envisioned a society of equality of economic opportunity. All were utopian in their visions of the new society and their attempts to create it through small-scale experiments of the great society.

These theorists shared the Enlightenment faith in science and reason to bring great progress to humanity. They sought to apply the spirit and method of the physical sciences to the science of "man" and society. They also shared the belief that character is a product of the environment. Evil conditions and bad training create evil individuals. Thus, their solution was to create new social institutions and teach the principles of "brotherhood," industry, and character building.[32]

Like the Romantics, utopian socialists believed in the primacy of the social group to the isolated individual. They especially objected to the system of economic individualism and free competition that exploited an economic underclass, and they sought to replace it with "cooperation" and "association." The feminist inclusion of women in this underclass creates a strong link between feminism and socialism. In their collectivist and socialist aims, socialists assumed "brotherly" love, not independent individualism, as the basis for social reform.

The central feature of utopian socialism is the utopian community envisioned. Some desired vast, sweeping reforms in society at large. Others sought to prove their vision to the world through small-scale experiments. Yet despite these differences, their utopian visions were similar in their desires to end the oppression of the lower classes by setting up a more equitable distribution of goods and to promote the happiness, freedom, and equality of every individual in an atmosphere of love and support. These experiments were especially important for feminism. In their communitarian division of labor they often, though not always, broke through the traditional division of tasks according to sex. The sharing of tasks also freed women from the burdens of domesticity to follow other pursuits.

Unlike any precedents in either the Enlightenment or Romanticism, the utopian socialists did not seek merely a natural or essential equality of persons. Equality, as they defined it, was actual equality—economic equality, equality of opportunity, if not of condition. Fundamentally, equality was represented by an equitable distribution of goods and benefits, which for most was defined as each drawing benefits from society in proportion to the amount he or she gives to society.[33]

The utopian socialists were also some of the first men to advocate the full equality of women. Saint-Simon sought to do this by reforming the marriage relation; Fourier by abolishing marriage and advocating sexual freedom. All sought to incorporate women fully into all the tasks of the community.[34]

The conception of freedom developed by the utopian socialists is very much akin to that of the Romantics. This stems from their common assumption of the primacy of society in relation to the individual. The freedom they sought was not the political liberty of individual rights and governmental limitations that was developed by liberalism, but rather a more personal freedom of self-expression and self-development, a theme that appears consistently in feminism. They desired freedom not *from* society, but *for* society. Real liberty consisted, in the words of Saint-Simon, "in developing without hindrance and with every possible extension, a temporal or spiritual capacity advantageous to society."[35]

Perhaps another reason for their lack of emphasis on political liberty is that their utopian visions were, for the most part, anarchistic. None envisioned much of a role for government in this utopian community. That which did exist would perform primarily administrative matters of economic organization. With the development of self-fulfilled human beings and a cooperative society, government would be at best unnecessary; at worst, oppressive.

The utopian socialists presented an indictment of the economic and social system of their day and believed that a remedy could be found in some form of social ownership and equitable distribution of goods. They believed human beings are basically good and are capable of developing to the highest perfection. Thus, they advocated a society that would afford each individual—and the utopian socialists, significantly, did regard women as individuals—full and free physical, intellectual, and moral development.

Anglo-American Radical Sectarianism

The emphasis on individual perfectibility is also a major strain in Anglo-American radical sectarianism. This tradition in America has its roots in the Anabaptism of the 1500s and 1600s and the English Dissenters of the 1600s and 1700s. It is not a single body of thought, but rather encompasses a wide variety of radical, dissenting sects, including Quakerism, abolitionism, nonresistance, come-outerism, perfectionism, and spiritualism. These sectarian traditions are associated together not only because of their interlocking memberships, but also because of certain common themes.

The central core of these sects was strong individualism. In contrast to the Enlightenment emphasis on the atomistic individualism of blank slates, this tradition emphasizes the dignity of human nature and reliance on individual conscience.[36] The individual is the final arbiter of moral decisions. Each individual is wholly and solely accountable for his or her actions.

To this emphasis on individual accountability is counterposed the sovereignty of God. The individual is ultimately accountable to God's will, as he or she discovers it through conscience, or inner light, or spiritual revelation. Only God's laws and God's government are supreme, which implied for many of the radical sects a form of antinomianism. Especially come-outerism, perfectionism, and nonresistance abolitionism expressed opposition to any form of government—social, political, or ecclesiastical—that attempted to mediate between the individual and God.[37] The very meaning of come-outerism is for the individual to "come out" from these oppressive institutions and rely on his or her own conscience and beliefs. From this arises a distaste for and rejection of political activity, because it is tainted by the laws of men, a theme that carries over into American feminism.

A theme prevalent in the perfectionism of John Humphrey Noyes and others is that if the individual were to follow the dictates of his or her conscience he or she might be able to achieve holiness. The individual is indeed perfectible. As Blanche Hersh has pointed out, this belief in human perfectibility underlies the American feminist idea that men and women not only could, but *should* change, in a way that would minimize sex differences.[38]

Despite this strong individualism, an undercurrent of communalism runs through Anglo-American radical sectarianism, as evidenced by the numerous utopian communities that grew out of the sectarianism (though these communities felt no kinship with utopian socialist doctrines such as Owenism).[39] Staughton Lynd offers an explanation that though the sectarians rejected government, they did not reject community. They tried to achieve a simultaneously free and communal society, through individual reliance on conscience but communal decision making of all individuals.[40]

Still, the predominant theme of Anglo-American radical sectarianism is the strong and radical emphasis on the autonomy and the accountability of the individual. It is this strain that was most influential on American feminism, particularly that of Grimké.

Quakerism more than any other sect has been associated with United States feminism for several reasons.[41] The Quaker belief that any man or woman might minister to the congregation as he or she was moved to do so gave many women their first opportunity to speak in public. The doctrine that in Christ there is no male or female broke down sexual stereotypes. The emphasis on inner light and fidelity to conscience encouraged the self-reliance of many women. Indeed, many of the nineteenth-century American feminists were Quakers.[42] Still, Quakerism was only the most prominent of a whole tradition of sectarianism that encouraged the moral autonomy not only of man, but also of woman.

These brief sketches of the major philosophical tenets of the nineteenth century cannot do justice to the variety and complexity of the ideas represented therein. But they provide a general frame of reference for the ideas discussed in the rest of the book.

All of these theories combined do not constitute feminism. They are part of its intellectual heritage. They are necessary to an understanding of feminism, but not sufficient. I do not argue, like Sabrosky, that United States feminism consists solely of female interpretations of male theories.[43] Certainly, all political philosophies are to some extent interpretations of those that came before, but they also contain distinctive elements. That aspect which makes feminism a unique interpretation must be examined and its essence distilled. Original concepts, like sorority, must be acknowledged and explored. The following chapters explore the heritage *and* the originality of feminist political thought.

THREE

Frances Wright

"[A] friend to humankind, zealous for human improvement, enamored to enthusiasm, if you will, of human liberty."[1] Thus did Frances Wright describe her character and her ideals. She was a reformer by vocation and avocation, and she dedicated her life to improving the lot of the poor and the oppressed, the laboring class and women in particular.

Frances Wright was born in Dundee, Scotland, in 1795, the second child of James and Camilla Campbell Wright. She never really knew her parents; they died when she was two years old. Still, Wright was her father's daughter. James Wright had been a militant advocate for Thomas Paine, whose *Rights of Man* he had been circulating throughout Scotland. He even changed the motto of the family crest from *"Pro rege solpe"* ("For a king sometimes") to *"Patria cara carior libertas"* ("Our country is dear, liberty dearer"). Later in her life, on reading through some of her father's notes, Wright was amazed at the considerable similarity in their political views.[2]

Frances and her younger sister Camilla were raised in the aristocratic home of her mother's sister. Frances continually rebelled against her conventional upbringing, eventually breaking with her aunt. The sisters spent the next few years with their father's uncle and close friend, James Mylne, a professor of moral philosophy at the University of Glasgow.

Her years in Glasgow were filled with excitement, new ideas, and intellectual challenges. She was exposed to the fervor of the Scottish Enlightenment. She had free run of the extensive college library and read voraciously. It was in Glasgow that she did her first writing: *A Few Days in Athens*, a Socratic dialogue exalting Epicurean philosophy; and a three-act play, *Altorf, A Tragedy*, written in Shakespearian verse.

At the age of sixteen, Wright came across one book that opened a completely new phase in her life—Bocca's history of America. Wright described her awakening: "From that moment she awoke, as it were, to a new existence. Life was full of promise; the world a theatre of interesting observation and useful exertion. There existed a country consecrated to freedom, and in which man might awake to the full knowledge and full exercise of his powers."[3] So began Wright's love affair with the philosophy of the American Revolution. She spent much of her life challenging the United States to live up to its ideals.

Wright's interest in the United States developed through a close friendship with Mrs. Craig Millar, who had spent two years there in political exile with her husband during the last years of the Washington administration. As Alice Rossi stated, this friendship was crucial for Wright. It satisfied her need for a loving mother, and it provided a source of detailed information on the United States as well as personal references should she go there.[4]

In 1818, Frances and Camilla set sail for New York. They spent two years traveling throughout the northern half of the United States. On their return home, Wright published a glowing tribute to the new republic, *Views of Society and Manners in America*, which was widely read and admired. She was to form significant and lasting associations with two of her admirers, Jeremy Bentham and General Lafayette.

For the next few years she became an intimate member of the social and intellectual circles surrounding these two men, frequently traveling between England and France. She became a favorite of Bentham's, to whom she was "the strongest sweetest mind that ever cased in a human body," while he was her "good old Socrates."[5] At Bentham's she came to know and exchange ideas with such other "philosophical radicals" as James Mill, Francis Place, George Gate (author of *History of Greece*), and the jurist John Austin.

In France, Wright became prominent in Lafayette's circle, even holding her own salon. She was also for a time involved in the Carbonari movement in Paris, a group that had adopted and implemented the views of Saint-Simon. Most important, however, was her deep personal and intellectual relationship with Lafayette himself. He was like a father to her, and the two spent several years together, even traveling to the United States in 1823.[6]

On this second trip to the United States, Wright decided to make the U.S. her home and the object of her crusade for reform. In America, she joined forces with Robert Owen, a mutual friend of Bentham's. She admired many of Owen's ideas about social reform. At the time, Owen had set up a utopian community in Harmony, Indiana, and Wright applied the principles of Harmony to what she felt to be the gravest problem in the United States—slavery.

The antislavery movement was just building steam. Though she sympathized with their cause, Wright did not approve of the abolitionists' methods. She felt emancipation had to be a more gradual process that liberated the slaves not only from their physical bondage, but also from their mental bondage.[7] The black population, she argued, needed a period of adjustment, as well as education and training. Free them unprepared, and they would not survive. She devised a scheme for the gradual emancipation, which she put into effect in her utopian community in Nashoba, Tennessee.

In 1825, Wright, with the enduring support of her sister and a few other backers, bought a plantation and five slaves, with the intention that the slaves would pay for their freedom from the proceeds of the plantation, while the whites, working alongside the blacks, provided education and training. The rule of moral practice in the community was human happiness. They considered virtuous whatever tended to promote happiness, and vicious whatever counteracted it. The marriage laws had no force at Nashoba, and religion occupied no place. Children were encouraged to examine all options and accept or reject them on the basis of their factual and moral soundness.

The experiment failed miserably. Due to disease and poor land, the blacks did not work and the whites fought over doctrine and division of labor. During Wright's absence, one of the managers, James Richardson, wrote a detailed article on the "free love" practiced at Nashoba,[8] and the community lost its financial backing. Wright eventually took thirty slaves to freedom in Haiti to start new lives there.

Wright moved to New York, where she joined with Robert Dale Owen (Robert Owen's son) in editing and publishing a radical journal, *The Free Enquirer* (originally *The New Harmony Gazette*). During her eight years as editor, she and Owen published articles advocating, among other things, the abolition of capital punishment; social, economic, and political equality for women; equal civil rights for all; and a national system of education free from sectarian teachings.

During this time in New York, Wright was involved in several other reform measures. She was a leader of the first workingman's party, called the Fanny Wright party. The party advocated more leisure, more education, and more control over government by the workers. She also organized a day school for the workers' children and established a dispensary.

By far her most significant and famous activity during these years was her lecture tour of New York, Boston, Philadelphia, Cincinnati, and other major cities. She lectured to packed houses and practically empty halls in defense of reason and free inquiry, in support of a national system of republican education, on behalf of the political and social rights of women, in opposition to the hypocrisy of clerics, and for the benefit of the oppressed everywhere. Her outspoken and radical views earned her such a reputation that her name became derogatory, and any radical was disapprovingly labeled a "Fanny Wrightist."

Whether her views were condoned or condemned, she always sparked excitement and controversy—not only because of the content of her speeches, but because she, as a woman, dared to speak in public. She was one of the first women in America to break the social stricture against speaking in public, and to mixed audiences! The newspaper reviews severely criticized her "unwomanly" activities:

> Miss Wright . . . has with ruthless violence broken loose from the restraints of decorum, which draw a circle around the life of a woman, and with a contemptuous disregard for the rules of society, she has leaped over the boundary of feminine modesty, and laid hold on the avocations of man, claiming a participation in them for herself and her sex. . . . Miss Wright stands condemned of a violation of the unalterable laws of nature, which have erected a barrier between the man and woman, over which neither can pass, without unhinging the beneficent adjustments of society, and doing wanton injury to the happiness of each other.[9]

The press and the public ridiculed and condemned Wright for her lectures. Wherever she went, attempts were made to prevent her from speaking; halls were locked, lights turned out, vegetables thrown, speeches boycotted. Once, in New York, someone set garbage on fire in the hall in an attempt to smoke out the audience. Wright kept on.

Many of the reviews of her lectures found nothing objectionable in the content, but neither did they find them particularly original or provocative. "But we do not recollect a single novel doctrine or argument that has not been declared and reiterated a thousand times from the pulpit or the press. . . . There is nothing to excite 'special wonder,' except that so many people should crowd to hear from Miss Wright, what they may hear and read every day of their lives."[10] Yet Wright did have her admirers, who occasionally came forward. "Throughout her Lecture, Miss Wright was listened to with the most profound attention. Occasionally, some beautiful sentiment, original thought, or striking illustration, drew forth a powerful response from the whole house. The purity and elegance of her language, her correct pronunciation, and eloquent and fervid manner, were acknowledged and applauded by all."[11]

The topic that seemed to evoke the greatest response, both of approbation and condemnation, was her support of the rights and the dignity of women. Though in an overall perspective, Wright's feminism was only part of a larger concern for reform of society as a whole, its importance should not be underestimated. Her thoughts on women were so original, provocative, and revolutionary that the press urged husbands and fathers to keep their wives and daughters from her lectures. It took a lot of courage and conviction to be one of the first to advocate equality for women, a topic that to this day arouses passion. Moreover, she showed what women could be and encouraged others to fulfill their potential. She was an inspiration for many.

After her lecture tour, Wright left the United States for a few years to live with and, against her own counsel, eventually to marry Phiquepal D'Arusmont in Paris. Their first child died, but they had a second, Frances Sylva, born in 1832.

It was a difficult time for Wright, not only because of the marriage, but also because of the death of her sister in 1831. She had always depended on Camilla to provide her with moral support, to be her companion, and to take care of her daily domestic needs. They were not close in a "sisterly" way—in fact, Camilla took on the role usually associated with that of a wife—but there was a strong bond of union and dependence that Wright found difficult to do without.

Wright traveled a lot after her marriage, leaving her husband to care for their daughter. She returned to the United States between 1835 and 1837 to do more writing and lecturing. During this time she met Lucretia Mott, but she never had much involvement in or sympathy for what she felt to be a middle-class women's movement.[12]

In 1844, Wright became heir to the Wright holdings in Scotland. Under the common law of both Great Britain and the United States, marriage stripped a woman of all rights to hold property; all her property automatically became her husband's. Much of her time until her death was spent in legal battles of one kind or another stemming from this event. She placed her property in a trust that excluded her husband, who then tried to secure all her property in his name. This ultimately ended in Wright obtaining a divorce and regaining her property through a bitter struggle. D'Arusmont fought the divorce, accusing Wright of not getting along with the family, of always forcing them to live around her life, and of just going mad. Their daughter became the pawn in their battles, with her father trying to set up a lasting barrier between Sylva and her mother, and her mother trying to keep her from her father.[13]

In 1852, Wright slipped and broke her hip. She died ten months later, quite alone.

Frances Wright spent her life fighting causes—for the poor, for the laboring classes, for women. Though often ridiculed and blocked in her efforts, she steadfastly pursued the calling of reform. The struggle itself was important.

The events in Wright's life tell only part of the story. Just as important are the people and ideas that shaped her intellectual life.

Intellectual Environment

Unlike most women of her day, Frances Wright was both well educated and well read. She was familiar with the history of philosophy, as well as the political and social debates of the time. She was the friend and intellectual companion of several of the leading educators, philosophers, social reformers, and statesmen of the early 1800s. Her intellectual background is rich and diverse. The challenge is to pull from it a framework of major influences.

It is certainly easier to pick one obvious source of influence and interpret all of Wright's thought as an application of that source. Several analysts have done this. But whom are we to believe? According to one source, she was an Enlightenment feminist; according to another, most of her principles stemmed from Epicurean doctrine; yet another sees her as a female copy of Robert Owen.[14]

Wright's thought is in fact a unique amalgam of several different philosophies. Certainly in many of her underlying ontological and epistemological precepts, Wright drew heavily on Enlightenment thought, especially that of Locke and Berkeley. Wright accepted the Enlightenment belief that human beings are born as blank slates and their characters impressed onto them by the society of which they are a part. She believed the character of humanity to be plastic, able to be shaped by circumstances and education.[15] According to Wright, human beings are just a bundle of habits.[16] This is the basis for Wright's emphasis on education as a tool for reform and on the equality of men and women. In order to change society, to reform it, one must first change individual habits. Wright sought to give people similar, equal, and just habits through similar, equal, and just education.[17]

In addition, Wright occasionally referred in her writings to such Enlightenment theorists as Voltaire, Condillac, and Condorcet.[18] She corresponded briefly with Mary Shelley, who introduced her to William Godwin.[19] And among the books in her estate was a copy of the great Enlightenment feminist work, Mary Wollstonecraft's *A Vindication of the Rights of Woman*.[20]

Specifically, it is possible to trace three major influences in Wright's thought: the Scottish Enlightenment, or moral sense philosophy; Epicurean utilitarianism; and utopian socialism.

Practically from her birth, Frances Wright was raised and nurtured in the Scottish school of moral sense philosophy. Though she did not know her father, who was a regular correspondent of Adam Smith, she had studied his papers and correspondence. As mentioned, her uncle was a professor of moral philosophy and a colleague of Dugald Stewart, who had studied with Thomas Reid. Though not permitted to enroll, Wright spent many years at Glasgow University, where the Scottish school of philosophy was at the height of its influence. She could not avoid being immersed in the ideas of Hume, Smith, Hutcheson, Reid, and others.

In addition, Wright revered Thomas Jefferson. "He—the Apostle of the Religion of Humankind promulgated that one, true, everlasting Principle of which the mind of the savage, equally with that of the sage, acknowledges the self-evidence. He pronounced the word *Justice* and the light of moral truth first broke upon the world."[21] Here Wright shows her affinity for the moral sense principles of Jefferson's thought, such as the emphasis on justice and on *moral* truth, and the recognition of the equality inherent in the self-evident nature of moral truth. According to Wills's interpretation, Jefferson's phrase "all men are created equal" refers to this capacity, equal in all, to discern moral truths.[22] As is discussed later, this notion of inherent moral equality is very important in Wright's feminism.

Wright felt that Jefferson's principles opened the possibilities of liberty and happiness to all humankind and said the source of her principles was the same as Jefferson's—self-evident truth and justice.[23] Wright was particularly impressed by Jefferson's Declaration of Independence and did not give a speech without invoking it in name or in principle. It was the self-proclaimed ground on which she stood as a public speaker[24] and was often her ground as a feminist, as she sought to include women under its rubric.

That Wright and Jefferson drew their principles from the same sources is reinforced by Wills's argument that the Declaration is a product of the

Scottish moral sense philosophy of Hutcheson, Reid, and Stewart. Since Wright read the Declaration at a time when its interpretation as a moral sense document was more prevalent, and because of her own particular philosophical background, she most likely viewed it as a moral sense argument. This brings us full circle to Wright's Scottish beginnings.

Though much of Wright's writing on moral theory is apparently utilitarian, her initial foundation in moral sense philosophy often surfaces in references to such standards for moral judgment as "an internal faculty," a "natural sentiment," an "internal moral sense," or "an instinctive human sentiment."[25]

In her assessment of her philosophical inclinations, Wright clearly indicated her preference not for utilitarianism, but for moral sense. "I incline to the opinion of those philosophers who trace within us the existence of a moral instinct, which when we have learned by experience to distinguish good and evil, pain and pleasure, in our own case, prompts us, without any process of reasoning, involving a reference to self, to desire the imparting of good and the averting of evil from others."[26] She was most apt to invoke moral sense to justify political principles, particularly justice, which is central to her concept of equality. She argued that we perceive justice by our internal faculties, just as we perceive light as a natural physical sensation, and that its simplicity and self-evidence make its effect tremendous. Her ultimate justifications for her feminist principles of equality and liberty are their inherent rightness, as discernible through the moral sense.[27]

Nevertheless, utilitarian thought was a significant influence in Wright's intellectual development. Her interest began with a fascination with Epicureanism, which was a forerunner of utilitarianism. While at Glasgow, Wright read Bayle's *Classical Dictionary*. This so excited her interest in Epicurean philosophy that she wrote her own philosophical tract, *A Few Days in Athens*, which extolled Epicurus and his doctrines. Speaking through the character of Theon, she wrote: "If ever I saw simple, unadorned goodness; if ever I heard simple, unadorned truth; it is in—it is from Epicurus. . . . Do you doubt the way? Let Epicurus be your guide."[28]

Though Waterman's generalization that all of Wright's philosophy stems from the principles she developed in *A Few Days in Athens*[29] is a bit too sweeping, one can certainly see the imprint of Epicurean doctrines in many of her most basic philosophical assumptions. Her beliefs that knowledge must be based on sensory evidence, that in discovering knowledge we also discover happiness and virtue, that happiness is the ultimate goal of life, and that religion is the major impediment to that happiness are all Epicurean doctrines.[30]

The impact of Epicureanism on Wright's thought was underscored by the strong tie between Epicurean doctrine and utilitarianism. Wright's interest in utilitarianism grew with her friendship with Bentham and the other utilitarians in his social and intellectual circle. She was a regular participant in the discussions of this philosophical group, and just as many utilitarian thoughts are incorporated into her writing, undoubtedly many of her thoughts, especially on women, are incorporated into theirs.

Compare, for example, Wright's statement that the condition of women affords the best criterion by which to judge the character of men[31] to Mill's "the elevation or debasement [of women] is on the whole the surest and most correct measure of the civilization of a people or an age."[32] Terence Ball has argued that this sentiment in Mill comes from his father, James Mill.[33] This may be true, but I think it is likely that James Mill first got the idea from his colleague, Frances Wright. Or J. S. Mill may have read it directly in *Views of Society and Manners in America*, a popular book of his day.

The other current of Wright's ethical theory is Epicurean/utilitarian. Like many of her contemporaries, Wright viewed morals as a science of human life, based not on religious prescriptions but on fact. The study of society and the individual's place in it should, according to Wright, be governed by the same rules of inquiry as any of the other physical sciences.[34] Because of its reliance on a quantifiable calculus of pleasure and pain as a measure for moral judgment, utilitarianism is suited to this conception of ethics as a positive science.

Wright's definition of morals is in line with utilitarian thought. "Morals," she stated, "is a rule of life deduced from the consequences of actions as ascertained through our own sensations and our observations of the sensations of others."[35] Wright argued that the standard of moral action must be based on its consequences. Moral actions are those which produce beneficial results; immoral, those which produce mischievous results.[36] These are clearly utilitarian sentiments.

Like the utilitarians, Wright stated that all affections of the soul and body could be reduced to two: pleasure and pain. Not only did she feel that it is natural to shun pain and follow after pleasure, but also that it is proper to do so, since pleasure is happiness and happiness is a virtue, a thesis she stated in *A Few Days in Athens*. "Why do you enter the Garden? Is it to seek happiness, or to seek virtue and knowledge?—Attend, and I will show you that in find one, you shall find the three. To be happy, we must be virtuous; and when we are virtuous, we are wise."[37]

Wright believed that all social practices should be judged by their utility.[38] Her condemnation of religion was in part due to its alleged uselessness, as was her praise of education based in part on its utility. This is also the ground of some of her justifications for her feminist precepts, which, foreshadowing Mill, argued that elevating the status of woman would benefit society as a whole.

However, utilitarian liberalism did not provide a sufficient basis for Wright's feminism, for two reasons. First, it relied on the individual's perception of self-interest to justify a demand for liberty and equality for all. Wright believed that people were so blinded by stupefying myths and religions that they were ignorant of their own self-interest. Equality of education was necessary before people could recognize their self-interest. Her ultimate justifications for liberty and justice for all came from moral sense.

Second, utilitarian liberalism stressed liberty over equality. This had been sufficient for privileged men who were not as concerned to demonstrate their equality. This was not adequate for Wright, however, who had first to make the argument for the equality of women in order to justify the liberty of women. She had to revise liberalism to take equality into account.

Wright's ethical theory is a tricky balance between utilitarian and moral sense thought. She accepted as a fundamental moral principle the utilitarian maxim to judge moral action by its beneficial consequences. But she did not accept the utilitarian motivation for so doing. Utilitarianism may provide the basic formula for moral judgment, but for Wright it is our moral sense rather than a selfish desire to increase our own happiness that inclines us to seek the happiness and benefits of others.

Wright used utilitarian and moral sense theory for two different purposes. She made a distinction between theory and practice. She conceived of theory as a religion, in the original sense, meaning to tie in a bond of union. She viewed such common principles as necessary to bind together any community. She viewed practice as the machinery developed to carry out the principles. As the two work together smoothly, Wright argued, so will the polity exhibit order and greatness. As they are ill-proportioned, the polity will be subject to internal division and decay. At least as far as the peace and durability of a polity are concerned, it is better to have a defective principle skillfully squared with a political framework than a more correct principle with a defective political framework. For Wright, the United States held so much promise not only because of the greatness of its political principles as set forth in the Declaration of Independence, but because of its good fit with the working machinery of the Constitution.[39]

Wright relied on moral sense primarily to justify her moral, political, and many of her feminist principles. Justice, equality, and liberty all appeal to our moral sense as good and right. However, she found moral sense insufficient to guide humankind through the process of civilization into a wise course of just practice. For this, long experience, a vast accumulation of positive knowledge, and observation of the consequences of action are required.[40] Wright relied on utilitarianism to guide the actual practice of moral action and the implementation of her feminist principles.

The ultimate goal of Wright's moral theory remains constant—happiness is a fundamental right that should be secured to all. It was the end she sought to achieve for all of society.[41]

Another link in this Epicurean utilitarian philosophical chain was forged through Wright's friendship with Robert Owen, who shared her admiration of Bentham. Wright and Owen had a long association, first during her time in his utopian community of New Harmony and later through her collegial relation with Owen's son, Robert Dale Owen.

According to some interpretations, Wright merely absorbed and rewrote Owen's philosophy. For example, Sabrosky views Wright's thought as a female's version of Owen's thought. Certainly some of Wright's views and approaches can be called "Owenite," but I disagree with the extent to which Sabrosky ascribes Owen's influence over Wright. For instance, Sabrosky states that Wright draws heavily on Owen's distrust of religion. She does not acknowledge that Wright's religious skepticism was developing in her early years at Glasgow and that she publicly ridiculed religion as a moral force in *A Few Days in Athens*, written long before she had even heard of Owen. Sabrosky also states that Wright's criticisms of woman's status in society evolved from Owen's ideas.[42] Here, too, Wright wrote about her own experiences in this area in *Views of Society and Manners in America*, published long before her association with Owen.

Wright always had an independent mind, and by the time she met Owen she already had a broad background of knowledge and experience as well as an international reputation as a writer. Owen did push her ideas about human happiness and liberty farther. His collective approach to society appealed to her and provided a context for dealing with existing questions she could not resolve through the selfish, individualistic context of utilitarianism.

Owen's was not, however, the only collectivist philosophy that interested Wright. She was attracted to the whole body of utopian socialist thought.[43] She had been involved with the Carbonaris, a group of Saint-Simonians, in

Paris in the 1820s and was also a friend of August Comte, who was himself greatly influenced by Saint-Simon. In later years, editing *The Free Enquirer*, she expressed admiration for Saint-Simon (though she was not particularly enamored of his followers).[44] A. J. G. Perkins and Theresa Wolfson felt that Saint-Simon's and Comte's beliefs in human history as elucidator of great fundamental truths underlying human conduct had a deep and lasting impact on Wright's later thinking and writing.[45] Her writings contain other similarities to Saint-Simon and utopian socialists. Ideas such as the importance of a religion (as opposed to a theology) or similarity of moral ideas in bonding people into a society, the need to extend the positive spirit of the physical sciences to the science of "man" and society, the distribution of economic benefits based on social outlay—all are found in the thought of both Wright and the utopian socialists. Though her assumptions about the nature of humanity and of knowledge may be based in Scottish and utilitarian thought, Wright's prescriptions for social reform have a distinct socialist tone.

This inclusion of collectivist principles in Wright's thought creates a tension with the utilitarian/liberal belief in individualism, a tension that lies at the core of her feminism. On the one hand, she believed that our existence as independent, individual human beings was primary to all other associations, especially the state, which she viewed as an artificial contrivance.[46] On the other hand, Wright felt that although as individuals we may be weak, as one collective being humanity is omnipotent.[47] She would have seen all of humankind bound together as one family by similar habits, pursuits, views, feelings, and interests.[48] This tension is evident in Wright's concept of interest.

The underlying thrust of Wright's concept of interest is that the interests of each individual are in unison with the interests of all. Though she maintained that each individual is the best judge of his or her own interest, by this she intended that the individual by nature (moral sense) or education (utilitarianism) is able to distinguish the means by which the greatest happiness may be produced to the whole population.[49] Furthermore, though Wright stated that the great task of government was the balancing of individual interests, she intended not a mere Benthamite mathematical calculation, but rather a perfect accord of interests, a unison of interests.[50] In the last analysis, Wright assumed all have the same general interest—to unite as a family, as equals.

Wright also sought to balance the autonomy of the individual with what she believed to be the mutual concerns and interdependence of individuals in society. She was concerned that each individual have the right and be permitted to develop, inquire, and behave according to the dictates of his or her own being. She believed that every individual can act wisely only according to the information of his or her own experience, and that a person's beliefs or actions should never be dictated by what someone else says is true, only by one's own truth. No individual, whether parent, legislator, or (especially) minister, should be able to dictate the thoughts and actions of another. Here was the root of Wright's concern for women, whom she saw being deprived of their capacity to think and act as individuals and being forced to depend on husbands, fathers, and clergy. This dependence she called the worst of all evils.[51]

However, though she sought independence of mind in the sense of relying only on one's own authority, she did not seek a disregard of others in society. "Yet, when I speak of independence, I mean not indifference; while we make ourselves sufficient for ourselves, we need not forget the crowd around us."[52]

Wright did not view society—collective humanity—as a threat to individual independence or rights. Individual and social interests were essentially harmonious, with no basis for antagonism.[53] Given enlightened education and similar habits and training, all will come to see that their interests must include everyone's interests. Wright believed that our lives are intimately interwoven, and as long as one member of society is oppressed, so are all. The inequality of one necessarily denies the equality of all. We are all part of a great humanity and it is only as humanity that we can reach ultimate happiness. "The separating of our individual happiness from that of others is, as I conceive, at the root of all ills of society. Certainly, every man must desire his own, but if he seeks his without reference to that of others, he can never secure his first desire."[54]

Wright sought freedom of the individual from authority, but within the context of naturally harmonious social relations. This presents problems for her analysis. How does she know that the interests of each are the same as the interests of all, and how does she ensure this without dictating individual beliefs? She respects individual inquiry, yet she wishes to give everyone similar habits, similar views, and similar interests. It seems that at some point she runs the risk that her harmonious society will become as authoritarian, if not more so, as the religious and political rule of the few that she seeks to escape. This tension between the individual and society is reflected in her contrasting emphases on liberty and equality, and this presents a real challenge for her feminism.[55]

Wright's Feminist Thought

The juxtaposition of all of the contrasting philosophical backgrounds and assumptions of moral sense, utilitarianism, and utopian socialism creates a complexity and richness in Wright's feminism. From the Enlightenment Wright drew the importance of education in shaping character and thus in defining the equality or inequality of the sexes. From utilitarian liberalism she gained her appreciation of the liberty of individual thought and action. She drew her passion for justice and equality from moral sense and utopian socialist thought. As a moral sense theorist, she justified her feminism with moral righteousness; as a utilitarian, she justified it as a useful solution to a practical problem.

Wright was a liberal feminist, a minimalist who saw no significant differences between men and women with regard to their physical, mental, moral, and sexual capacities. Along utilitarian liberal lines, Wright argued that the emancipation of women was called for by the right of self-determination and just treatment, and would result in the happiness and improvement of the individual and society. She was also a feminist socialist, believing that the freedom and the equality of both sexes would best be established and enhanced through equal and communal education and living and working conditions. Along utopian socialist lines, Wright argued that women claim equality as members of the common humanity and that liberty, happiness, and all other benefits of society were contingent on first achieving equality. She sought the moral autonomy of all as guaranteed through free inquiry, which is in turn guaranteed through equality. In essence, in her feminism Wright sought the full inclusion of women into every aspect of society, to the point that little or no distinctions would be drawn between the sexes. She sought the liberty of women primarily through their equality to men, not through their sorority to one another.

Liberty

Frances Wright was a champion of free inquiry, the unfettered pursuit of knowledge and truth. All other aspects of freedom followed from this. She believed that most people led lives of submission and domination out of fear, fear grounded in lack of knowledge. Educate people, give them the knowledge of facts and the principles of reason and understanding, and they would be able to rule their own lives.

While valuable in and of itself, the freedom to search and to question and to discover one's truths is essential to the development of moral autonomy. Through knowledge, individuals could understand the consequences of their actions, giving themselves a basis on which to make moral decisions. Further, a portion of the populace so enlightened would mitigate the oppressive intolerance and ignorance of popular prejudices and public opinion. As an entire society became educated, individuals would be free to think and to act without restraint of public law or popular opinion.

Thus it is that Wright's concept of freedom is strongly associated with autonomy and independence. To be free is to depend only on one's own senses and reason. Dependence on anything or anyone else was the worst evil, and the dependence of women was especially deplorable.

> Alas for the morals of a country when female dignity is confounded with helplessness and the guardianship of a woman's virtue transfigured from herself to others! . . . Of the two extremes it is better to see a woman, as in Scotland, bent over the glebe, mingling the sweat of her brow with that of her husband or more churlish son, than to see her gradually sinking into the childish dependence of a Spanish donna.[56]

The dependence of women was fostered primarily by three causes: the neglected state of the female mind, lack of sufficient economic reward, and marriage. Women were deprived of education, and thereby deprived of the resources on which to base rational decisions. They were left dependent on those who dispensed formulas of belief and actions, and they were particularly vulnerable to the quackery practiced in the name of religion.[57]

Wright felt that the main stumbling block to knowledge, especially to free inquiry, was religion. She objected to religion as taught and practiced not only because it was not true knowledge (empirically based) and was therefore useless,[58] but also because it was the cause of much suffering. Misery and evil, she claimed, are always conjoined with ignorance, and religion is willful ignorance. Its indifference to the visible causes of tangible evil and the visible sources of tangible happiness were the primary causes of suffering. "[The problem] is not that religion is merely useless; it is mischievous. It is mischievous by its idle terrors; it is mischievous by its false morality; it is mischievous by its hypocrisy; by its fanaticism; by its dogmatism; by its threats; by its hopes; by its promises."[59] Wright was especially concerned about the subjection of women by religion.⁶⁰ Women were particularly vulnerable to the sway of religion because they had not developed their reason. The liberation of women from the domination of religion is a recurrent theme in her feminism.

Wright found two reasons for women's lack of education. First, women were viewed by fathers, who made those decisions, as nothing. Even if women could learn, fathers would argue, they could not apply it in a trade or profession. Whatever earnings they might have would become their husbands'. In the eyes of the law, married women did not exist. In the eyes of educators, they had no value. Second, men thought women were more useful ignorant. Ignorant women would be more likely to accept complacently their subservient position. Deprived of reason and thereby of autonomy, women would be dependent on men, who desired women's dependence to flatter their own egos. Wright countered this view by arguing that this principle, to hold up, must hold for *all* cases, not just for women, and since no one would argue that a man is more useful when ignorant, it must not be true of women. More likely, men simply do not want the competition of women.⁶¹

Deprived of a proper education, most occupations were closed to women. Those that were available did not pay a living wage. Then as now, men were paid higher wages "because they had a family to support," and the only viable option for women was to depend on that support for survival.

Driven into marriage by economic and social pressure, the dependence of women was assured. By law they were deprived of all rights to property and person; by sheer drudgery they were deprived of any means of improvement. In marriage women became economically, physically, legally, and morally dependent on their male partners.

Wright attacked the legal institution of marriage on three fronts: it is unnecessary, unjust, and the cause of much suffering of women.

Wright felt that the affections between a man and a woman are personal in nature. They can't be regulated like traffic or contracted like any other business relation, and it is unwarranted that the state should try to do so. It was ludicrous that men and women had to be given permission to live together, or apart, and that relations formed without this sanction, no matter how loving and caring, were regarded as morally evil; just as relations given this sanction, no matter how miserable and mean, were thought to be morally blessed. Even louder did she decry the travesty of the state declaring illegitimate the children of such unsanctioned unions.

Wright found the whole notion of state permission and regulation of adult relations paternalistic. She argued that men and women should be treated as autonomous beings and that their affections should be their private concern only. Love should be sufficient reason to bring men and women together, and lack of love sufficient reason for them to part. Legal and public sanctions of marriage and divorce were unnecessary and undesirable. Their only purpose was to fill the coffers of the priest with a fee of union and those of the lawyer with a fee of parting.[62]

In her condemnation of the role of the state in regulating relations between adults, Wright made explicit the political nature of the marriage institution. She recognized it as just one more tool to suppress women. She viewed the marriage contract as a means for the law and the government "to deprive the female of *all defense*, by abrogating all her natural rights as a human being, and all her artificial rights as a citizen."[63]

Wright criticized the absurdity and injustice of the common law of England, adopted by the United States, whereby a married woman was deprived of her very personhood. Under these laws of coverture, a woman at marriage literally ceased to exist in the eyes of the law. All her property and earnings belonged to her husband; all contracts and other legal associations had to be made through him. Her husband was even responsible for any criminal actions on her part (and often for whatever punishment ensued as well). Wright condemned a system of laws that so completely abrogated the rights of women as to make every woman a slave.[64]

She argued that women were by marriage deprived not only of their rights, but also of any possibility of peace and happiness.[65] Further, their mental bondage was secured. Entering into marriage ignorant and naive, women were soon submerged in the never-ending drudgery of domestic chores and child producing. Marriage left women at the disposal of their partners. Deprived of their rights, of economic self-sufficiency, and of opportunity for improvement, they were dependent on and defenseless against the whims of their husbands and were often the victims of neglect, misery, and brutality.

> The unfortunate dependence of women too often makes them . . . victims to all evils which the error of their partner entails.[67]

> See her, moreover, compelled to endure the company of her destroyer, experience its vitiating example, and entail its evils on a yearly multiplying progeny![68]

Wright advocated better divorce laws, primarily so that a woman could get out of a bad situation. She argued that all states should adopt the divorce laws of Rhode Island, which permitted an annulment of the marriage contract on the grounds of a simple declaration of incompatibility and two years' separation.[69]

In her discussion of marital relations, Wright indicated that the problems originate in the legal stipulations of the marriage contract, rather than in the more fundamental association of women with men. She clearly felt that men and women were capable of tender and loving relations outside of the bonds of a legal contract. The marriage laws had no force in her own community of Nashoba, and yet she encouraged love relations between men and women. Thus it would appear that Wright believed that the marriage laws, by ensuring the dependence of women, fostered a situation in which men would take advantage of the powerlessness of their partners.

Men, Wright argued, finding women's dependence flattering to their egos, fostered that dependence. After all, it was men who determined the laws, men who determined wages, and men who determined the scope of the educational system. It was well within the power of men to grant women independence, but they had consistently refused. Given the political liberties available to the men in the United States, Wright felt reforms were possible. American men had the right of popular sovereignty. They needed only to exercise that right to bring about changes in the laws that would assure liberty, equality, prosperity, and happiness to all.

Paradoxically, in calling on the enfranchised citizenry—men—to exercise their liberty of popular sovereignty to invoke liberty and equality for all, Wright was suggesting that men relinquish the very dependence of women that they found so flattering. It is not clear how men would be persuaded to do so.

The freedom Wright claimed for women is their intellectual and moral independence and autonomy. This required above all the free pursuit of knowledge. And in order for this liberty to be secured, it must be shared equally. In that knowledge is power, as long as it is distributed unequally, some will be more powerful and others will be dependent and submissive. In particular, men, who monopolized knowledge, would ensure the submission and dependence of women. Thus we come to the subject of equality.

Equality

Equality of all humankind is the central tenet of Wright's thought. All are born with equal mental, moral, and physical capabilities. We bring with us no inherent female or male traits. Each comes into the world equally blank. Any distinctions that occur are the result of education and circumstances.

Also, relying on moral sense principles, Wright argued that regardless of whatever privileges or distinctions, intelligence or talents, circumstances may have brought our way, they have no relevance to our capacity to act morally. The moral faculty is inherent in all. Separate from our physical powers, it is not circumscribed by merely physical differences of sex; separate from our intellectual powers, it is not affected by differences in intelligence or education. With respect at least to moral truth, Wright argued that "the mind of the savage, *equally* with that of the sage, acknowledges the self-evidence."[70] All are equal in the moral sense notion that all are capable of being useful and happy, of being guided by reason and senses in a course of practice consistent with their own and the common good.[71]

Finally, Wright's assumption of equality stemmed as a necessary corollary from the utopian socialist assertion of our common species. We are first and foremost human beings—not citizens, not sects, not lawyers or merchants, and particularly not men and women. Our humanity is fundamental. It overrides and mitigates any distinctions between the sexes.

However, Wright was acutely aware that differences in education and environment create inequalities of privilege and condition. She felt keenly the wretchedness and squalor of the masses of humanity. She knew well the oppression of the working classes and of women. Believing strongly in the right of every human being to equal chances for development, reward, and happiness in this life, she dedicated her life to promoting educational and economic reforms. She sought

> the equal claim of all the members of the human family to equal chances; to equal care in infancy, equal protection and equal opportunities for mental and physical development in childhood and youth; equal credit according to the powers of his or her individual industry and genius in manhood or womanhood; equal certainty of reward in precise accordance with his or her services thro' life; equal security in the present and for the future of enjoying what his or her services may have fairly earned.[72]

An equal chance depends primarily on two conditions: equal educational opportunities and fair reward for labor. In pursuing the first condition, Wright developed a plan of national republican education that she promoted on every speaking tour. Her plan called for a government-supported and government-run system that would take responsibility for the care and education of *all* children, from the age of two years on up. The pattern of equality was to be set in the nurseries, in which all would be fed at a common board, wear common clothes, and be given similar duties, habits, and training, and would continue from infancy to adulthood.[73]

Wright was particularly concerned with equalizing the benefits, powers, and privileges of the sexes, and she saw a system of equal education as the key. Wright was severely critical of the lack of education for women. The facilities and the subjects of study for men were far superior to those for women. What education some women did receive was of little value. Women were usually educated in the European tradition, obtaining knowledge of only those things necessary for polite amusement—French, Italian, dancing, and drawing.

Since women had been educated only in the moral aspects of their nature, Wright was especially concerned that the two other aspects—the intellectual and the physical—be given equal cultivation. Whereas many did not regard women as rational beings, and were skeptical that women's intellect could be developed at all, Wright asserted that the mind has no innate characteristics of sex—or any other distinction—but only those characteristics that habit and education give it.[74] Women's intellects had been stifled. Even "in the happiest country, their condition is sufficiently hard. Have they talents? It is difficult to turn them to account. Ambition? The road to honorable distinction is shut against them. A vigorous intellect? It is broken down by sufferings, bodily and mental."[75]

However, that women did indeed have intellects, which were equal of any man's, Wright herself was proof, an argument she frequently advanced in speeches to challenge her male taunters.[76] Given that women's intellectual capabilities were equal to that of men, Wright argued that they should be equally developed, with equal education in philosophy, history, political economy, and sciences.

Even those who advocated the equal intellectual education of women often did not believe women should receive the same physical training. Though she occasionally referred to women as "the weaker sex," Wright felt that any physical differences between the sexes could be minimized by women being taught to race, swim, and shoot. The physical aspect of human character was just as important as the moral and intellectual, and Wright emphasized the need to exercise it equally with them. "I often lament that in rearing of women so little attention should be commonly paid to the exercise of the bodily organs; to invigorate the body is to invigorate the mind, and Heaven knows that the weaker sex have much cause to be rendered strong in both."[77]

Unlike many of her contemporaries, who sought the education of women so that they might be better mothers and teachers of men, Wright felt that the education of women as complete human beings was of the utmost importance for themselves, as individuals.[78] Education would enable women to reason, to fulfill their capabilities, to become autonomous.

It is important to remember that for Wright knowledge was the one key to all other societal goods. Without knowledge a woman could not be free or equal; she could not progress; she had no power. Moreover, Wright adopted the Epicurean belief that knowledge is the foundation of all other virtues. Thus, without education a woman could attain neither virtue nor happiness. Deprived of knowledge, women were deprived of all that is worthwhile in life. One cannot say of Wright that she *merely* sought education for women. In seeking education she sought all.

Wright also presented a very utilitarian argument (presumably addressed to men, to whom all of her utilitarian arguments seem to be addressed) for the education of women. Not only would education equalize benefits to women, it would extend these benefits to the nation as a whole. "The wonderful advance which this nation has made, . . . may yet be doubly accelerated when the education of women shall be equally a national concern with that of the other sex."[79]

In its equalization of knowledge, equal education would serve the Epicurean/utilitarian purposes of the extension of other equal benefits to all individuals and society as a whole. Wright also thought that equal education would serve the utopian socialist purposes of establishing a sense of community and equality of condition by providing similar habits, views, and interests. She argued "that a nation to be strong, must be united, to be united, must be equal in condition, to be equal in condition, must be similar in habits and in feeling, to be similar in habits and feelings, must be raised in national institutions as the children of a common family, and citizens of a common country."[80] By providing similar habits, pursuits, views, feelings, and interests, education would serve to bind individuals together in the common interests and the equality of a family.[81] This is an important notion for her feminism, for as all would come to recognize their common interests and bonds, the degradation of women by men would cease.

We do, however, encounter here the tension in Wright's thought between individual liberty and the collective good. Wright seems to be suggesting that equality and unity can be achieved by educating everyone to think alike. She tries to argue that given the proper education, each would independently recognize his or her responsibility to the community.

> Practical equality, or, the universal and *equal improvement of the condition* of all, until, by the gradual change in the views and habits of men, and the change consequent upon the same, in the whole social arrangement of the body politic, the American people shall present, in another generation, but in one class, as it were, but *one family—each independent* in his and her own thoughts, actions, rights, person, and possessions, and all *co-operating*, according to their *individual* tastes and ability, to the promotion of the common weal.[82]

The predominant question this raises for her feminism is how the nature of this similar education is to be determined. Perhaps constrained by the male bias in utopian socialism, Wright implied that this sense of community is ultimately male-defined. She had no concept of female awareness or self-definition. Rather, we get the impression that women should be able to become equal to the best of men.

Wright was equally concerned with achieving equality for all, but especially for women, through a fair reward for one's labor. Again, following in the utopian socialist tradition, Wright felt that the monetary system of rewarding the rich for idleness while the hard labors of the masses went unrewarded was immoral and unjust and was at the basis of the evils of society. Only by securing to all equal opportunity and affording them useful occupations and full and fair fruits of their labors would happiness and abundance be attainable by the whole of humanity.[83]

Wealth, as Wright defined it, is the fruit of industry and, in justice, should be owned by those who create it—the laboring classes. The estimate of value should be based on the average time employed in the production of an article, and workers should be rewarded according to the labor they invest. The substitution of just for unjust money and the fair reward of labor would lead to reform in all of society, equalizing the condition of humankind, bringing plenty to each, as well as honesty, ease, independence, and "brotherly" love.

Wright was particularly concerned with ensuring a just reward for women's labor. Women were deprived of economic equality in several ways. To begin with, they were not given sufficient training or skills to pursue a career. Their rights to property were denied by laws of marriage and primogeniture. Most significant, their labor was not rewarded equally to that of men. This economic discrimination rendered women incapable of supporting themselves, leaving them the choice between living independently in poverty or trading their independence for survival. Wright stated her case eloquently.

> We might ask if the brightest half of our race whose wisdom best might guard and guide the interests and happiness of the whole, could ever be found selling their persons for a subsistence, weighing in useless idleness on their relatives or male help-mates, or struggling in want and wretchedness under unrequited toil, if the fruits of industry, and not metal from the bowels of a mine were accounted wealth, if all were trained to create those fruits, and if, by whomsoever created, they bore ever their own value, and could neither be depreciated nor exalted below nor beyond the same.[84]

Wright believed that the labor of women is not inferior to that of men, and in any case, sex is not a legitimate basis of distinction. The labor of women should be rewarded equally to that of men,[85] and the labor of all should be rewarded according to the amount of service rendered. As a practical course to the achievement of equality of condition, Wright sought to institute what she called the "self-evident axiom: *To every man, woman, and child, according to his and to her works.*"[86]

In sum, Wright sought to put the principles of equality and justice into effect through equal educational opportunity and a fair reward for labor. Both were particularly important to women, who had consistently been denied them. She believed that women and men were equal in their mental, moral, and physical capacities and that women needed only be given equal opportunities in order for that equality to be realized. For Wright, the standard of excellence, privilege, and power was male. Equality of the sexes meant the extension of male opportunities, privileges, responsibilities, and rewards to women. Her goal was that women be equal to men—and this brings us to sorority.

Sorority

The concept of sorority is not as central to Wright's feminist thought as are the concepts of liberty and equality. Her utopian socialist collectivism was strong, and she sought not so much the identity and unity of women as the identity of humanity.

Wright believed any differences between the sexes to be minimal. She made little mention of sex-related behavior or sex roles. She discussed the educational and economic distinctions that society imposed on the sexes, but had no further discussion of the effects of such distinctions on behavior or attitudes. Unlike most of her contemporaries, including Fuller and Grimké, Wright made no mention of masculine/feminine character traits, or sexually separate "spheres."

One important reason for this lack of emphasis on sex roles and sexual distinctions is that Wright did not develop a concept of womanhood. Her concern was humankind. The equality and liberty she sought for woman was that of humanity in general.

I believe that Wright's inattention to sex roles stemmed in part from her allegiance with and concern for working-class women. It was one thing for middle-class women to address the issue of sex roles because their lives of domesticity were so far removed from their husbands' and brothers' professional lives. It was quite another to expect working-class women to regard their roles as unique, when they went to work in the factories just as their husbands and brothers did. Neither did working-class women need solitude for reflecting on their nature as women so much as they needed a decent wage. Better for them to aspire to the lives of middle-class men than to those of middle-class women.

Another reason Wright did not focus on sex role differences is that she did not regard women as first and foremost wives and mothers. She questioned the institution of marriage and family by her very acceptance of divorce, by her advice that women not marry, by her suggestion that men and women could sustain loving and committed relations outside of marriage, and by her advocacy of taking children out of the home and placing them in common nurseries. Thus Wright made a new perception of the role of women possible. No longer viewed solely in terms of domestic functions, women would be regarded as human beings, with all their potential and possibilities. Because Wright went beyond the restrictive assumption of the family unit, she viewed women as something other than wives and mothers. Able to break through this most basic of women's roles, she did not view any roles whatsoever as significant.

Another reason for Wright's lack of emphasis on culturally defined sex differences may be her belief that there were no significant differences between the sexes in their sexuality. Unlike her contemporaries, Wright did not condemn or deny sexuality. Wright was irritated by the dictums of propriety that rendered the mere mention of an arm or leg indecent. She condemned the fact that women were afraid of their own bodies, and were, in fact, often viewed as having no bodies at all.[87] Wright advocated that rather than shrouding their bodies, desires, and faculties, women address them openly.[88]

That men had healthy appetites and passions was readily acknowledged. Wright, however, was among the first to acknowledge that women have any sex drive whatsoever, let alone one that is as "healthy" as a man's. Wright viewed both men and women as sexual beings, and felt the temperate expression of their passions was a natural outgrowth of their nature as human beings.[89] It was the denial of these feelings that was undesirable. "Let us not teach that virtue consists in the crucifying of affections and appetites, but in their judicious government," Wright admonished. "Let us not attack ideas of purity to monastic chastity, impossible to man *or woman* without consequences fraught with evil, nor ideas of vice to connections formed under the auspices of kind feelings."[90]

Wright believed that men and women were each other's equals, even in their most sex-defined relationships. This underscored artificial distinctions between the sexes. The one exception to this is that, like her contemporaries, she sometimes argued that women are morally superior to men. At times she made the distinction between "brute males" and "the brightest half" of the species.[91] Wright felt that women were more noble and generous than men, and exerted a special moral influence over all of society.[92] In fact, the moral character of a whole society is determined by the influence that women have in that society. The position of women is a gauge for the morals of a country.[93]

Wright made a passionate argument that the current depravity of the human condition was a direct result of the degradation of the nobler instincts of women.

> The first master of measure employed for the more certain enslavement of the species was the subjugation of woman in her body and her soul. She—the intellect, the soul, the providence of society—being made a tool of that sex which looks to individual conservation and selfish gratification—the nobler instinct enshrined in her—that which looks to the conservation and happiness of the species—was necessarily made subservient to the baser. The consequence has been what we witness at this hour: brute force quelling the inspirations of the mind; noise drowning reason; disputation knowledge; fraud subtracting from weakness what violence may have failed to rob; law usurping the place of

justice; selfish interest that of generous friendship; prostitution, contraband or legal, that of love; theology of religion, and rapacious government that of benign administration.[94]

Wright went so far as to argue that all of human improvement is contingent on the position of women. Her belief that men will ever rise or fall to the level of women is put forth in her most famous statement.

> However novel it may appear, I shall venture the assertion, that, until women assume the place in society which good sense and good feeling alike assign to them, human improvement must advance but feebly. It is in vain that we would circumscribe the power of one half of our race, and that half by far the most important and influential. If they exert it not for good, they will for evil, if they advance not knowledge, they will perpetrate ignorance. Let women stand where they may in the scale of improvement, their position decides that of the race. Are they cultivated?—so is society polished and enlightened. Are they ignorant?—so is it gross and insipid. Are they wise?—so is the human condition prosperous. Are they foolish?—so is it unstable and unpromising. Are they free?—so is the human character elevated. Are they enslaved?—so is the whole race degraded.[95]

If one is looking for consistency in Wright's thought, the question must be asked, Why, if women are in all respects equal to men, do they exert such a unique influence over the morals of society? This may be answered in part by her own statement that "the fate of the sexes is so entwined that the dignity of the one must rise or fall with that of the other."[96] So, as women were then denied their full dignity, so were men; and as women came into their own, so would men and thus society.

This may also be answered in part by her observations that women, though receiving no physical or intellectual training, did receive moral training whereas men did not. Thus women may be more moral than men simply because their moral faculties have been enlightened and developed.

However, it may also be true that Wright is inconsistent. It may be that she was presenting the cultural stereotype of her day. Or perhaps in these affirmations of women's moral nature are the seeds of a bolder affirmation of womanhood in general and an incipient notion of sorority.

Wright occasionally hinted at a sisterhood among women. Certainly she affirmed her sisterhood with working-class women in a way that most middle-class feminists did not. She also recognized the common suffering that all women endured as a class. Wright separated the afflictions of humanity into those of men and those of women, the latter always being more burdensome. "It is difficult, in walking through the world, not to laugh at the consequences which, sooner or later, overtake men's follies, but when these are visited upon women I feel more disposed to sigh. Born to endure the worst afflictions of fortune, they are enervated in soul and body lest the storm should not visit them sufficiently rudely."[97]

Wright made occasional reference to women's oppression by men. In general, however, she did not regard the relations between women and men to be that of the solidarity of the oppressed versus the oppressors. Wright did not view the relations between the sexes as antagonistic. She felt that women were oppressed by clergy and bankers and lawyers and husbands; not by men *as men*, but by men as representatives of institutions—the church, the bank, the state, marriage. In the utopian socialist tradition, it was institutions, not people, that were responsible for the character of society, and in her evaluation of male/female relations, Wright viewed the problem as one of institutions, not sexes, and not persons.

Far from urging an independent struggle for women, Wright urged men and women to cooperate to achieve the goals of collective humanity.[98] Wright viewed our humanity as fundamental, and she denied the significance of subdivision by sex, race, or any other category. Humanity, with its inherent equality, takes precedence over sorority.

For Wright to believe in and affirm a unique nature of womanhood would be to go against her Enlightenment assumptions that human character is shaped by education and environment, rather than by such physical characteristics as sex. For Wright to affirm a sisterhood of women separate and apart from men would be at odds with her utopian socialist beliefs in the essential commonality and solidarity of all humanity.

But beyond the issue of Wright's beliefs, her own life story gave her little experience of sorority on which to draw as a feminist. Wright's life and work were not within the common world of women, but among the world of men. Unlike most women, she was highly educated and her intellectual companions were men; unlike most women, she traveled extensively; she chose and pursued what was typically a "man's" occupation and her working relationships were with men. Indeed, all of Wright's closest and best relationships were with men—her uncle, General Lafayette, Jeremy Bentham, Robert Owen, Robert Dale Owen.[99] Men were her peers, and they treated her as such.

Wright had relatively few correspondingly close relationships with women. Except for her brief association with Mrs. Millar, who was more like a mother, and her reliance on her sister, who was more like a wife, there were no women with whom Wright related as a sister.

Wright felt much more at home with men than with women. Men and their lives and works were more familiar to her. So estranged from the lives and the world of most women, it is no wonder that Wright did not develop a stronger notion of sorority.

Rather than being an appeal to women to recognize and affirm their autonomy and identity as women and their sisterhood with other women, the whole tenor of Wright's feminism is an appeal to men. She wrote and spoke as though by far the more important and certainly the more influential members of her audience were male. Her arguments for improving the condition of women so as to improve that of men were addressed to the interests and concerns of men. Her appeals for equal education, fair wages, and just marriage laws were addressed to fathers and husbands, not to those she hoped would benefit. The general argument put forth by Wright is for men to take the yoke of servitude off of women, rather than encouraging women to do so themselves. Unlike Fuller and Grimké, Wright trusted and relied on men to help women, who she felt were not in a position to help themselves. This position is consistent with the rest of Wright's philosophy. She felt that unless a person were educated, he or she was powerless. To address her argument to women would have been futile, for women were incapable of doing anything to improve their situation. Wright had to appeal to those who were capable of changing society, and at that time, this meant addressing her arguments to men.

Once freed from their yoke, women would enter equally into the lives and knowledge and power and work of men, as Wright had, rather than affirm their own particular identity and vision.

Only in her later life, after years of bitter marriage, divorce, and being cheated and lied to by her husband and her attorney, did Wright change her sentiments. She openly admitted that she was afraid of men, that she would not trust them, and with what she believed to be good reason.[100] I suggest that had Wright written after this point in her life, she might have been hesitant to address her feminism to men, and the approach of her feminism might have been based more on the concept of sorority.

Conclusion

Wright's feminism is a balanced tension between liberty and equality. As she wrote, "equality is the soul of liberty, there is, in fact, no liberty without it."[101] She sought free inquiry only in conjunction with equal education for all; she sought equality of economic condition only in conjunction with political and legal liberties. For Wright, the liberty of free inquiry was guaranteed only by the equal distribution of that inquiry. If knowledge was held as a monopoly of a few, then the masses would lead lives of submission and domination to the knowledge keepers—priests, doctors, lawyers, governors. The lives of all would be restricted by the ignorance and prejudices of all. The purpose of providing everyone with an equal education is so that each can discover his or her own truths, not to enforce conformity. It is the equality of the education that guarantees its liberty. Liberty unaccompanied by equality is nonexistent. Similarly, women's independence could be guaranteed only through a fair and equal wage for their labor. Without this, women would continue to depend on men for economic support, usually through marriage.

Whereas liberty and equality are well balanced in Wright's thought, there is no corresponding tension with the concept of sorority. The value of this for Wright's feminism is that it helped to break down the stereotypes of female behavior and roles prevalent in the 1830s. She broke from the view of women as wives and mothers—and, ironically, as asexual or antisexual beings. Her feminism is liberating, stressing the liberty of women to exercise fully their physical, moral, intellectual, and sexual capacities.

However, Wright's feminism also suffers from this lack of balance with sorority. Her standard of virtue becomes maleness. She wanted women to be able to think, work, run, shoot, act like men. She sought the liberty of women to be like men; she sought the equality of women to men. Wright failed to see the paradox in her thought. She recognized the oppressiveness of certain institutions and sought to eliminate them. However, she did not make the connection that these oppressive institutions were shaped by the very men to whom she thought women should aspire. She did not recognize that these institutions were outgrowths of a patriarchal culture and male-defined reality. She did not see that in encouraging women to be like men, she was encouraging the perpetuation of male-defined institutions.

Nor did Wright recognize how the knowledge she sought to convey had been defined, recorded, and interpreted by men. Or if she did, she did not regard this as a problem. Neither did she recognize the limitations in a male-defined "truth," a truth discernible only through reason. She did not see that her rejection of "women's ways of knowing," that is, intuition and personal knowledge,[102] was perpetuation of a male-defined reality that denied the equality of women's experiences and perceptions.

Contemporary feminist critiques of the academy show the male bias in the existing knowledge base. They show as well how the questions and concepts and even facts of academic disciplines have necessarily, though often reluctantly, changed in response to challenges raised by a feminist perspective.[103] For example, feminists have challenged the validity of traditional theories of moral development such as those of Freud and Kohlberg, because women have been excluded from these studies.[104] Similarly, in political theory, the liberal theory of justice has been challenged by the feminist ethic of care.[105]

To Wright's credit, this feminist challenge of the canon of knowledge could not have begun without the inclusion of women in the academy, which Wright demanded. However, generations of women have passed through the academy simply following in the male tradition. It took more than the inclusion of women in the academy to change it. It took the challenges of those who valued women's experience and women's perspectives.

Thus, Wright's notions of liberty and equality are limited. Without the inclusion of women's experiences and unique knowledge base, without the acknowledgment of a "woman's reality,"[106] women's true liberty is denied. They are free to be like men. They have equal pay, but are they free to pursue those aspects of their nature that are regarded as traditionally feminine? Will women who choose to be homemakers or mothers be considered of less worth than those who pursue an education and a career? Will women's truths, based on intuition and personal experience, be regarded as of little or no value? How can women be free or equal with their experiences and perspectives denied? I argue that in a society that regards maleness as the standard for the liberty and equality of women, women—and men—continue to be oppressed by male-defined institutions and a male-defined reality.

Wright made necessary and important strides for women. She helped break the path for women escaping the traditional molds that had been in part designed by men to serve their purposes. However, the alternative molds she proposed are male-defined as well. Wright herself was a victim of this. Her feminism is more deeply rooted in male traditions than the more gynocentric feminism of Grimké and Fuller.

The whole notion of sorority was at odds with her deep sense of the collectivity of humanity. For Wright, women could not be *just sisters*, because they have *brothers*, who are as important. The importance of the equality of humanity for Wright could not be superseded by the division inherent in sorority. Wright's feminism is first and foremost an eloquent appeal for independence as individuals and equality as human beings.

FOUR

Sarah Grimké

When, in 1835, Angelina Grimké wrote and *signed* a letter to appear in the *public* press (*The Liberator*), her sister Sarah was appalled. She felt Angelina was acting immodestly and going beyond the bounds of propriety for her sex. Yet three years later, Sarah was not only publishing her name in the press, but was taking on the church establishment in the process. Beneath her timid exterior lay a heart burning with righteous indignation at the wrongs of slavery and to women. She was sensitive and reflective, and subject to depressions. A single rebuff from Theodore Weld silenced her for years. But she was also a fighter, dedicated to her cause, approaching everything with enthusiasm and energy. In the cause of women's rights, though she might be occasionally silenced, she would never be suppressed.

Sarah Grimké grew up in a Southern slaveholding patriarchal family in Charleston, South Carolina. Her mother's family was part of the wealthy governing plutocracy; her father, chief judge of the South Carolina Supreme Court, owned hundreds of slaves. It was this youthful experience of slavery that fostered her abolitionism. At the age of five, Sarah witnessed the whipping of a slave and became from that moment opposed to slavery.

Sarah's father did much to encourage her intellectual development, but the strongest influence on her was her older brother, Thomas. He taught her Latin, Greek, mathematics, and geography. When he returned home from Yale he brought with him many new ideas, including the dangers of the Enlightenment and the truths of the Bible, which Sarah found fascinating. Yet her aspirations toward the higher education pursued by her brothers were discouraged and her schooling was changed to the more typical fare for a young woman of her day—French, watercolors, harpsichord, and embroidery.

Sarah's mind and spirit were stifled. She felt that her calling was to be a lawyer, and she studied law secretly on her own. Her father is said to have told Sarah that she would have made the greatest jurist in the land—had she not been a woman. She learned very early what it meant to be denied something because of her gender, a lesson that shaped the course of her life, both in what she did not become and in her life's testimony to the liberty and equality of women.

Well into her sixties this experience was still vivid. "Had I received the education I wanted and been bred to the profession of the law, a dignity to which I secretly aspired, I might have been a useful member of society, and instead of myself and my property being taken care of I might have been a protector of the helpless and the unfortunate, a pleader for the poor and the drunk."[1]

Instead, she plunged into the life of the stereotypical Southern belle—balls and parties and picnics. Looking back she called that time the "prostitution of my womanhood . . . the utter perversion of the ends of my being."[2]

Her years of gaiety were followed by years of somber solitude and meditation. Under the influence of Rev. Dr. Kolloch, the Presbyterian minister who warned her that her frivolity would lead to everlasting punishment, she tried to atone through works and self-deprecation. Her diaries are filled with despair of ever achieving salvation.[3] The one bright spot in all of this was her sister Angelina. When Angelina was born, twelve-year-old Sarah requested that she be allowed to take care of the child. She became part sister, part mother to Angelina, forging the most important relationship of her life.

In 1819, Sarah accompanied her father to Philadelphia, where she attended him in his final illness. This was a turning point for her, as she encountered the frailty of the person who had heretofore been the single most important source of order and authority in her life.[4]

While in Philadelphia, Sarah made her first acquaintance with the Society of Friends. She was impressed with the Quaker idea that women and men are equal through inner light, and felt a calling from God to go north and become a Quaker minister. Thus began a fifteen-year period in Philadelphia (where she was joined by Angelina in 1829) of personal growth, intellectual development, and theological study. Life was not easy for her with the Society. She was constantly opposed by elder Jonathon Evans. Intimidated and condemned, she spoke in meetings only with intense suffering.[5] She became increasingly dissatisfied with the society's theological doctrines and principles of action, especially its racial prejudice and opposition to abolition. In her "Letter on the Subject of Prejudice Amongst the Society of Friends in the United States," she described in detail her disappointment at the blatant prejudice in the Society of Friends. She related that Friends were unwilling to associate with blacks and had even set up a separate bench for them in the meeting (on which Sarah and

Angelina sat in protest). She also expressed her sadness over the fact that to become an abolitionist was to lose caste in the Society.[6]

After reading a few antislavery publications, Sarah began to feel a strong sympathy with the abolitionist cause. Though she had initially mourned Angelina's letter to William Lloyd Garrison and tried to get Angelina to abandon the cause, Sarah was now converted. She knew that to become an abolitionist was to forfeit all hopes of usefulness in the Society of Friends, but she felt that she was doing so on the undoubted evidence of the will of God.[7]

The Grimké sisters dedicated the years from 1833 to 1840 to the American Anti-Slavery Society, painting slavery as it was, as they had lived with it, and expounding on the antislavery character of the Constitution and the Bible. They were the first women among the seventy abolitionist agents who toured the Northeast, promoting the cause of abolition. In 1837, they addressed the first Anti-Slavery Convention of American Women, the first public assembly of non-Quaker women in America, addressed by American women. The convention brought together one hundred women from ten states, including Lucretia Mott, Mary Grew, Sarah Pugh, Sarah Douglass, Maria Chapman, Mary Parker, Lydia Child, and Abby Kelley. They resolved that it was "the province of woman and her duty . . . to plead the cause of the oppressed and to do all that she can by her voice and her pen, and her purse, and the influence of her example, to overthrow the horrible influence of American slavery."[8]

Urged on by their own sense of moral purpose and by Garrison and other male abolitionists,[9] the Grimkés remained undaunted in their struggle, despite the growing criticism of the clergy for stepping beyond the bounds of "woman's sphere." The most vicious clerical attack came in the form of the infamous "Pastoral Letter," published in *The Liberator* in 1838, which enjoined women no longer to take part publicly in the abolitionist cause.

Sarah's work as an abolitionist deepened her concern for women's plight and propelled her into the women's rights movement. There was the controversy, both in and out of abolitionist circles, over women speaking in public before "promiscuous" (mixed) audiences. Wherever they went they were criticized and harassed, asked what right women had to hold public meetings.[10] To this Angelina responded:

> Every citizen should feel an interest in the political concerns of the country, because the honor, happiness, and well-being of every class are bound up in its politics, government, and laws. Are we aliens because we are women? Are we

bereft of citizenship because we are mothers, wives, and daughters of a mighty people? Have women no country—no interested stake in public weal . . . no partnership in a nation's guilt and shame?[11]

Finding their rights as women denied, they asserted them even more vigorously.

Sarah saw a strong parallel between the condition of the slaves she defended as an abolitionist, and the condition of women. Both were treated as inferior and deprived of basic human liberties. The plight of the slavewoman was especially grave, since she was called on to gratify the appetites of her male masters. Sarah could not plead the cause of slaves without also pleading the cause of women.

Finally, Sarah confronted the subordination of the women she encountered in her abolition work. In her later life she reflected: "It was when my soul was deeply moved at the wrongs of the slave that I first perceived distinctly the subject condition of women."[12] She was referring to the frequent occurrence in the antislavery petition campaign of women who wanted to sign the petitions being forbidden to do so by their husbands. Until then Sarah had not realized the extent to which women sacrificed their consciences to the opinions of husbands, brothers, and fathers in order to preserve domestic tranquility.

For Sarah, the "woman question" was of paramount importance.[13] She had given it much thought and study ever since her parents denied her the same education as her brothers, and now she had the opportunity to do something about it. After the "Pastoral Letter," Sarah became an active speaker and writer on women's behalf.

The Grimké sisters' activity came a decade before any organized movement for women's rights. By the time of the Seneca Falls Convention (1848), they had retired into domesticity. In 1838, Angelina had married fellow abolitionist Theodore Weld, and Sarah, who chose not to marry,[14] lived with them, helping Angelina with housekeeping and child rearing. The enormity of this task grew especially burdensome during the five years (1840-44) in which they singlehandedly ran a boarding school for more than twenty children in their own home.

In 1853, the Welds joined Raritan Bay Union, a cooperative community based on the principles of utopian socialist Charles Fourier. Largely at the urging of Angelina, Sarah did not accompany them. It appears that over the years, Angelina had come to resent Sarah's mothering of herself and of her children, as well as her dependence on Angelina for any domestic life of her own. At the age of sixty, Sarah found herself on her own for the first time.

Uneasy in her aloneness, Sarah rejoined the Welds six months later and remained with their household the rest of her life. Her retreat into domesticity was not, however, a withdrawal from her active concern for women's rights. She kept in touch with the feminist movement, subscribing to *The Una* and *The Lily* and occasionally publishing articles, as well as her translation of Lamartine's biography of Joan of Arc. She even wore the Bloomer costume for a while. At the age of sixty, she wrote fragments of manuscripts on marriage, divorce, the role of women, and women's history.[15] She compiled laws pertaining to women in different states in order to expose their unfairness and arouse the conscience of the nation. Had it not been for her home duties, she would have undertaken some form of missionary work, especially among poor and working women. Even in old age she remained an undaunted activist. She spent her last years marching for women's rights and going door-to-door selling copies of Mill's *The Subjection of Women*. The tragedy is that she was not peddling her own book.

I agree with Lerner that to a large extent, Sarah Grimké's feminist concerns developed from years of repressing and thwarting her own talents.[16] As a child and young woman, she was denied the education she desired simply because of her gender, which affected her the rest of her life. As a crusader for abolition, she was condemned by the New England clergy and silenced by Theodore Weld's harsh criticism of her public speaking abilities. She never had an opportunity to put her talents and energies to the productive service of which she was capable. Her experiences with several, though not all, men—her father, brother-in-law, ministers in general—had been ones of domination. She found she was better able to develop and express herself with women—her sister Angelina and her friends Elizabeth Pease and Harriot Kezia Hunt.

Many of her thoughts lie buried in archives, undoubtedly many lied buried in her grave, but in the record she left the world, Sarah Grimké gave full vent to those thwarted talents and left a proud legacy as a feminist philosopher.

Intellectual Environment

Unlike Wright and Fuller, Grimké was not well educated or well read. She had attempted to make up for the deficiencies in her education by learning some Latin and Greek and reading much of Shakespeare and Byron, but she lacked a broad grounding in philosophy from which to develop her own ideas. Accordingly, much of her feminist thought is an outgrowth of her own experience and that of other women. However, two major strains of thought are apparent in her intellectual environment: the tradition of "Anglo-American radical sectarianism," along with interpretation of Scripture;[17] and other feminist thought.

The tradition of radical sectarianism in America was made up of a variety of strains of thought, three of which were especially important for Grimké: Quakerism, perfectionism, and abolitionism. On her first trip to Philadelphia, Grimké had been impressed with the Society of Friends, to which she eventually returned and joined. After that time she read and reread John Woolman's works, in which she found great insight and inspiration. Indeed, Woolman's journals read much as do Grimké's, with an early period of vanity and frivolity, followed by deep despair and spiritual distress, followed by spiritual enlightenment and comfort.[18] Both she and Woolman found a common source of support and inspiration in Quaker doctrine. She became for a time absorbed in Quakerism, her only source of current information being *The Friend*, a weekly newspaper of the Society of Friends.[19] Grimké was to spend many years with the Society of Friends and the influence on her thought was profound. This is evident, for example, in her denunciation of vanity and concern with appearances, in her principles of nonresistance to violence, and in her emphasis on good acts. Quakerism was perhaps most significant as her first introduction to the more general Puritan idea that each person must read and interpret the Bible for himself or herself and take responsibility for his or her own soul. This idea formed the foundation on which Grimké built much of her early feminism. It impressed on her the notion that God created both men and women as moral beings, responsible for their own actions. Women must be free to discover this moral nature by themselves and be free to act on its incumbent duties as they saw fit.

In her early writings, Grimké implied that one comes to know one's moral duty through an experience akin to the Quaker doctrine of "inner light." By turning inward and opening ourselves to God's light, we will find our way.[20]

In her later writings, Grimké developed a kind of Kantian principle of practical reason.[21] She argued that we know what ought to be intrinsically through our practical reason, and this needs to be brought to coincide with what we know to be desirable through our feelings and emotions.

Finally, Grimké believed in the possibility of knowledge through direct revelation from God. The primary example of this is in the Bible, which she viewed as a testament of written revelation. She also experienced periods of revelation in her own life, which gave her grounds that others have lacked for asserting its potential.

Whereas scriptural knowledge was important to Grimké throughout her feminist thought, it is only in her later writings that she developed a real concern for the type of knowledge that can be achieved through education. She adopted views very similar to those of Wright, stating that knowledge is "the power which has civilized, elevated and dignified humanity,"[22] and that education would lead to freedom of thought, which would in turn engender self-reliance.

In both instances, she viewed knowledge as important to women as a means of self-discovery, of discerning their true nature. The difference is that in her earlier works she felt that nature was defined by God, and in her later works, that it was defined by woman herself. Hence, she relied on two different modes of discovery. She continued to believe in a Creator, but as her thought evolved, she decreasingly felt that God plays a direct role in our lives. She believed that God created us not only as moral creatures, but also as rational creatures. We are endowed with reason, and with this reason we can discover Truth, which provides us with a rule of conduct independent of God's will.[23]

Grimké wrote a small tract in which she outlined the basic principles of her moral theory. She argued that people tend to value most those actions which produce feelings that are pleasant. However, she rejected this utilitarian notion as an adequate basis of moral judgment. Rather, she felt that we should prefer those feelings which arise from actions that are intrinsically valuable. (This intrinsic value presumably is to be determined by our reason, though Grimké failed to clarify this point.) The great question was how to make the intrinsically and the actually preferred coincide. She felt we could come actually to prefer the intrinsically valuable feelings three ways: by the influence of truly virtuous persons—their kindness, justice, and compassion; from ideal creations of the brain; and from ideal representations originating in other minds and discussed in books.[24]

Grimké rejected any utilitarian or positivistic approach to a moral theory. Rather, a moral standard exists that is transcendent to humanity and a priori to humanity's laws. Grimké's ideas of this standard evolved from the divine will of God to a natural law independent of God's will. The important point that undergirds her feminist principles is that this standard is revealed in the Scriptures and is made known to persons through their own individual interpretations and revelations. Her own interpretation of the Bible is her primary source for her feminist principles elucidated in *Letters on the Equality of the Sexes*.

Grimké's abolition work brought her into frequent and close contact with some of the leading abolitionist thinkers—William Lloyd Garrison, Henry C. Wright, Gerritt Smith, and Theodore Weld. Grimké did not consider herself a "Garrisonian." She found the circle of New England nonresistants as constraining as the Quakers. "They wanted us to live out William Lloyd Garrison, not the convictions of our own souls; entirely unaware that they were exhibiting . . . the genuine spirit of slaveholding, by wishing to curtail the sacred privilege of conscience."[25] However, Grimké did tend toward Garrison's brand of radical abolitionism, with its roots in nonresistance and perfectionism.[26]

Like Garrison, Grimké was impressed by John Humphrey Noyes's *The Perfectionist*. She felt that Noyes's views on civil government, public worship, ministry, and the Sabbath were the expression of her own.[27] She found in his work a wonderful release from the *duty* of public worship, as well as sound arguments for opposing civil government. She found the no-government arguments of nonresistance and perfectionism compelling. These argued that civil government is based on physical force, which is forbidden by the Law of Love. If we have no right to resist evil ourselves, then we have no right to call on another to resist it for us. If we have no right to call on a magistrate for aid, then he has no right to render us aid.[28] Grimké increasingly acknowledged God as the only lawgiver and judge. She wrote to Gerritt Smith: "Dear brother, the more I contemplate this sublime doctrine of acknowledging no government but God's, of loosing myself from all dominion of man both civil and ecclesiastical, the more I am persuaded it is the only doctrine that can bring us into the liberty wherewith Christ hath made us free."[29]

In keeping with her Perfectionist tendencies, Grimké believed that God is the one and supreme lawgiver. His Law of Love is the only rule of conduct to which people should submit. Men should not submit to the canons of civil government, and women should not submit to men. All should become as little children and trust in God to show the way.[30]

She was encouraged in this by her friend Henry C. Wright, who advocated the abolition of all governments—civil, ecclesiastical, and familial—so that divine law, interpreted by each for himself or herself, might have free course. He failed, however, to make a convert of her. Grimké was convinced of one great truth—that God is love—but she was troubled that God could issue commandments at one period and then change them. Before she could dedicate herself to no-government doctrine, Mosaic and Christian principles must be reconciled to her.[31]

Theodore Weld tried to discourage Grimké's Perfectionist tendencies, but she privately continued her interest in, if not acceptance of, Perfectionist doctrine, as well as other "forbidden" subjects such as women's rights.[32] The influence of radical abolitionism and Perfectionist thought runs throughout her feminist works, especially in her concern that no man be an intermediate government between woman and God, as well as in her conviction of her right to interpret the Bible for herself.

Grimké's thought evolved away from the Perfectionist stands against government, and she eventually sought full political rights and privileges for women. Hersh argues that the source of this feminist tenet was the Enlightenment ideology of human rights.[33] However, it is important to distinguish the idea of having rights from the governing rules or moral principles that define the substance of those rights.[34] Certainly the rhetoric of rights emerged from the Enlightenment, and Grimké borrowed the idea and terminology, but it is not clear that the rules on which Grimké's concept of rights is based come from the Enlightenment. The source of Grimké's concept of rights is found not in the term *rights*, but in the governing rules and principles. During the period in which she wrote *Letters on the Equality of the Sexes*, her principles were of quite a different source than the Enlightenment. Whereas for the Enlightenment the governing principle of human rights was a natural law discoverable only through our senses and our reason, Grimké's governing principle of human rights was a divine law discernible in the immutable truths of the Bible.

Twenty years later, Grimké came to distinguish from divine will a natural law discernible through reason, which served as the basis of human conduct.

> ... the will of *any being* ought not to be assigned as a rule of conduct for a rational creature. Truth should be the only standard of Right, and Truth stands alone, independent even of the will of Jehovah. . . . God never designed to make his arbitrary will the standard of our actions, he endowed us with reason and in these oracles received as his revelation to man, he says, "come now let us reason together saith the Lord."[35]

Yet even in justifying the use of reason, she relied on revelation. The difference between Grimké's governing principles and those of the Enlightenment is that Grimké's are inextricably bound with the notion of a Creator and must find their ultimate justification not in reasoned principles but in the divine revelation of scripture. The basis for Grimké's concept of human rights remains fundamentally scriptural.

Grimké wrote in the Anglo-American Protestant tradition, a tradition that sought to break with medieval organicism to affirm instead the primacy of the individual[36] and that questioned the authority of anyone to champion his or her interpretation of the Bible and God's will as being "the Truth." According to this tradition, it is "the solemn duty of every individual to search the Scriptures for themselves, with the aid of the Holy Spirit, and not be governed by the views of any man, or set of men."[37] Thus, every individual is responsible for his or her own conduct. An individual cannot blame anyone else for his or her sins, nor can anyone else redeem him or her. Grimké had no notion of society's responsibility to the individual. The individual may owe some responsibility to society, but he or she alone is responsible for himself or herself. Grimké quoted the Bible as her authority for this belief: "None can by any means redeem his brother, or give to God a ransom for him, for the redemption of the soul is precious, and man cannot accomplish it."[38]

Thus Grimké believed that no intermediary between God and the individual should presume to have authority over or take responsibility for individual souls. God is the only authority, and each individual is responsible only to God.[39]

Despite this strong strain of individualism in her thought, Grimké was not advocating an abandonment of societal concerns. Her idea of the individual, contrary to Hobbes's vision of an egoistic, pleasure- and power-hungry beast, was a moral and responsible being, whose individual moral duties included an active concern for the well-being of others. This implies that we must ensure the rights of all to fulfill their duties as moral beings to guarantee that the final authority and responsibility for all individuals comes from the individual.

This theme of the moral autonomy of the individual forms the basis of much of Grimké's feminism. Her feminism is an argument for the equality of women, the freedom of women to develop, and the dignity of women as moral and intelligent beings.

The other major influence in Grimké's intellectual environment was other feminists. It is unlikely that she would have read Frances Wright, since Wright was condemned by the Quaker community of which Grimké was a part at the time; and Grimké did the bulk of her writing before Margaret Fuller had written *Women in the Nineteenth Century*.[40] However, Grimké was involved with the early Female Anti-Slavery Societies, where she came into contact with Lucretia Mott, Lydia Maria Child, Mary Parker, Anna Weston, and others. She later came to know the cousin of her friend Gerritt Smith, Elizabeth Cady Stanton, and they developed a lasting friendship. She frequently corresponded with the British feminist Elizabeth Pease. One of her most significant relationships was with Harriot Kezia Hunt, an active feminist and one of the first women doctors in this country.[41] And of course Grimké derived constant inspiration and support from Angelina. Unlike Wright and Fuller, Grimké was dedicated to the women's movement and, though not always able to participate, had an active exchange with the women involved in that movement. Much more than for Wright or Fuller, the central concern of Grimké's entire life was women and their cause.

In sum, Anglo-American radical sectarianism and other feminists shaped Grimké's feminist thought. The first provided the justification and some direction for her interpretation of Scripture; the second provided the subject around which to focus that interpretation.

Grimké's Feminist Thought

Grimké's feminism is a cry of outrage, a protest against the humiliations, deprivations, and indignities suffered by women at the hands of men. It is a plea for men to "take their feet from off our necks" and for women to stand upright in our full dignity and self-respect. It is a claim for the equality and the autonomy of women as moral agents and creatures of God.

Grimké's feminism is rebellious.[42] She was saying yes and no simultaneously, at once rejecting the oppression of women by men and affirming the dignity of women as moral and responsible beings. The two combined to form a strong argument for women and women's roles and natures to be valued equally with men, and for women to be awarded the same respect, duties, responsibilities, opportunities, and privileges as men, especially in fulfilling their moral duties.

It is difficult to define Grimké's feminism as one particular set of beliefs, for as she grew, so did her feminism evolve. Part of this evolution is from a feminism based on scriptural beliefs to one based more on reason and experience. Perhaps more significantly, it is also in part a movement from resentment to rebellion,[43] from a potentially self-destructive envy of what women do not have to a creative affirmation of who women are.

While the affirmation of the dignity of women as moral and responsible human beings is clear throughout her feminism, her earlier writings are also filled with resentment toward men. Men had what she wanted—education, vocational outlets for their talents and abilities, respect for their intelligence and ambitions, freedom of movement in the world, power. And it was men who denied these to women. Thus her earlier writings are angry and often hostile claims for women to share equally in those powers and privileges of men. At times, Grimké remonstrated herself for her anger toward men.

> Woman must not, cannot rightly, take an antagonistic position to man, they must labor together for the benefit of the race, they are a unit and can only make progress by working harmoniously—she ought to feel, every true woman does feel, in the depths of her being, that to do herself good, she must do good to man. As soon as man sees, that every injury inflicted on woman is inflicted on the race, he will come to her aid nobly, generously.[44]

In her later writings, Grimké is still angry, but this anger takes the form not so much of a resentful envy as of a rebellious affirmation of the dignity of womanhood. As she grew, Grimké came to focus more and more on who women are and of what women are capable, rather than on what women lack and are denied. As her feminism evolved, it became more and more a statement of the strength and beauty and bond of women.

The relationship among liberty, equality, and sorority in Grimké's feminism changes through this evolution. It is valuable to look at each separately, then in relation.

Liberty

Grimké likened women's bondage to that of slaves. Women were constrained physically, mentally, and morally. They were deprived of physical autonomy by continual pregnancy and nursing, and were often subject to physical abuse. (Grimké was particularly sensitive to the physical abuse suffered by black slavewomen.) Denied educational and vocational opportunities, women lost their intellectual freedoms. And treated as dependent children by the laws and the church and by men in general, women were denied their moral autonomy. The freedom Grimké claimed for women entailed all of these elements—physical, mental, and moral.

Grimké knew well that women's basic freedoms must include physical autonomy. Grimké regarded women as victims and slaves of men's passions. She knew full well of the sufferings of women who were forced into motherhood against their will, who were burdened by the cares of multiplying children, or who, unable to care for more, were broken in body and spirit by abortions.[45] She knew also of the physical abuse and battering that often accompanied sexual abuse. She condemned the treatment of women as means to men's ends not only because it deprived them of their status as moral beings, but also because it raised a threat to their physical safety. Regarded as things rather than as persons, women were much more likely to become instruments of man's brutality, and when that man was a woman's husband, she had no protection.

The sad thing, in Grimké's eyes, was that women had been taught to expect such treatment. They had been taught to regard themselves as instruments. They regarded themselves as inferior to men, and this notion was the real cause of their suffering and degradation in marriage.[46]

Grimké explicitly stated the right of women to physical autonomy. She claimed a woman's right to decide when, how often, and under what circumstances she would become a mother. Since the woman had the responsibility of nurturing the child both within her and after it was born, Grimké argued that she ought to have the freedom to control her sexual relations. Too often Grimké found women subject to the lust and licentiousness of men and forced into motherhood. Women must claim autonomy over their own persons, which only an equality in the relations between sexes can assure. Otherwise men, claiming some superior right, will assert themselves on women. "Woman must be conceded an *equality of rights* thro'out the circle of human relations, because she can be emancipated from that worst of all slaveries—slavery to the passions of Man."[47]

From the time Grimké was a child, she was well aware of the obstacles placed in the way of women's intellectual development. Women were denied entrance to institutions of higher learning, and even if they were self-educated, few vocations were open to them to apply that knowledge. Through her life Grimké increasingly stressed freedom of the mind, and to this end advocated equal educational opportunities for women and women's self-reliance and self-discovery. She sought this intellectual freedom so that women might be able to explore and discover their capabilities and to fulfill their potential. She also valued the autonomy that intellectual development enables. It was important to her that women as well as men be able to rely on their own knowledge and resources to think and act in the world and that they be responsible for their own conduct.

This brings me to the essential element in Grimké's concept of freedom—moral autonomy. Grimké stressed the fact that God created man and woman as "free agents."[48] By this she meant that we are endowed with free will—moral choice. Our destinies are not predetermined by God. Although we are aware of what God desires, we are free to choose to follow or not. Our actions follow from our own will, not that of any other being.

While Grimké stressed free will, the central tenet of her notion of moral freedom is that we are morally free when we discover and choose to fulfill the duties that God has assigned to us. God has given us duties as moral and responsible beings, and it is in fulfilling these that we achieve freedom. "Freedom," Grimké wrote to Henry C. Wright, "is the sweet and voluntary subjection of our entire being to God."[49]

The essential problem for women is that even though God had created spheres and duties for women, men and their institutions and laws have prevented women from discovering these duties. Deprived of education and economic resources, women became dependent on men and remained, in a sense, childlike. Male pride kept women from moving into the spheres where they would perform their duties. Men's laws absolved women of their responsibilities as moral agents.

Nothing contributed to this erosion of women's moral autonomy as much as marriage. Ideally, Grimké argued, marriage is the union of two halves in a whole; an internal marriage of souls; a divine ordinance, rather than a civil contract.[50] The purpose of marriage should be to increase the happiness and dignity of the individuals, not to debase them.[51] Yet more often than not, the woman was debased in marriage, and Grimké devoted a great deal of her feminist analysis to an examination of the suffering of women in the marriage relation.

According to Grimké, the problems with marriage start long before a woman marries. They begin the moment a woman regards marriage as not only necessary and the one avenue to distinction, but also as the sine qua non of her existence, the ultimate fulfillment of her being. When a woman defines her future solely in terms of marriage, the chief business of her life becomes attracting men. She focuses on those traits which she thinks men find alluring rather than those which fulfill her as a moral being.[52]

This situation is only aggravated after marriage. In marriage a woman loses her individuality, her independent character, and her responsibility as a moral being. She becomes absorbed into her husband. As Grimké had encountered in her abolitionist petition drives, many women secretly suffered in submission to the opinions and judgments of their husbands. The crime of marriage in Grimké's eyes was that it denied woman's autonomy as a moral and intelligent being accountable only to God, not to her husband.[53]

Grimké singled out two other elements of marriage that support this denial of woman's personhood and moral responsibility: the laws regarding marriage, and the husband's functionalist attitude toward his wife.

Grimké regarded the laws concerning married women an outrage. Like those regarding the slave, they absorbed the woman, her rights and her possessions, into the master. The laws deprived woman of both her financial and moral autonomy.[54]

First, woman lost all rights to property in marriage. All of her personal property and earnings during marriage were her husband's, and he could do with them as he wished—even will them away. Thus wives became dependent on the goodwill of their husbands for their material needs. This financial dependence served only to underscore and guarantee the wife's moral dependence. How could she realistically go against her husband's wishes when he controlled her material well-being?

The laws assured this moral dependence. By the law of coverture, the woman on marriage ceased to exist. All acts performed, all contracts entered into by a woman during marriage were considered null and void. She could not even be found guilty of a criminal offense if she had been commanded to commit it by her husband. She was not regarded as capable of independent thought and action, and was entrusted to her husband as though he were her legal and moral guardian. Indeed, the law gave the husband the right to restrain, judge, and punish the actions of his wife. Women "being made by civil law inferior to their husbands, has a debasing and mischievous effect upon them, teaching them practically the fatal lesson to look unto man for protection and indulgence,"[55] rather than relying on their own consciences. The insidious effect of the marriage laws was to destroy not only woman's autonomy, but also her sense of self-worth.

The destruction of women's autonomy and sense of self-worth was furthered by men's functionalist attitude toward woman in marriage. Men regarded their wives not as moral and intellectual companions, but as instruments for their domestic comfort and physical pleasure. Other feminist writers had mentioned this attitude, but Grimké was one of the first to regard it as a central problem. Woman's inferior status was in large part a result of man's disregard for her as a human being, with all the potential and rights and responsibilities of that humanity.

> [T]hat state which was designed by God to increase the happiness of woman as well as man, often proves the means of lessening her comfort and degrading her into the *mere machine* of another's convenience and pleasure.[56]
>
> O! how many women who have entered the marriage relation in all purity and innocence ... have too soon discovered that they were unpaid housekeepers and nurses, and still worse, chattel persons to be used and abused at the will of a master, and all in a cold manner of course obey.[57]

Yet despite her condemnation of the current marriage relation, Grimké supported the institution of marriage. She did not feel that a woman must marry to fulfill her duties as a woman. However, once a man and a woman had made the commitment, they were honor bound to it. Though well aware of the horrors of a bad marriage, she felt divorce could only be worse.[58] Nor did she condone male/female relationships outside of marriage.[59] In fact, she explicitly denied the accusation that the women's movement would destroy marriage. If a man's independence after marriage does not destroy the marriage, why then should a woman's? Rather, the women's movement would strengthen the marital relations by placing both partners on an equal footing and allowing women to exist as independent moral beings. She did not regard the fault of marriage to lie in the institution itself, but in the individuals. If individuals come to marriage as moral, autonomous beings, marriage serves to increase their happiness and dignity.

The fact that woman is a moral being is at the center of Grimké's notion of the equality, the freedom, the nature, and the destiny of woman. Based on her belief that each individual is ultimately responsible for her or his own soul, Grimké emphatically claimed the moral responsibility of woman for her own actions. "On all moral and religious subjects she is bound to think and act for herself."[60]

In order to do this, women needed to break the bonds placed on them by men. Thus physical and intellectual freedom—the ability of women to control their own bodies and minds—are integral to women's moral freedom. One cannot be claimed without the others. Free to think and to act and to grow, a woman would become "the arbiter of her own destiny."[61]

Equality

Grimké's feminist writings are a thorough cataloguing and condemnation of unequal economic, legal, educational, and political status. Her earliest concerns were for the economic status of women. She was disturbed by the disproportionate value set on time and labor of men and women. Women doing the same work as men were always paid less. But more than this, Grimké was among the first to point out that "woman's work" paid less than "man's work." "In those employments which are peculiar to women, their time is estimated at only half the value of that of men. A woman who goes out to wash, works as hard in proportion as a wood sawyer, or a coal heaver, but she is not generally able to make more than half as much by a day's work."[62] One hundred fifty years ahead of her time, she introduced the notion of "comparable worth" into the arguments about economic equity of the sexes.

Grimké also decried the unequal treatment of women, especially married women, by the law. In marriage, only the woman, not the man, lost her property rights, her rights to make contracts, her very right to be treated as a responsible human being.[63]

Grimké deplored the inequality of women's education. Women, and she among them, were deprived of the kind of education given to their brothers. Women were expected to sacrifice, and did, so that men of the family could go to school. In fact, women spent their time in sewing circles and bazaars raising money for men to go to school.[64]

Though at one time glad that women had not been involved in the immorality of politics,[65] Grimké came to view with indignation a system of government from which women were denied any means of representation or participation, except the paying of taxes. Nothing paralyzes a class more than to be labeled unfit for self-government.[66]

> Since the legislative body is the medium of communication between the government and the various classes of society, it would seem but justice that women who form one half of every class should be participators in it, otherwise the government cannot open a healthy channel of reciprocal intercourse with one half the persons over whom it claims to exercise authority and for whom it enacts laws. Hence it seems self-evident that until women share the burdens and responsibilities of government it never can arrive at that perfection of which it is capable, or maintain an equipoise between the sexes. It is as true of government as of the marriage relation. God designs to unite the sexes. Let us beware how we put them asunder.[67]

Toward the end of her life she developed more of an interest in suffrage. She and Angelina shared the vice presidency of the Massachusetts Woman Suffrage Association from 1870 until their deaths. And in 1870, at the ages of seventy-eight and sixty-five, Sarah and Angelina led forty-two women in a suffrage demonstration, marching through a snowstorm to cast their ballots in an election despite the restrictions against them doing so. Each woman dropped her ballot into a special container that the election officials had prepared, and then all marched back as they had come. While this did not win them the right to vote, it did gain significant amounts of publicity for their cause.

Women were denied equality in every arena, and Grimké declared her condemnation of it.

> It cannot be said that there is more difference in the capabilities of men and women than there is between men and men. Why then impose educational, social, civil, and political disabilities on woman. Education, human rights are hers by the improscriptible decree which created her a moral and intellectual being. To obstruct her highest development, to render it difficult to useless for her to acquire property, to crush her industry, eclipse by stern behest her talents, coerce her activity and energy is to commit an infinite wrong on society.[68]

The recurrent argument in Grimké's feminism is a direct confrontation of this unequal status of women, based on a profound belief in the essential equality of men and women. Much of her thought is dedicated to an examination of the bases, the nature, the methods for achieving remedies, and the justifications of the equality of the sexes.

Grimké did not believe the burden of proof should be on women to demonstrate their equality. She did, however, provide two bases for her assumption of the fundamental equality of the sexes: Scripture and common sense.

Grimké made a vital contribution to feminist thought in taking as the basis for her concept of equality the same document that for hundreds of years had been used to demonstrate the *in*equality of the sexes. She took scriptural verses that had been used against women and provided new interpretations that demonstrated the essential equality of men and women.

According to Grimké, the first account of the creation demonstrates the equality of the sexes in two ways. First, both male and female are created in the image of God. This is clearly stated in Genesis: "So God created man in his own image, in the image of God created he him, male and female created he them." If both are created in the image of God, then there can be no differences between them.

Second, God gave man and woman dominion over all other creatures, but not over each other. Men and women were created in perfect equality, neither one to be subservient to the other.

> Authority unsurped from God, not given.
> He gave him only over beast, flesh, fowl
> Dominion absolute: that right he holds
> By God's donation: but man o'er woman
> He made not Lord, such title to himself
> Reserving, human left from human free.[69]

Grimké provided other scriptural evidence that God granted no supremacy to man. For example, God gave Noah dominion over all the animals, but not over woman. The commandment that "Thou shalt worship the Lord thy God, and *Him only* shalt thou serve" was given the same to man and woman. If God wished woman to be subservient to man, he would have commanded instead, "Man shall have no other gods before ME, and woman shall have no other gods before MAN."[70]

The second account of creation provides a third justification of the equality of man and woman. According to this account, God created woman to be a companion to man. "It was to give him a companion *in all respects* his equal; one who was like himself *a free agent*, gifted with intellect and endowed with immortality; not a partaker merely of his animal gratifications, but able to enter into all his feelings as a moral and responsible being."[71] The only way woman could be a true companion of man in all his endeavors was to be his equal in all respects. *Helpmeet* means a helper like unto himself. Thus it is impossible for woman to fill this station assigned to her by God unless man treats her as an equal moral being.[72] Still, the argument that this second account raises, which Grimké did not address, is that woman was created to be a helpmate *to* man, not *with* man. Nor is there mention of man helping woman. Regardless of the fact that woman is man's moral and intellectual equal, this could lead to the assumption that the primary responsibility for human endeavor on earth lies with man. Indeed, this seems to be Grimké's approach in her earlier writings. Her concept of equality stresses the notion of woman's equality *to* man, and her concept of sex roles stresses woman's helping role as wife and mother.

Perhaps most important, Grimké took the story in the Bible that has been used for centuries to condemn women—Eve eating first of the forbidden fruit, bringing sin and evil into the world—and turned it around. Grimké accepted the fact that Eve had sinned, but she asserted that so did Adam. He, too, ate of the fruit, though both were equally commanded not to. The difference in their sin is that whereas Eve was beguiled through a supernatural agent and thus easily fooled by a satanic influence of which she was ignorant, Adam sinned through the instrumentality of his equal, a free agent, like himself, able to transgress the divine command. If Adam had tried to make Eve repent rather than share in her guilt, we could accord man the moral superiority he claims. But Adam was as weak as Eve; both were equally guilty. "They both fell from innocence, and consequently from happiness, *but not from equality*."[73]

Grimké found evidence of the equality of the sexes in the New Testament as well. Taking the verse, "There is neither Jew nor Greek, there is neither *male* nor *female*; for ye are all one in Jesus Christ," she argued that there are no distinctions among people as Christians. All are equal because they are brought together in a unity. All are one. Moreover, God regards all individuals as souls, and all souls are alike, for all are capable of receiving the influence of the Holy Spirit.[74]

Grimké found the principal scriptural support of the dogma of woman's inferiority in Paul's letters, but she held no particular respect for these. She did not regard them as revealed Scripture. Rather, she felt that Paul wrote his letters under the influence of the Jewish culture's prejudice against women.[75]

Grimké found much more scriptural evidence for the assumption of the equality of the sexes, but her main arguments were these: God created men and women equally in his image; God gave dominion to *both* over other creatures, but not over each other; God created woman as a helpmeet for man, which implies her moral and intellectual equality; Adam sinned equally with Eve; all, including male and female, are one in Christ, and all souls are alike in the eyes of God.

Grimké's main argument was that a scriptural basis could be found for the fundamental equality of men and women. However, the notion of the equality of the sexes also had a basis in plain old common sense. On its very face, she found absurd the idea of the superiority of man to woman. Such a notion would place the most morally depraved man above the highest woman. This just did not make sense. Grimké argued that there are not more differences between men and women than there are between men and men;[76] thus, any policy of discrimination against women had no basis in the logic of common sense.

For Grimké, there was no area of legislation or activity in which the unequal status of women could be viewed as acceptable, because she viewed men and women to be equal in all respects.[77] Women are equal to men not only, as the Quakers believe, on the ground of spiritual gifts, but as she put it, "on the broad ground of *humanity*."[78] Women are equal to men as moral and intellectual beings; they are potentially equal physically; and they are equal in their rights as human beings.

The theme that runs throughout Grimké's work is that men and women are moral equals. Both were created as moral beings by God and both have equal moral duties and responsibilities to fulfill. "Men and women were CREATED EQUAL; they are both moral and accountable beings, and whatever is *right* for man to do, is *right* for woman."[79]

Men and women are also endowed with the same intellectual capabilities. Grimké built her case to prove that "intellect is not sexed"[80] from numerous historical examples of leading and capable women. She provided instances of women rulers, women poets, women priests, women lawyers, women professors, women writers—all of the highest caliber—to show that men are not the sole intellectual power on earth.[81]

While Grimké's primary concern was to demonstrate that God made no distinction between men and women as moral and intelligent beings, because women's physical weakness had been used to justify their exclusion from certain spheres of activity, as well as their general dependence on men, Grimké was also concerned to demonstrate the potential for women's physical equality to men. Though she conceded the actual physical superiority of most men, she provided evidence that women are capable of achieving the physical capabilities of men.[82] She pointed to women who throughout history, and in various cultures, have been regarded as the laboring classes and given the responsibility for such tasks as cultivating the land, reaping and threshing grain, dragging the plows, and carrying water and manure.

Finally, Grimké assumed the equality of the sexes in their human rights and civil rights. Human rights are sacred, inalienable, and God-given.[83] God grants these rights to every human being, without distinction. "Human rights are *not* based upon sex, color, capacity, or condition. They are universal, inalienable and eternal, and none but despots will deny to Woman that supreme sovereignty over her own person and conduct which Law concedes to man."[84] Grimké did not detail what these rights included. Since she felt that our main responsibility is to recognize and fulfill God's design and to act as moral beings, it could be inferred that our rights include everything that is necessary to fulfill that duty—our life and our liberty.

Civil rights are those political, legal, and economic rights which are guaranteed through legislation. Grimké insisted that in establishing civil rights the polity must never violate human rights.[85] Because women and men are equal with respect to their human rights, they must be guaranteed the same in their civil rights. She sought to achieve this equality in civil rights and other areas through laws and legislation and through education.

Grimké argued that equal laws were among the most efficient means of elevating and developing the latent powers of all of humanity.[86] Arguing that it was "laws which blight and stultify their [woman's] being and render them comparatively useless members of Society,"[87] she sought legal reform in the areas of marriage and divorce, inheritance, education, and suffrage, in every area in which law denied women equality.

The other major means of achieving equality was equal education (which implied equal opportunities in adulthood since future prospects affect the effect of education).[88] Grimké argued that education opens up new theaters of action, introduces new trains of thought and reflection. Most important, it gives the mind a just appreciation of itself. When women are given the education they require and deserve, they will be able to unfold their nature and fulfill their potential. Only then can women rise above the world of fashion and drudgery and fulfill their duties equally with men.

> It is because we feel that we have powers which are crushed, responsibilities which we are not permitted to exercise, duties which we are not prepared to fulfill, Rights, vested in us as moral and intellectual beings, which are utterly ignored and trampled upon. Woman had been so long used as a means to an end and that end the comfort and pleasure of man, her intellect has been so little taken into account *when* her value in society has been estimated, she has been for so many ages regarded as the *property* of man that we must not marvel if it is long before she realizes the dignity of her own nature. It is because we feel this so keenly that we now demand an equal education with man, to qualify us to be coworkers with him in the great drama of human life.[89]

Grimké often justified her claim for the equality of women in terms of the benefits that would thereby accrue to men and to society in general. Women would be more valuable to men as their equals than as their inferiors.[90] They could better serve as companions and helpers. They could help support the family and relieve the toil of their husbands. Indeed, the equality of women would benefit all of society. Like Wright, Grimké argued that in proportion as equality prevails, will civilization increase, and in proportion that it does not, so will civilization decay.[91]

However, Grimké's primary justification for equality is in terms of women's own development and fulfillment. Although born free and equal moral agents, women were prevented from discovering and acting on their duties as moral and responsible human beings by their unequal treatment by the laws and institutions of society. Equal education, equal economic and vocational opportunities, equal privileges and responsibilities in the realms of church and state, equal relations within marriage—all are necessary so that each woman may fulfill her potential as a moral human being. Only conscious equality would engender the self-respect necessary to base her life on the grounds of her own being,[92] which brings me to the concept of sorority.

Sorority

Central to Grimké's feminism is her rejection of the notion of the inferiority of women and her affirmation of the dignity of women as moral and responsible beings, as creatures of God, as immortal souls—and as women. She respected women and felt strongly the bond and unity of all women in sisterhood.

In many ways, her affirmations were angry, rebellious protests against the indignities and oppressions women suffered at the hands of men. Grimké definitely viewed men as the oppressors of women. Far more vehement than Wright or Fuller, she argued that man is fundamentally misogynist. "From the days of Eve to the present time," she asserted, "the aim of man has been to crush her [woman]."[93] The first effect of man's fall from grace was the lust of dominion, and woman was the first victim.

> All history attests that man has subjected woman to his will, used her as a means to promote his selfish gratifications, to minister to his sensual pleasures, to be instrumental in promoting his comfort; but never has he desired to elevate her to that rank she was created to fill. He has done all he could to debase and enslave her mind; and now he looks triumphantly on the ruin he has wrought, and says, the being he has thus deeply injured is his inferior.[94]

Grimké argued that man has denied to woman the full growth of her intellectual potential through education. He has subverted her intellect and rights by appealing to her vanity. He has, by means of law and the church, denied her of her autonomy as a moral being. He has prevented her from going forth in the world to fulfill her moral and God-given duties. She scoffed at the idea that all of this was done in the name of protection.

> How has he protected and cherished us? Let her faded youth, her shatter'd constitution, her unharmonious offspring, her withered heart and *his* withered intellect answer these questions.[95]

> Ah! how many of my sex feel in the dominion, thus unrighteously exercised over them, under the gentle appellation of protection, that what they have leaned upon has proved a broken reed at best, and oft a spear.[96]

Grimké regarded men's oppression of women to be universal, knowing no boundaries of race, class, or culture. She wrote at great length of the oppressed condition of women in the United States, Asia, Africa, and Europe. Whether their subjection took the form of Hindustani women being forbidden to read or write, or of Siberian women being forbidden to step across the footprints of men or reindeer, or of American women being forbidden to speak in public, all were manifestations of the same male oppression. Similarly, much of Grimké's abolition work stressed the sexual, physical, and emotional abuse female slaves suffered at the hands of their male masters and called on white women to recognize their sisterhood with black women.[97] And though she felt that any women's revolution would be based in the middle class,[98] her concern extended to the plight of poor and working women. Their sex was especially burdensome to them not only because their low pay and lack of training drove them to starvation and unworthy occupations,[99] but especially because they were more likely to suffer from the brutality of their husbands.[100]

It is this common plight of women that binds them together in a sisterhood. The unity of womanhood, expressed so passionately in Grimké's thought, is primarily the unity of common suffering. Women suffered together in the school of affliction,[101] in the denial of their moral autonomy, and in their degradation and abuse by men. Though Grimké certainly experienced the positive bonding of women with her sister and friends, the emphasis in her earlier writings is on women unified by their oppression rather than by a positive feeling of womanhood. Grimké referred not to "the *bond* of womanhood," an expression of positive unity and solidarity, but to "the *bonds* of womanhood," an expression of their common bondage. We are given the impression of women being bound together with the same rope, rather than bound in a common embrace.

Particularly in her *Letters on the Equality of the Sexes*, Grimké presented conflicting views of the nature of womanhood. She was struggling, torn between the notion that women and men are equal in every respect and the notion that women have a special destiny to fulfill, separate from that of men; between the need boldly to mark out new worlds for women and the need to assure women of their worth as wives and mothers; between her rebellion against her upbringing, which limited woman's sphere to the home, and her very real need to accept that upbringing. The result is that Grimké's ideas about female and male natures and roles vary from no spheres to dual spheres, to a suprasphere, to separate spheres.

Based on the scriptural dictum that there is neither male nor female, but rather all are one in Christ, Grimké felt that all social relations are harmed by viewing men and women primarily with regard to their male/female characteristics. Such distinctions are based solely on physical differences and negate the moral and intellectual worth of human beings. All male/female distinctions are false because all are one in Christ. God does not assign virtues or duties on the basis of sex. Christian principles were laid down without reference to sex or condition. Both man and woman were equally commanded to bring forth love, meekness, and gentleness.[102]

By implication, it would appear that Grimké was rejecting the notion of separate and distinct female and male natures and roles, that is, notions of women as more gentle and nurturing and moral and delicate than men; of women's sphere being the private domain of home and family and men's sphere being the public domain of work and politics. Indeed, Grimké explicitly rejected the pervasive argument of her day that woman's influence should be private and man's public.[103] Women's morality and sphere of action are defined not by their sex, but by God, and they are alike in the public realm as they are in the home. She urged women to go forth in the world not as females but as messengers of God.

Yet, at least in her earlier *Letters*, Grimké backed away from this argument and accepted the traditional view that women would be shamed and tainted by entering the sphere of politics. She was willing to act out her moral duties in every public sphere but this one, which she regarded as immoral and corrupt. "I had rather we should suffer any injustice or oppression, than that my sex should have any voice in the political affairs of the nation."[104]

Presumably she would even forego her moral duties to prevent entering the political arena, which would certainly destroy her as a moral being.

As her feminism evolved, Grimké came to recognize that women should play a role in the political realm. However, rather than breaking the barriers between public and private morality[105] by following the consequences of her thesis that men and women have the same sphere of action as moral beings, she felt that women would bring their private morality to the public sphere, rather than establish a public morality.[106] "The acquaintance which women naturally acquire of the workings of the human heart, of the unfoldings of the passions, of the affectional nature, by *virtue of their office as mothers* renders them peculiarly fit to select those who are to represent and watch over the interests and legislate for a Christian community."[107]

This bifurcation in the sphere of woman is a result of the contradiction between Grimké's notion of no spheres and her concept of dual spheres and dual roles. The result is that she saw male/female roles as two overlapping spheres.[108]

In their public affairs and relations, the functions and roles of women and men are the same. Thus, men and women should receive the same education, have the same job opportunities, and participate equally in the government of their society and in the ministry of God's word. However, in their private affairs and relations, in particular their relations as husbands and wives and mothers and fathers, men and women have separate functions and duties.

> As moral and responsible beings, men and women have the same sphere of action, and the same duties devolve upon both; but no one can doubt that the duties of each vary according to circumstances; that a father and a mother, a husband and a wife, have sacred obligations resting on them, which cannot possibly belong to those who do not sustain these relations. But these duties and responsibilities do not attach to them as men and women, but as parents, husbands, and wives.[109]

But this does not explain the special influence of *all* women, not just married women, on politics. Nor does it explain why Grimké regarded the home as the special province of *woman*, not just wives and mothers, or man.

It does not explain why Grimké did not follow through on her own statement that men, as well as women, had been commanded to bring forth love and gentleness, traits usually associated only with women's private morality. She could have used this to restructure significantly the expectations of men and what has been traditionally defined as their realm of the public. But she failed to do so.

I think a truer conceptualization of Grimké's concept of dual roles is not overlapping spheres, but a suprasphere for women that encompasses all of men's roles as well as sets aside specific functions and roles as the special province of woman.[110] We know this phenomenon today as the "superwoman."

Grimké believed that women should be able to perform all the functions and roles of men, in addition to being solely responsible for all domestic functions. Woman's traditional sphere was confining and women should enlarge their sphere. At the same time, women alone have responsibility for the home. Women's claim to equality could be substantiated only by scrupulous attention to their domestic duties.[111]

This raises a paradox. Grimké claimed that she desired to define woman's sphere on the basis of woman's nature and potential—on her personhood. She wanted to define what woman *is*, not what woman *is for*.[112] Yet in isolating the domestic sphere as "woman's sphere" she was doing what she deplored in men—treating women as domestic instruments, rather than as persons. She regarded her own retirement into domesticity as proof to the world that women can be successful in both their public and private functions. She was in effect arguing that women must first justify themselves (to men) as women, and the functions equated with that, before they can be accepted as human beings. She took upon herself, and upon all women, the burden of two spheres—"let her fulfill in the circle of home all the obligations that rest upon her, but let her not waste her powers on inferior objects when higher and holier responsibilities demand her attention";[113] but she did not ask that men share in the burdens and responsibilities, so neither could they share in the joy.

In some of her later writings, Grimké seemed to be moving away from the idea of overlapping spheres. She became more concerned with relieving women of their domestic duties, and with women defining their own sphere, than wholeheartedly engulfing man's sphere as their own.[114] At the same time she wrote, like Fuller, of the needs of women and men to find masculine and feminine elements in each other, and of the need for the unity of masculine and feminine elements in society.[115] It seems that she was approaching a vision not unlike Margaret Fuller's, in which women and men, having separately defined their natures, would join together in a unity. She had come full circle to a concept of unity. This unity, however, was not the dissolution of masculine and feminine in the unity of Christ, but rather the counterpoint of masculine and feminine in the harmony of the whole.

Such a counterpoint requires a woman-centered definition of femaleness. In Grimké's earlier writings, her notion of womanhood is either male-defined or a reaction to that male definition. Like Wright, her notion of equality was of an equality *to man*, not an equality of men and women together. She knew that women lacked what men had, and she sought to obtain that for women, but she had little idea of what women lacked as women. Similarly, her conception of sex roles is based on a societal definition imposed from without, rather than a woman's definition. Instead of defining woman's identity from an inner notion of the nature of womanhood, Grimké appropriated society's definition of both men's and women's identities to define the nature of womanhood. The very notion of sisterhood within her concept of sorority focuses on women's common oppression *by men*, rather than the common experience and the unity of womanhood.

Yet, in her later years, Grimké more vigorously rejected male-defined notions of femininity and urged women to explore their own natures.

> The debasing and unsatisfying babble of representation through another, of the beauty of feminine delicacy and dependence, has had time to echo and reecho itself . . . she has listened to it, paid homage to it—she is weary of it. She feels its emptiness with reference to that inward life which is not yet extinguished. . . . She can no longer receive the superstitions whose death warrant her reason has signed but she is awakening to higher and clearer ideas of her own nature and capacities and responsibilities.[116]

Grimké had initially appealed to men to lift the burden of oppression from women. "All I ask of our brethren is that they will take their feet from off our necks, and permit us to stand upright on that ground which God has designed us to occupy."[117] She had long believed that women could gain equality through the equal and just legislations of men. But as she grew older, she became more and more disenchanted with the nature and motivations of men, finally coming to believe that because of their different experiences, they were incapable of recognizing and affirming women's place in society. "Man never can legislate justly for women because 'he has never entered the world to which she belongs.' "[118]

Grimké came to believe that women must rely only on themselves for their own education.[119] They cannot expect men to come to their aid. Her new theme became self-reliance. "Woman by surrendering herself to the tutelage of man many in many cases live at her ease, but she will live the life of a slave, by asserting and claiming her natural Rights she assumes the prerogative which every free intelligence ought to assume that she is the arbiter of her own destiny. . . . Self-reliance only can create true and exalted women.[120]

Grimké had hinted at the potential of womanhood, especially in her discussion of freedom, in which she sought the freedom of woman to fulfill God's duty in her as a woman, or to fulfill her potential as a woman. She came to realize that this nature of womanhood was not something that could be defined by man, but only by woman, on her own.

> Thus far woman has struggled through life with bandaged eyes, accepting the dogma of her weakness and inability to take care of herself not only physically but intellectually. She has held out a trembling hand and received gratefully the proffered aid. She has foregone her right to study, to know the laws and purposes of government to which she is subject. But now there is awakened in her a consciousness that she is defrauded of her legitimate Rights and that she never can fulfill her mission until she is placed in that position to which she feels herself called by the divinity within. Hitherto she has surrendered her person and her individuality to man, but she can no longer do this and not feel that she is outraging her nature and her God. There is now predominant in the minds of intelligent women to an extent never known before a struggling after freedom, an intense desire after a higher life. Let us not imagine that because superstition, blind faith in unexamined and untenable dogmas are losing their power over the mind of woman, that her religious nature will be swept away. Far from it. The fact that woman has eaten the bitter fruits of slavery to the will and selfishness and passions of man has prepared her to receive the truth of her own selfhood revealed to her by the spirit of God. Hitherto there has been at the root of her being a darkness, inharmony, bondage and consequently the majesty of her being has been obscured, and the uprising of her nature is but the effort to give to her whole being the opportunity to expand into all its essential nobility.[121]

Conclusion

The concepts of liberty, equality, and sorority push and pull in Grimké's feminism. They are in a living dynamic with one another, especially as her thought changes and develops over time. Occasionally cracks and bulges appear as she stresses one concept to the detriment of another. The contradictions *and* the integrity of liberty, equality, and sorority become apparent.

In one sense, Grimké's concepts of liberty and equality and sorority are very much at odds. She at once sought the equality of women *to* men and the freedom of women *from* men. She sought to define woman's nature and woman's sphere as simultaneously the same as man's and different and unique from man's, thus her development of the notion of woman's suprasphere that did more to impinge on women's freedom than to enable it.

The relationship among liberty, equality, and sorority changes in Grimké's feminism as her concept of sorority evolves. In her earlier writings, she posed the concepts of equality and sorority as mutually exclusive. She viewed equality solely as equality *to* men, of women having all the rights, privileges, opportunities, responsibilities, and duties of men. Her notion of sorority, however, focused on women's unity vis-à-vis men, who denied women equality. In other words, women were united because they were all oppressed by men, united by their inequality to men. This poses problems for Grimké, because it offers two contradictory attitudes of women's view of men: men are everything women would like to become, and men are oppressors of everything women are. More important, however, is the contradictory relation this creates between equality and sorority. By this conception, inequality creates sorority. Thus, sorority would dissolve on the achievement of equality.

In her later writings, Grimké recognized the need to affirm the nature and dignity of womanhood. She came to conceive of sorority not solely as a manifestation of oppression but also as the positive affirmation of womanhood. As she came to see the fallacy of women trying to achieve freedom through the same male system that enslaved them, Grimké redefined that freedom more in terms of a woman's reliance on herself and on other women. Similarly, her concept of equality evolved to encompass not an equality of women to men, but rather the equal affirmations of individuals as unique beings.

Though potentially contradictory, the concepts of liberty, equality, and sorority are also necessarily linked in Grimké's feminism.

Grimké argued that all persons are equal in the sense that all are free, in the sense that all have free will and are autonomous, moral beings. She also argued that women could be free to discover and fulfill God's will as well as to discover and develop a sense of their womanhood, to act in the world only *through* equality. Equal education, equal laws, equal opportunities, and equal affirmation are the bases on which women can achieve freedom.

Liberty and sorority also go hand in hand. In being free to discover their own natures, women would simultaneously discover their womanhood, their qualities held in common with other women. Grimké also felt that a woman's freedom rests on her self-reliance and valuing of her womanhood. Thus, liberty and sorority enable each other.

Finally, sorority and equality complement each other. Equality allows a woman the resources and opportunities in which to explore and determine her own being. Sorority helps to define a womanhood that allows women the opportunity for an equal affirmation with men, rather than a submergence into men's being. Rather than dissolving on the achievement of equality, sorority becomes the true foundation of equality.

Thus it is the counterbalancing of liberty, equality, and sorority that provides the dynamic and the integrity to Grimké's feminism.

FIVE

Margaret Fuller

Margaret Fuller was a woman of intellect and deeply felt emotion, of introspection and social action. Known primarily as a member of the Transcendentalist circle, a critic of art and literature, and a philosopher of feminism, she was also a reformer among the women inmates at Sing Sing and a revolutionary in the political upheavals of Italy of the late 1840s. Margaret Fuller was a visionary. She gave voice to the inner struggles, intelligence, and dignity of women. The seeds of her feminism were sown in her childhood and in her later association with the Transcendentalist circle.

Fuller was the first daughter of Timothy and Margaret Fuller. Her father, a Harvard graduate, was a Jeffersonian Democrat, who served in Congress and in the House of Representatives in Massachusetts, of which he was the speaker in 1825. He was a stern patriarch and Fuller's biographers tend to agree that he dominated the Fuller household.[1]

Fuller had the following memory of her mother:

> She was one of those fair and flower-like natures, which sometimes spring up even beside the most dusty highways of life—a creature not to be shaped into a merely useful instrument, but bound by one law with the blue sky, the dew, and the frolic birds. Of all persons whom I have known, she had in her most of the angelic,—of that spontaneous love for every living thing, for man, and beast, and tree, which restores the golden age.[2]

Fuller's father was the main force shaping her early intellectual life. He put her under a strict regimen of study. He exposed her to classical and modern languages, philosophy, literature, and history, and he deliberately cut her off from the female subculture of etiquette books and sentimental novels.[3] He pushed her hard, too hard in Margaret's view. "The consequence was a premature development of the brain, that made me a 'youthful prodigy' by day, and by night a victim of spectral illusions, nightmares, and somnambulism, which at the time prevented the harmonious development of my bodily powers and checked my growth."[4]

Her father's rules—do not speak unless the meaning is intelligible, do not express a thought unless you can give a reason, do not make a statement unless sure of the particulars—polished her intellect to a glowing shine but neglected the development of her imagination and feelings. Even at a young age she felt that her natural character was being suppressed, and she sought refuge in her mother's garden. "Within the house everything was socially utilitarian; my books told of a proud world, but in another temper were the teachings of my garden. There my thoughts could lie callow in the rest, and only be fed and kept warm, not called to fly or sing before the time."[5]

She emerged well educated from her father's tutelage. Though not allowed admission to the university because of her sex, she was the intellectual equal of her friends and companions in the Harvard class of 1829, among them William Henry Channing and James Freeman Clarke.

In 1833, her family moved from Cambridge to a farm in Groton, Massachusetts, where Margaret spent her days teaching her four younger siblings and writing. After her father died in 1835, she supported the family by teaching in Bronson Alcott's school in Boston and Providence.

It was also during this time (1830-44) that she became a member of the Transcendentalist circle in Concord, participating in a discussion group known as the Transcendentalist Club with Ralph Waldo Emerson, George Ripley, George Putnam, Frederick Henry Hedge, Elizabeth Peabody, and others. She found in Transcendentalism a chance to express and develop her inner nature and to explore the ideas of the soul and her experiences of mysticism. Especially important to her was her relation with Emerson. They challenged each other to develop intellectually and personally, and became close friends.[6] It was also during this time that Fuller discovered Goethe. She spent several years studying his work, and was thought to be the foremost Goethe scholar of her day. From 1840 to 1842 she was editor of *The Dial*, a Transcendentalist literary quarterly.

While still in the Transcendentalist phase of her life, she forayed into feminism. In 1839, she began her series of "Conversations," a lecture series she held for women in an attempt to share her own education with them. Fuller was a sparkling speaker, renowned much more for her Conversations than her written work. Her Conversations attracted women from the most prominent Boston families: Emerson, Peabody, Parker, Lowell, Quincy, Channing, Shaw, Whiting. Her series lasted for five (some say six) years, covering mythology, fine arts, ethics, education, and the influence of women.[7] In 1843 she published her first major essay on women, "The Great Lawsuit. Man v. Men,

Woman v. Women," which she two years later expanded for her book *Woman in the Nineteenth Century*.

In 1844, Fuller took a trip west that greatly influenced her life.[8] Away from the confines of Concord, she gained a new perspective on the world. She witnessed firsthand the opening of the West, including its consequences for the abuse of Native Americans and the sufferings of pioneer women. She became increasingly aware that the preeminence of America was based on the exploitation of various classes of people—blacks, immigrants, women, Native Americans. This awareness was deepened by her exposure to the poor and immigrants in New York City, during her years there as the literary critic for the *New York Daily Tribune*. She took on the role of a muckraking journalist, with special concern for oppressed women, especially prostitutes and female inmates in Sing Sing.

In 1846, she traveled to Europe, where she befriended Richard Carlyle, George Sand, Adam Mickiewicz, and Giuseppe Mazzini. This last friendship was especially important as it intimately involved her in the Italian Revolution of 1848-49. In that revolution she cast her allegiance, principles, and fate to the democratic partisans, actively working, mostly as a nurse, for their cause. Her letters to the *Tribune* at this time are some of the most vibrant she wrote.[9] It seemed that she had truly found her cause and her role in it. Had the revolution succeeded, she might have been an important part of the Italian republic. In Italy, her incipient socialism, woven throughout *Woman in the Nineteenth Century*, and her radical democratism found expression in action.

In Italy Fuller met and married Angelo Ossoli, and they had a son.[10] Though caught in the turmoil of the revolution, her experience of marriage and motherhood was filled with contentment and tenderness. She felt fulfilled in her relation with her son and was devoted to him. In one of her last letters to her brother Richard she wrote, "I feel impelled to try for good for the sake of my child."[11]

In a letter to Elias Hicks in 1848, prior to her involvement in the revolution, Fuller had expressed her willingness to die. "I have wished to be natural and true, but the world was not in harmony with me—nothing came right for me. I think the spirit that governs the universe must have in reserve for me a sphere where I can develop more fully, and be happier."[12] But two years later she appeared to have found her sphere. She had finally come into her own. In giving birth to herself in the revolution and in giving birth and care to her son, she seemed to have found the self she had been seeking. But just as the promise was being fulfilled, it was lost. Fuller drowned with her son and husband in a shipwreck within sight of Fire Island, New York, on July 19, 1850, at the age of forty.

Unlike most women of her time, Margaret Fuller was the intimate associate and valued colleague of men. She was also the close friend of and passionate advocate for women. She struggled with that masculine/feminine dialectic all of her life. The androgyny that surfaced in her feminism is an androgyny she played out in her own life. Fuller could not grasp her identity, but she found within herself both masculine and feminine. The problem tortured her, but it also led her to develop within her feminism the creative idea that there is not a pure masculine or pure feminine, but a blending of the two in every individual.

Margaret Fuller's feminism was to a large extent an outgrowth of her personal experience. Her father educated and treated her like a son, so that when she grew older she also outgrew her "woman's sphere." She could not become the person she had been trained to become. Among her Transcendentalist friends she was accepted as an equal intellect, and she found solace throughout her life in strong, close relationships with women. She was personally surrounded by the sorority she was later to express so eloquently. Most important, her feminism was an expression of her inner longing and desires, of her truths.

Intellectual Environment

To discuss the influences of Margaret Fuller's thought is akin to discussing the contents of the card catalog of a good library. Fuller was known to be not only the most well-read woman, but also the most well-read person of her day. Besides being extremely well read in philosophy, literature, and history, she was also literary critic for the *New York Daily Tribune* for years and was considered the leading scholar of German literature in the country. Her scholarship ranged from Confucius to Kant, Lammenais to Locke, Plato to Perfectionism. In addition to her scholarship, Fuller was intimately associated with some of the leading thinkers, writers, and activists of her day. Whole volumes have been written on the influence of these on Fuller's life and thought.[13]

It is generally acknowledged that Fuller was a Romantic philosopher.[14] Beyond that there is widespread disagreement. Most analysts of Fuller's thought distill one or both of two major influences: Transcendentalism and

German idealism, which are farther distilled to two persons, Emerson and Goethe. Some argue that Transcendentalism, especially Emerson, was the most influential factor in Fuller's thought; others that German idealism, especially Goethe, was most influential; others that Fuller's thought borrowed from both Transcendentalism and German idealism, and still others that Fuller brought Goethe's influence to Transcendentalism.[15] I argue that Fuller blended and interpreted, as well as influenced, a wide variety of thought, and was not merely "the Transcendentalist most concerned with women."[16]

Another of Fuller's reviewers brings a wise perspective to his study. Frederick Braun stated that, "The most beneficent influence that any great poet or thinker can exercise on us, is not to cause us to follow vassal-like in his train, but to stimulate, to inspire in us great and noble thoughts, to call out all the latent energies and powers of the soul, and to develop them to a greater degree of perfection and independence. This is chiefly what Goethe did for Margaret Fuller."[17] This can be fairly said for all the various influences on Fuller. She adopted, discarded, and interpreted philosophies as they inspired or enhanced her own thought, rather than simply choosing a Transcendental or Goethean mold and fitting into it.

Of those philosophies that did stimulate Fuller's feminist thought, four are particularly important. Fuller was first and foremost a Romantic. Her favorite philosophers, writers, composers, poets, and friends were all Romantics. Her Romanticism drew primarily from German idealism (especially Goethe) and Transcendentalism (especially Emerson), though she had a great fondness for British Romantic poets as well. Another important, though often disregarded, influence on Fuller was utopian socialism. She was well acquainted with Alcott's utopian experiment at Brook Farm and just before her death expressed interest in the North American Phalanx at Red Bank, New Jersey. She was particularly interested in the thought of Fourier. Also, Fuller read much of the early feminist literature and was acquainted with some of the leading feminists of the day. She did not adopt their specific arguments, but she was inspired by their words and deeds. Finally, Fuller was subtly yet profoundly influenced by Jefferson. Many agree that much of Fuller's social thought is grounded in Jeffersonian values.[18] There are several other scattered influences on Fuller's thought, such as Unitarianism, Quakerism, and the Republicanism of both Mickiewicz and Mazzini,[19] but Romanticism—with its component Transcendentalism and German idealism, utopian socialism, early feminist thought—and Jefferson were the most important.

Before exploring these elements of Fuller's intellectual environment, it might be helpful to examine those philosophies which Fuller did not find inspirational, specifically Enlightenment and utilitarian thought. Fuller certainly had a good understanding of Enlightenment thought, having read Locke, Berkeley, and others; and she appreciated and admired certain Enlightenment thinkers, such as Jefferson, Godwin, Wollstonecraft, and Rousseau. However, she was not, as Rossi has characterized her, an Enlightenment theorist.[20] She rejected the basic premises of the Enlightenment—mind-body dichotomy, empiricism, individualism, the preeminence of reason. These doctrines failed to explain her experience.[21] If the Enlightenment was predominantly the Age of Reason, then Fuller, who thought reason was an "inferior faculty which the Deity gave for practical, temporal purposes only,"[22] was hardly a part of it. Her rejection of the utilitarian strand of the Enlightenment was even more explicit. On several occasions she expressed her disdain of utilitarian thought, finding the notion of the greatest happiness for the greatest number especially crude.[23]

In rejecting the Enlightenment, Fuller found kinship in the major nineteenth-century challenge to the Enlightenment, Romanticism. Fuller's basic philosophical assumptions were Romantic.[24] She regarded the fundamental striving of humanity to be for harmony, of both the individual and the universe, and viewed the soul as the main vehicle to that end. Fuller did not accept the mind-body dichotomy of the Enlightenment.[25] She viewed the individual as an organic whole, in which intellect, body, passions, emotions, and spirituality all define the human character. She felt we must affirm our experiences both of life and activity and of intellect and spirituality. She argued, "Man is a being of two-fold relations, to nature beneath, and intelligences above him."[26] The important thing is that every aspect of the individual be developed for the individual to grow as a whole. One capacity should not be developed at the expense of another, for physical desires unchecked by reason, and intellect uninformed by emotion, are equally impediments to the realization of one's true nature.

> Whenever man remains imbedded in nature, whether from sensuality or because he is not yet awakened to consciousness, the purpose of the whole remains unfulfilled, hence our displeasure when man is not in a sense *above* nature. Yet when he is bound so closely with all other manifestations, as duly to express their spirit, we are also displeased. He must be at once the highest form of nature and conscious of the meaning she has been striving successively to unfold through those below him.[27]

The intellect and the passions, the spirit and the body, should balance each other harmoniously. "Sight gives experience of outward faith, faith of inward. We then discern, however faintly, the necessary harmony of the two lives."[28]

Fuller sought first the harmony within each individual of all his or her various capacities and development of the whole human character, but all individuals also extend beyond themselves into a more universal harmony. All individuals are organic and grow according to their own laws, but they also seek and fulfill greater laws of the universe.

Fuller agreed with the Romantic conception of divine harmony or all-encompassing unity. For her, the fundamental character of human nature is that each individual wishes to embrace "the whole" in which all lives are linked and all destinies are unfolded.[29] She viewed "the whole" as an uncontainable spirit in which we discover total comprehension and unity. Fuller defined this harmony lyrically: "When we feel ourselves the microcosm, the whole is known. This is the true music which binds necessarily spheres together. Man should be the key-note to the universal harmony."[30]

The only comparable idea with which most people are familiar is that of God. Indeed, Fuller spoke of the All as God, but by this she did not intend the traditional Christian interpretation of a being who separates himself from and transcends all human experience and knowledge, but rather a Beauty and Perfection that is manifested in all creation.[31] Fuller believed that this idea of God was manifested in Jesus Christ, but so was it manifested in the laws of Confucius and Moses, in the ideals of the Brahma, in the eloquence of Apollo. Fuller reverenced all religions, and felt that multiple faiths were various approaches to and expressions of God.[32] She believed in Christ not because he was some ultimate fulfillment of the grand design, but "because I can do without him: because the truth he announces I see elsewhere intimated; because it is foreshadowed in the very nature of my being." She reverenced all things and beings that helped her develop in harmony with the All. It made no difference to her whether Christ had actually spoken the words and performed the deeds attributed to him. Had they been presented to her as a poem, the ideal truths they offered would have been as real. While the spirit of Christ kindled her faith and attested to the justice of her desires, so did "Apollo, and the beautiful infant, and the summer's earliest ease. It is only one modification of the same harmony . . . it is a part of the All."[33]

Fuller was a mystic, believing in clairvoyance and reincarnation and "miracles." She did not feel the need, as she believed most people did, for an outward church which, she felt, tended to limit the inner. She had her own individual worship and church.

> Let others choose their way, I feel that mine is to keep my equipoise as steadfastly as I may, to see, to think, a faithful skeptic, to reject nothing but accept nothing till it is affirmed in the due order of mine own nature. I belong nowhere. I have pledged myself to nothing. God and the soul and nature are all my creed, subdivisions are unimportant.—As to your Church, I do not deny the Church. . . . I have my church where I take these simpler modes, if the world prefers more complex, let it. I act for myself, but prescribe for none other.[34]

The primary vehicle of both individual and universal harmony for Fuller is the soul, a central idea in her feminism. The soul, like harmony, exists on two levels simultaneously—that of the individual and that of the universe. On the individual level, the soul is neither animal nor intellect, but a separate essence of the individual. On the universal level, the soul is synonymous with the All. In referring to the soul, Fuller meant both the individual soul and the universal soul, both separate and yet both one. Our soul is both the primary expression of our individual personhood and the immortal link with universal harmony. Thus we can see how Fuller used her notion of the soul to underlie not only her ideas of individual development and freedom, but also equality and the organic society.

In both senses, the soul is dynamic, continually growing and manifesting itself in new ways. "The next step in the soul's upward course shall interpret man to the universe as he now interprets those forms beneath himself; for there is ever evolving a consciousness of consciousness, and a soul of the soul. To know is to bring to light somewhat yet to be known. And as we elucidate the previous workings of spirit, we ourselves become a new material for its development."[35]

The primary characteristic of human nature is thus to grow and to develop. It is never satisfied with its current level of development, but is always seeking higher expressions of its essential nature. This theme forms the basis of Fuller's feminism.

Fuller accepted reason only as a limited tool of discovery. She believed, rather, that true knowledge came from the intuitive and personal knowledge of self-discovery and the discovery of nature. She believed that each individual in his or her own process of self-development and becoming unfolded an inherent social harmony. Her feminism relied to a great extent on this notion of self-development. Susan Conrad has concluded that, "Feminism was accordingly a romantic imperative: for Margaret Fuller feminism *was* romanticism—and vice versa."[36] Her Romanticism was shaped by both Transcendentalism and German idealism.

Margaret Fuller is most widely known as a member of the literary, social, and intellectual circle of the Transcendentalists and as editor of their relatively short-lived journal, *The Dial*. She had a long and close association with many in the Transcendentalist "club," and in their frequent exchange of ideas it was inevitable that she should come to share some of their thoughts and they some of hers. This was especially true of her close friendship with Emerson, who came closest for a time to being a sort of mentor to her, though she always maintained her independence. She was at the height of involvement with the Transcendentalists when she wrote "The Great Lawsuit," and the Transcendentalists' influence on that work is apparent.[37] Her notions of the dynamic soul as part of one universal soul, of the importance of acquiring knowledge through intuition, and of the need of woman to grow as a nature and develop as a soul are all reminiscent of Emerson and Transcendentalism in general. But as strong as these similarities are, Fuller differed from Emerson and Transcendentalism in several important ways.

Perhaps the best overall view of the differences between Emerson and Fuller is that whereas Emerson sought permanence and beauty in the Ideal, Fuller sought beauty and happiness on earth among persons and created works.[38] She was probably referring to Emerson when she said:

> What is done interests me more than what is thought and supposed. Every fact is impure, but every fact contains in it the juices of life. . . .
> Climb you the snowy peaks when come the streams, where the atmosphere is rare, where you can see the sky nearer, from which you can get a commanding view of the landscape? I see great disadvantages as well as advantages in this dignified position. I had rather walk myself through all kinds of places, even at the risk of being robbed in the forest.[39]

Or, as she later states, "Waldo must not shake me in my worldliness."[40]

Fuller differed essentially from Transcendentalism as to the nature and role of our physical existence.[41] Transcendentalism regarded humanity's physical nature as the seat of original sin and thus rejected it. Fuller, on the other hand, was trying to develop a philosophy of the whole person, of which the physical was a very real part. "I agree with those who think that no true philosophy will try to ignore or *annihilate* the material part of man, but will rather *seek to put it in its place*, as a servant and minister to the soul."[42]

Both Fuller and Emerson sought the same end of divine harmony and pervading unity, but in different ways. Emerson was a "Puritan spiritualist" and Fuller a student of "broad humanity."[43] A participant at one of Fuller's Conversations observed:

> Mr. E. served only to display her [Fuller's] power. With his sturdy reiteration of his *uncompromising idealism*, his absolute denial of the fact of human nature, he gave her opportunity and excitement to unfold and illustrate her *realism* and acceptance of conditions. . . . She proceeds in her search after the unity of things, the divine harmony, *not by exclusion*, as Mr. E. does, *but by comprehension*,—and so, no poorest, saddest spirit, but she will lead to hope and faith.[44]

This later found expression in including her real concerns for the lives of pioneer women, prostitutes, women in prison, poor and working-class women in her otherwise often introspective feminism.[45]

Recognizing her differences with Emerson, Fuller wrote: "We agreed that my God was love, his [Emerson's] truth."[46] Fuller sympathized with the Transcendentalist strivings for a freer and nobler humanity, but she differed with them on some fundamental philosophical beliefs and methods. Unlike the Transcendentalists, who believed the highest laws for individual growth were determined by a principle or law imposed from outside our being, Fuller believed we must discover these higher laws in the determinations of our inner heart and self.[47]

Fuller found in Goethe the appreciation of social and physical reality that Emerson lacked. Fuller's first acquaintance with German philosophy and literature came through her friend James Freeman Clarke, who was a student of Charles Follen, the first instructor in German at Harvard.[48] Fuller and Clarke met every day for over a year to read and discuss German literature. Her appetite was voracious, and during a period of one to two years she had enthusiastically devoured Tieck, Korner, Novalis, Richter, Schiller, Kant, Lessing, Fichte, Jacobi, and nearly all fifty-five volumes of Goethe's works.[49]

Goethe was Fuller's "sunny morning or rosy afternoon reading."[50] In him she found communion of thought and feelings. Over and over again in her writings she referred to her love of Goethe: "He comprehends every feeling I have ever had so perfectly, expresses it so beautifully."[51] But by her own admission, Fuller was not a blind admirer of Goethe.[52] She was disturbed by his character, his aversion to pain and isolation of heart, his conservative and aristocratic politics, his lack of heroism. But she did appreciate Goethe's sensitivity to spiritual beauty, his appreciation of what is rather than what might be, his fine observation of human nature, his lyrical command of the German language, his ability to bring his life into harmony with his thought, and his willingness to let her disagree with him. She most admired Goethe's reconciliation of individual character with universality of thought, a problem that is central in Fuller's feminism.

The influence of Goethe on Fuller was greater in her religious doctrines. Here the distinction with Transcendentalism is clear. Whereas the Transcendentalists thought that a person's aim was to live a religious life, Fuller, like Goethe, felt the aim was purity and harmony of character, to develop our being to the highest possible expression. Her emphasis on life and activity is quite Goethean, as are her conceptions of the phenomenon of all-encompassing unity. She also shared with Goethe an interest in mysticism and the occult.[53]

The most prevalent view of Goethe's influence on Fuller is that Goethe liberated her from the stifling restrictions of New England morality and prescriptions of femininity.[54]

> Goethe was the great liberator for Margaret Fuller. Through him she formed and remained true to the humanist ideals at the heart of her endeavors: her literary criticism and social thought, her personal relationships, her philanthropy and political activity. Through Goethe, her individuality came to light, and she discovered who she was and what she might become. From Goethe came the sustaining vision toward which her thought and life unfolded.[55]

In Goethe, Fuller found support for her appreciation of the whole human being, for the development of the truly human through experience in life rather than solely through the elevation of thoughts into the higher realm. She found common expression for her value of human life and experience.[56]

Fuller also found in Goethe an appreciation of women. His variety of roles and characters showed a clear understanding of their potential. Fuller appreciated this and was indebted to him for his role in developing a positive vision of female experience.[57]

Fuller regarded Goethe as one of three male writers (the two others are Swedenborg and Fourier) who had done much to elevate the status of women. She felt that Goethe had three aims in his expression of woman. First, woman should seek pure self-subsistence and full development of her powers. Second, he regarded women as souls. Thus, any meeting between women and men is equal and noble. Finally, a world of natural harmony within each and among all women and men arises when Truth and Love are sought in the light of Freedom.[58] We see many of these same aims in Fuller's feminism.

Fuller found in Goethe a common soul, who helped her to shape a philosophy independent of her Puritan upbringing and supported her need to develop as a whole human being. Yet despite the fact that Fuller and Goethe shared some basic philosophical assumptions, politically Goethe was conservative and Fuller was revolutionary. She found greater inspiration and support for her political and social concerns in socialism.

Fuller's active interest in socialism emerged strongly in the years after she wrote her major feminist work, *Woman in the Nineteenth Century*. While in Europe she followed the progress of Fourierism and other socialist movements, writing home of her increasing interest in socialism.[59] Just before her return home, she reported in a letter to Marcus and Rebecca Spring that she had become an "enthusiastic Socialist" and expressed a real interest in the North American Phalanx at Red Bank, New Jersey, which she might have joined had she lived.[60]

Yet this was just the culmination of a commitment to socialist ideals that had been developing all of her life. In her early studies she had taken an interest in Sismondi and Saint-Simon.[61] In the memoirs of Fuller written by her friends, Emerson acknowledged that Fuller was very attracted to French socialism, especially its attitude toward women.[62] The most important of the French socialists for Fuller's thought was Fourier.

Fuller probably encountered Fourierism in practice at the utopian community of Brook Farm, which was remodeled as a Fourier phalanx in 1844 and which she visited frequently. She at first found the place desolate, but soon delighted in the freedom. She agreed with the division of labor, but did not believe in the utopian hopes of excluding evil. Though finding herself conservative in comparison, she admired the pervading spirit of mutual tolerance and gentleness and the great development of mind and character.[63]

Fuller had studied Fourier in her youth and admired his purposes. She felt some of his methods were incorrect, particularly making the soul the result of a healthy body rather than the body the clothing of the soul, but generally she respected his love of humanity.[64] She was especially impressed by his views of women. He sought to place women on equal footing with men, giving both independence, and he sought to give women the means for self-help, so that they could dignify and unfold their lives for the happiness of themselves and society. Though Fuller found Fourier's views of women and society somewhat superficial because of his emphasis on outward rather than inward needs, she still regarded them as significant.

Fuller viewed Fourier as a complement to Goethe, Fourier choosing the path of changing institutions to change individuals; Goethe of promoting individual growth, with society to follow. Both ways were legitimate and should be tried.

Some analysts of Margaret Fuller have argued that Fourier did not play a significant role in her thought.[65] Others have labeled her a Fourierist.[66] I think it is more appropriate to say that Fuller had Fourieristic sympathies that grew stronger as the years passed.[67] The most important aspect of Fuller's interest in socialism is that it provided a philosophical basis for her political and social concerns, which she had not found in either German idealism or Transcendentalism. As her feminism developed, she was increasingly concerned with the social problems of women, as well as their need for self-fulfillment. In her practical concerns for the status of women, Fuller increasingly emphasized socialist solutions.

Fuller could not, and did not, rely on Emerson, Goethe, or Fourier for the core of her feminism. For this she had to draw on her own experience and that of other women. She drew much of her inspiration for this from the lives and works of feminists who came before her. She had read de Staël early in her study of German and found her "brilliant." She was a friend of Lydia Maria Child and was acquainted with the British feminist and sociologist, Harriet Martineau.[68] She was familiar with several other feminist writers—Charles Brockden Brown, Mme. Roland, William Godwin, Mary Wollstonecraft, Maria Edgeworth, Anna Brownell Jameson, and Catherine Maria Sedgwick. She considered the last three particularly helpful.[69]

Of all the feminist writers, however, her greatest inspiration was George Sand, whom she admired in her youth and came to know later in life. On meeting Sand, Fuller wrote: "It made me very happy to see such a woman, so large and so developed a character, and everything that *is* good in it so *really* good. I loved, shall always love her."[70] She felt that Sand was a person of strong passions, but with nobleness and love of right sufficient to guide them to the service of worthy aims. She protested, examined, assailed, cut to the very root of things to find reality. She was a genius—free, bold, and pure from suspicion of error.[71]

However amazed Fuller was with Sand's insight into the life of thought, she recognized Sand's limitations. Sand had had no better luck in solving the enigmas of free will, the problem of reconciling the life of the heart with that of the intellect, or of the Spirit with the world, than she had. Nor had she solved that most fundamental of problems for Fuller's feminism, the androgynous balance of male and female. "She [Sand] has genius, and a manly grasp of mind, but not a manly heart! Will there never be a being to combine a man's mind and woman's heart, and who yet finds life too rich to weep over? Never?"[72]

Of all the women who touched Fuller, probably none inspired her more than those who touched her with their lives. In a consideration of the influences on her feminist thought, it is important to remember the many women whom she encountered in her Conversations, her travels to the Great Lakes, her visits to Sing Sing, and in the streets of Boston and New York. These, above all, taught her the meaning of a key concept in her feminism—sorority.

The effect of Jefferson on Fuller's thought was not as pronounced and pervasive as some of the others, yet he was significant in shaping the premises of her political beliefs and in reconciling these with her feminism. She had read all of Jefferson's papers in her youth and was charmed with his mental activity, spirit of philosophical inquiry, freedom, and firmness in thought and action.[73] Perhaps most important, Jeffersonian values of republicanism shaped her political consciousness at an early age; they came to fruition in days of revolutionary struggle and political activism in Europe.[74]

Significantly, Jefferson helped Fuller to distinguish political activity that was consistent with her ideals and the dignity of the collectivity from the game of local politics.[75] This was especially important in reconciling her feminist vision of society as cooperative, tolerant, and gentle with political reality. "He [Jefferson] has given me a higher idea of what a genuine citizen of this republic may become. He may become a *genuine man*. He need not stoop to be a demagogue, he need not swagger his Demosthenian thunders on every petty local question, he need not be a narrow-minded braggart, he need not despise, he ought not to disregard general literature, nor elegant pursuits."[76] In other words, a feminist might engage in political activity without renouncing his or her dearest values. It was in such committed political action that Fuller finally felt at home.

It is hard to do justice to the breadth and depth of Fuller's background. Her intellectual environment was not the sum of these four elements. She could just as easily theorize on an aspect of Xenophon's dialogues of Socrates or wax poetic on a movement of a Beethoven sonata. The point is that her philosophy cannot be attributed directly to Transcendentalism, or Goethe, or Emerson.

She was an independent and multifaceted individual, and all of these shaped and inspired her thought, just as her own thought brought to these philosophies a unique character.

Fuller's Feminist Thought

In a paradoxical way, Margaret Fuller's feminism holds in tension a clear affirmation of the beauty and uniqueness of woman's nature and a vision of humanity as androgynous. Fuller played out the theme of androgyny both in her own sense of self as being intuitive, emotional, loving, *and* intellectual and ambitious and in her writings about male and female being sides of the great radical dualism. She is perhaps best known among feminists as one of the earliest exponents of androgyny. Hers is also an early voice of a radical woman-centered vision. Her poetic affirmation of woman as self-centered, self-defined, open to her own truths and the beauties of her soul foreshadow the writings of Mary Daly, Susan Griffin, Adrienne Rich, Audre Lorde, and others. Fuller's feminism is an expression of the freedom of women to grow and to become truly themselves and for all of humanity to develop as the potentiality of androgyny becomes reality.

Fuller's feminism also balances the concepts of liberty, equality, and sorority. Her main theme is the freedom of women to grow and become, and this is developed at once in women's discovery and celebration of womanhood—sorority—and in women's affirmation of their androgyny—equality.

Liberty

In writing of liberty, Fuller distinguished between inward and outward freedom. She defined outward or external liberty as "independence from the encroachments of other men."[77] This required such political guarantees for both men and women as elective franchise, tenure of property, and freedom of speech and the press, and provided the means for each individual to act out the dictates of his or her own conscience in accordance with the higher spiritual law.

However, "Political [external] freedom does not necessarily produce liberality of mind."[78] Inward liberty, liberty of the mind, the spirit, and the soul, was by far more important than outward liberty and is the central focus of Fuller's work. However, perfect freedom was not merely purified intelligence.[79] Fuller sought inward freedom for the whole person, the essence of which is freedom of the soul to grow and develop. "Give the soul free course, let the organization, both of body and mind, be fully developed, and the being will be fit for any and every relation to which it may be called."[80]

Fuller's concept of inner freedom bears a resemblance to more recent notions of identity, as well as to the ancient maxim to "know thyself." She argued that persons achieve freedom of the full development of their selves through first coming to know who that self is. We must listen to the voices of our souls, become attuned to them. When we understand who we are, as dictated to us only by our own inner being, then we are able to attain freedom by becoming more ourselves.[81] By becoming more ourselves, we free the essence of our being—the soul.

Fuller did recognize the connection between internal and external liberty, that certain external liberties are requisite to internal liberty. Although her main concern was the securing of inward freedom, she did speak of the extension of the political liberties of the vote and property rights to women. However, the main external obstacles to women's freedom were the details of running a household and raising children and their acceptance of society's norms of feminine behavior. It was the burden of domesticity and the constraints of social propriety that enslaved women, that kept them from realizing their full potential. She feared that many women were cut off from the possibility of self-development by the narrow confines of the home and incessant drudgery of housework. While Fuller respected those who enjoyed the tasks of running a home and did it well, she argued that these "functions" should not be a drudgery, but rather an ordinary part of life.[82] Comparing the lives of women on the American frontier, whose lives were comfortless and laborious, to those of women in Paris, whose time was freed for more uplifting pursuits by such arrangements as common laundries and day care centers, Fuller much preferred the latter.[83] She also felt that such household duties should not fall exclusively to women. Unlike Grimké, Fuller rejected women's domestic role along with the other sex-role stereotypes.[84]

Fuller contended that all opportunities should be open for women, not as ends in themselves, but as means for women to pursue their own natures. Women must be free to develop as whole beings, without society circumscribing the nature and scope of that being. She sought for women especially the freedom of the soul—freedom not to do what men do, or to act like men, or to think like men, but to develop their own nature as women, as souls.

> We would have every arbitrary barrier thrown down. We would have every path laid open to woman as freely as to man. Were this done and a slight temporary fermentation allowed to subside, we should see crystallizations more pure and of more various beauty. . . . What woman needs is not as a woman to act or rule, but as a nature to grow, as an intellect to discern, as a soul to live freely and unimpeded, to unfold such powers as were given her when we left our common home.[85]

All of the rest of Fuller's feminism draws on this central notion of the freedom of woman to grow and develop according to her own nature.

Equality

Fuller was not the champion of "equal rights" for women that Wright and Grimké were. She did not make sweeping arguments for the equality of humanity. She did not provide justifications for equal treatment, or detailed plans for achieving equality in practice. Her feminism focused on the uniqueness of women rather than on the equality of women and men. She did not seek to have women abandon their feminine characteristics to take on masculine ones, because she valued those feminine qualities in their own right.

Though she did believe women may be different from men, this is not to say that Fuller believed that women were either inferior or superior to men. Women and men were equal with respect to both their intellectual and physical capabilities. If women have been prevented from thinking deeply, it is not because of an inferior intellect, but because of their position and their duties. What person could study and reflect on her thoughts when plagued by inadequate training, household drudgery, and frequent pregnancies? Women have intellects equal to those of men and they should be equally cultivated.

Though Fuller occasionally referred to women as "the weaker sex," she forcefully argued against the assertion that women may be excluded from full participation in society because of their alleged weakness. "Those who think the physical circumstances of woman would make a part of the affairs of national government unsuitable, are by no means those who think it impossible for the negress to endure field work, even during pregnancy, or the sempstresses to go through their killing labors."[86]

Fuller was also concerned with the way the equality or inequality of women and men affects the quality of the relationships between them. She discussed this primarily in the context of marriage. Though having high ideals as to what an equal marriage could be, Fuller deplored the contemporary state of unequal marriage. She found fault with the form of marriage as it existed for four reasons: women married for the wrong reasons; women became their husbands' property; women were abused by their husbands; and women lost themselves in the sphere of domesticity.

First, Fuller felt people should marry out of mutual love, based on her Romantic notion of two halves finding in each other the elements of a whole. However, such marriages were rare. Women frequently married solely to achieve the wealth and status through a man that they could not achieve on their own. Others were nothing but heart, and married to have anybody devoted to them.[87] As long as marriage was structured as it was, women would for the most part not come to it seeking an equal partnership, let alone a spiritual union.

Second, Fuller felt that marriage, of all relations between the sexes, was harmed by the fact that the woman belonged to the man, rather than forming a whole with him.[88] In such a relation, the wife existed only to accompany her husband to social events, to cook his meals, to meet his sexual desires, to bear and raise his children—in other words, to serve as a tool, a toy, an ornament.[89] The woman, as a person, was absorbed by the relation.

This attitude toward women in marriage set the stage for their abuse and mistreatment. Wives suffered a great deal at the hands of their husbands.[90] They were robbed of their earnings, and if they tried to leave the marriage, they were robbed of their children as well. They were beaten by their sons and their husbands as a diversion after drinking. They were commanded always to indulge their husbands' brute sexual appetites, for not to do so was considered evil, if not insanity.

The point that Fuller stressed over and over again is that the greatest danger of an unequal marriage relation is that women center their lives outside of themselves—in their husbands, their children, their homes—and thereby lose all sense of self.

Fuller did not issue a blanket condemnation of all marriage. She saw some hope for an equal relation in four different forms of marriage: the household partnership, mutual idolatry, intellectual companionship, and religious union.[91]

The first marriage is essentially one of teamwork, though the roles in the team are assigned by sex. The man provides for the home and the woman cares for it. Their relation is one of mutual esteem, mutual dependence, and mutual kindness. It is a good relation, as far as it goes.

In the second relation, the man and woman see only each other. They are locked in their mutual cell of infatuation. In so narrowing the lives of each other, the relation is destructive for both.

In the third relation, man and woman find intellectual and emotional companionship in each other. The husband and wife enrich each other's intellectual lives and sustain each other's intellectual pursuits, as did M. and Mme. Roland and William Godwin and Mary Wollstonecraft.

The fourth and highest form of marriage relation is very rare. Fuller expressed it as a "pilgrimage towards a common shrine."[92] It includes elements of the three other types of relations, then moves beyond them to a perfect union of souls. The man and woman journey together in their common endeavor to achieve the All.

While physical and intellectual equality, and equality within relationships were important for Fuller, the real core of her concept of equality, like that of other Romantics, lies in her vision of the soul. Fuller conceived of the soul as both an individual and a universal phenomenon, and both aspects are important in her concept of equality.

On the individual level, Fuller regarded every person primarily as a soul. Unlike the body, which may be distinguished and classified by sex, or race, or strength, or height; unlike the mind, which may be distinguished and classified by intelligence, or mathematical aptitude, or poetic vision; the soul cannot be differentiated. Souls are souls. They are neither rich nor poor, black nor white, female nor male. They are fundamentally souls. The soul exists independent of temporal and spatial dimensions, and thus does not share in distinctions based in time or space. There can be no criteria for distinguishing souls. Every individual has a soul, and all souls are equal. Therefore, all individual human beings are fundamentally equal.

Fuller regarded all individuals as equal not only as individual souls, but as expressions of the universal Soul. Every individual is living out the dynamic of the All; every soul is a piece of the Soul. Regardless of how different the modes of expression may be, all individuals are ultimately equal because they express the same thing, the universal Soul.

This concept of equality of the soul cuts through all inegalitarian arguments based on anatomical differences or emotional differences or intellectual differences, because it asserts a more fundamental basis of equality. It lets feminist philosophy move beyond the emphasis on physical and biological differences between the sexes without falling into the equally narrow trap of conceptualizing woman as intellect. The soul provides a vessel in which the body and the mind may be subsumed without being destroyed. It allows feminists to discuss equality in terms of the whole essence of a person instead of the isolated characteristics of muscular strength or capacity to reason.

Fuller's feminism was quite distinct from that of the women's rights movement in that she did not speak in terms of "rights" or equal opportunities for women. This is consistent with her rejection of atomistic individualism in favor of the relatedness of individuals in the divine harmony. Contemporary research has shown that a responsibility orientation to ethics is more central to those whose conceptions of the self are rooted in relatedness, whereas a focus on rights is more common in those who define the self as separate and autonomous.[93] As Theriot has argued, this is also consistent with Fuller's Romantic conception of humanity.[94]

One usually considers rights vis-à-vis the rights of someone else. When all are linked, so that in denying another's right one denies oneself, the term is no longer useful. Rather, as we have a need and a responsibility for our own self-development, so do we have a similar need and responsibility for the growth of others. All our individual growth, freedom, happiness affects the whole. Fuller stated the point in this way:

> As the whole has one soul and one body, any injury or obstruction to a part, or to the meanest member, affects the whole. Men can never be perfectly happy or virtuous till all men are so.[95]

Fuller made another contribution to a feminist conception of equality in her development of the notion of what is now called androgyny. She believed masculine and feminine traits are of equal worth, and that both exist within male and female. "Male and female represent the two sides of the great radical dualism. But, in fact, they are perpetually passing into one another. Fluid hardens to solid, solid rushes to fluid. There is no wholly masculine man, no purely feminine woman."[96]

To define a woman only by her feminine characteristics or a man by his masculine characteristics is to deny the whole person. No person exists as purely masculine or feminine. Sex-role stereotypes collapse when subjected to scrutiny. Women may be brave leaders; men may be inspired poets. "Nature provides exceptions to every rule. She sends women to battle and sets Hercules spinning; she enables women to bear immense burdens, cold, and frost; she enables the man, who feels maternal love, to nourish his infant like a mother."[97]

She argued that masculine and feminine elements coexist in every individual, each finding his or her own unique harmony of male and female. Thus one of the main tasks in self-development is the full and free development of both masculine and feminine traits within each individual, not emphasizing one to the detriment of the other.

Fuller felt that the societal restriction of women to female roles and of men to male roles suppresses the masculine in woman and the feminine in man, and in so doing depresses the spirit and prevents the soul from discovering its true harmony. It creates in the individual feelings of discontent with the self and dissonance with the universe. Fuller saw this happening in girls, who, forbidden to pursue their tastes for woodworking or physical activity, became sullen and mischievous. She saw it in "the ennui that haunts grown women,"[98] who have been forced to submerge their natures into the narrow confines of domesticity without ever being allowed to bloom.

Fuller rejected the notion of "woman's sphere." All roles, all characteristics, all occupations should be open to women. She was probably best known for her then outrageous suggestion: "let them be sea-captains if you will."[99] Only full and free access to all spheres and employments would allow women to fulfill their destiny.

Just as each individual must seek the harmony of masculine and feminine traits within himself or herself, so must men and women learn from and balance each other. It is the desire of every spirit "to seek in another what is lacking in itself and thereby to form a whole."[100] In order to be complete souls, women and men need to learn from each other that which they could not discover on their own. The sharing and mutuality of the sexes is essential for the complete development of the androgynous soul.

Sorority

The concept of sorority is a central tenet of Fuller's feminism. It provides the uniqueness, the framework, and the direction for her feminist thought. She first suggested the notion of sisterhood in *Woman in the Nineteenth Century*, and, "ultimately, her quest was for the feminine principle."[101]

Fuller felt all women were united by common bonds that stretched across all barriers of class or race,[102] though certainly the objection can be raised that though Fuller believed that this bond stretched across race and class, she defined it within the limited perspectives of the white middle class. Perhaps in her search for the unity of a common bond, she neglected the voices of women from diverse backgrounds. A significant strand of this bond was women's shared experience of oppression and subjugation by men. Because man is vain and loves power, he teaches woman to depend only on him. But rather than protect woman, man deprives her of her freedom and inflicts wrongs and abuses on her.[103] "Woman is the flower, man the bee. She sighs out melodious fragrance, and invites the winged laborer. He drains her cup, and carries off the honey. She dies on the stalk; he returns to the hive, well-fed, and praised as an active member of the community."[104]

Fuller's expression of this common bond of oppression is best articulated in her concern for women being trampled by the brute appetites of men. Whether they be wives or prostitutes, all women are equally the victims of man's seemingly uncontrollable desires and demands.[105] Such a rude commonality could be a basis on which women could join together. Fuller called upon more fortunate women to reach out to their less fortunate sisters, to take in degraded women and prevent others from falling under the abuse of men by teaching them self-respect. In this regard, Fuller argued, women have a duty to protect and support one another.[106]

Women's shared experiences of inferiority and subjugation by men is an important element of Fuller's concept of sorority. However, the more fruitful element of her idea of sorority lies in the potential for a more positive bond of unity among women.

In laying the groundwork for this positive bond, Fuller rejected the notion that women should mistrust and compete with one another (especially for the attentions of men)[107] and asserted instead that women may indeed love one another. "It is so true that a woman may be in love with a woman, and a man with a man. I like to be sure of it, for it is the same love which angels feel. . . . It is regulated by the same law as that of love between persons of different sexes; only it is purely intellectual and spiritual. Its law is the desire of the spirit to realize a whole, which makes it seek in another being what it finds not in itself."[108]

Love is the motive force underlying Fuller's sorority. Indeed, it was love of women, "love for many incarcerated souls, that might be freed,"[109] that had prompted her to put her thoughts to paper. Fuller's journals and letters are filled with expressions of love and affection for women, both on a personal and a communal level, and it is this love that serves as the foundation for her concept of sorority.

In stark contrast to Wright, Fuller explicitly argued that men could not be trusted to improve the lot of women. She presented several reasons for this. In general, men believe that women are indeed inferior creatures. Historically, men have been more prone to regard women as slaves or children, assuming woman's soul and intellect to be somehow limited. Men simply do not see things from women's perspective. Indeed, it is men who have interposed the obstacles to woman's development and prevented her from discovering what is fit for herself. Given this, "can we feel that man will always do justice to the interests of women? Can we think that he takes a sufficiently discerning and religious view of her office and destiny, *ever* to do her justice?"[110] Accordingly, Fuller did not address her arguments to men, who would not and could not help women, but to women, who should be united in helping one another in the quest for independence and self-discovery.

Fuller's strong sense of the positive bonding of women flows directly from her clear affirmation of womanhood. She articulated a woman-centered vision of women's unique natures, capacities, and strengths. She affirmed the beauty of women's souls, the keenness of women's intellect, and the breadth of women's capabilities. The tragedy, as she saw it, was that women themselves did not believe this. Women are hindered in their own development not so much by legal, political, or social inequalities as by their own feelings of inferiority.

Fuller was concerned that throughout their lives, women were reminded of their "inferiority." Their education was of a lesser quality, their opportunities in life fewer, and their political and legal rights inferior to those of men. The highest praise given a woman was that she was "manly." Women were so indoctrinated by the myth of their inferiority that their minds were impeded by doubts. The challenge was to get them to the point at which they could naturally develop self-respect.[111]

Above all, Fuller urged women to respect themselves, to trust in their own intellects and impulses, to believe in the capacity of their own souls. She did so most effectively through her own deep respect for women as women. She respected the work they did, the people they were, and the virtues they represented. She found in woman, more often than man, a calm strength, a gentle wisdom, tenderness and faith.[112] She honored women by seeking out and making public noble images of women. Throughout her life and works, Fuller sought to impress upon women that it was good to be a woman, to respect in themselves the strength and dignity of womanhood, and never to wish to be anything else. "Were they free," she argued, "were they wise fully to develop the strength and beauty of woman; they would never wish to be men, or manlike."[113]

Hers was not a conservative vision of separate spheres or of sex-role stereotyping. Hers was clearly a vision of androgyny. However, this androgyny was based on distinctions between masculine and feminine traits. She tended to describe power and ambition as masculine, and love, beauty, and holiness as feminine. She believed "the especial genius of woman . . . to be electrical in movement, intuitive in function, spiritual in tendency." Such masculine and feminine traits evolve as we filter our life experiences through our different experiences as sexual beings. Though when completely developed, male and female souls are the same, as they are influenced by sexual experiences as men or women, they manifest themselves in masculine or feminine ways.[114]

Fuller departs sharply from her woman-centered vision with respect to women's definition as sexual beings, adapting male-defined paradigms of female sexuality. Rather than drawing a central core of feminine sexuality from female experience, she accepted the external view of women's sexuality as split between the sacred, pure, and chaste Mary and the profane and insatiate Eve. She drew on the biblical tradition in distinguishing the shameful and disgraced Eve from the holy and revered Madonna, and she opposed the two to each other. She appealed to women to develop their powers, so as "to live off the curse incurred by Eve" and to make the name "for her era Victoria, for her country and life, Virginia."[115]

She chose for her own ideal of womanhood that enforced by patriarchal society to ensure its control over the social structure as well as the passage of property—purity and chastity.[116] Fuller viewed virginity as the repository of female goodness. We see this particularly in the ballads that she felt expressed the idea of woman to a greater height and depth than elsewhere. In each the heroine is a maiden, or the Virgin Mary herself. In the first, a knight is protected throughout his life because he always has the name of the Virgin Mary on his lips. In the second, a maiden brings rushing dragons to reverence at her feet. In the third, a maid waits her entire life for the return of her betrothed from war. After years of waiting he returns, only to enter a monastery. She enters a convent to honor their love.

Fuller challenged the stereotype of male sexual behavior when she sought to extend this ideal of purity to men. Rather than viewing men as brutes, unable to control their passions, she felt that men also must aspire to the ideal of sexual purity. Women should be able to expect the same character of men as men do of women.[117] However, most women had been condemned either to decline or submit to men's rampant passions because they had accepted the myths of male sexuality, rather than being permitted openly to explore the facts of male and female sexuality.

It is in urging the full exploration of human sexuality that Fuller began to break through the Eve/Madonna stereotype. She believed that in the examination of their own sexuality, women might discover the rich fulfillment of sexual relations within marriage, or they might discover the equal fulfillment, not of enforced chastity, but of freely chosen and deliberate celibacy.[118] Fuller was on the verge of redefining female sexuality as emerging from woman's own sexual experience, rather than man's.

Indeed, Fuller was suggesting the redefinition of femaleness in general, as women discovered and experienced their own natures. Women had never had the opportunity to discover their true natures. Dominated by men, educated by men to serve men, absorbed in relationships with men, women's sense of self had historically been defined by men. Women were defined primarily by their relationships to others, as wife and mother. In radical departure from this, and at the core of her feminism, Fuller urged women to become self-centered. Then "Woman . . . would never be absorbed by any relation; it would be only an experience to her as to man. It is a vulgar error that love, *a* love to woman is her whole existence; she also is born for Truth and Love in their universal energy. . . . Ascertain the true destiny of woman, give her legitimate hopes, and a standard within herself; marriage and all other relations would by degrees be harmonized with these."[119]

What Fuller required for women was a time apart, a time to learn from themselves what their nature and destiny entailed. In this regard, Fuller viewed celibacy as a fruitful avenue to self-discovery. Undistracted by intimate relations with another, woman would be able to turn her thoughts to her center and gain a closer communion with the All.[120] She strongly suggested that the only way that women would be able to discover and assert their own identities and independence was to avoid marriage. She regarded spinsterhood as a positive step toward the freedom of self-fulfillment. "In this regard of self-dependence, and a greater simplicity and fullness of being, we must hail as a preliminary the increase of the class contemptuously designated as old maids."[121] A woman, on her own, unlimited by the concerns of one man, might center her thoughts on her own being for the benefit of all, rather than one. Only that woman who could provide the focus of her life herself could pursue her self-development.

It can be argued that Fuller urged woman's celibacy on a more metaphysical level as well. She believed that men in general had prevented women from discerning their own nature, and that women who seek that nature in conjunction with men will find the way distorted. So she called on women to purify themselves metaphysically to discover the soul of woman. She asked women to search their own experience and intuitions, to consider what *they* need, and to ascertain a standard within themselves.[122]

> It is therefore that I would have woman lay aside all thought, such as she habitually cherishes, of being taught and led by men. I would have her, like the Indian girl, dedicate herself to the Sun, the Sun of Truth, and go no where if his beams did not make clear the path. I would have her free from compromise, from complaisance, from helplessness, because I would have her good enough and strong enough to love one and all beings, from the fullness, not the poverty of being. . . .
>
> . . . and women must leave off asking them [men] and being influenced by them, but retire within themselves, and explore the groundwork of life till they find their peculiar secret. Then, when they come forth again, renovated and baptized, they will know how to turn all dross to gold, and will be rich and free though they live in a hut, tranquil, if in a crowd. Then their sweet singing shall not be passionate impulse, but the lyrical over-flow of a divine rapture, and a new music shall be evolved from this many-chorded world.[123]

Fuller urged women to become self-centered not only as individual selves, but also as one unified self of womanhood. She sought to develop a community of self-help and support among women in their common search for the essence of womanhood.

> I believe that, at present, women are the best helpers of one another.
> Let them think; let them act; till they know what they need.
> We only ask of men to remove arbitrary barriers. Some would like to do more. But I believe it needs for woman to show herself in her native dignity, to teach them how to aid her.[124]

Two difficulties exist with this aspect of Fuller's concept of sorority. First, it is not clear what she hoped to achieve in the metaphysical celibacy of women—individual discovery and identity or group discovery and solidarity. Her emphasis on self-centering and individual freedom seems to indicate the individual, yet she urged women to help one another in the discovery of womanhood.

The problem of individual versus group, recurrent throughout political philosophy, raises a false dichotomy for Fuller. She did not make such a sharp distinction between the individual and the group. All individuals are ultimately united in the universal Soul. But this raises another question. If *all* individuals, men and women, are linked through the Soul, then how are women to discover their *unique* characteristics by developing their souls? Will not they merge in a more general soul of humanity? Or did Fuller mean to suggest there is a female soul, separate from the universal Soul?

Fuller responded that in discovering the Soul, we do not lose the self; rather, our being is perfected and heightened. "By being more a soul, she will not be less a woman, for nature is perfected through spirit."[125] Thus each woman, in discovering the nature of her own womanhood, helps to define the womanhood of all. The individual is both defined by and helps to define the group.

Yet there is the suggestion that women share a common female soul. Fuller responded mystically to women. She believed that all women were a part of the woman she was and that she was a part of all women.[126] Though she never explicitly articulated this view, it was clear that she felt women were linked by a fundamental bond that went beyond shared experiences to a communion of souls.

Such a female soul, separate from the universal Soul, would be at odds with her fundamental assumption of divine unity. However, we may conceive of a female soul as *part* of the universal Soul. Fuller conceived of the individual soul and the universal Soul as being androgynous, as a whole formed of male and female elements. Thus in their individual quests for the universal Soul, women might also discover a universal female element.

Fuller's romantic assumption about the unity of individual souls through divine harmony provides a means of reconciling individual achievement with group solidarity. In the very process of *self*-development, one inherently comes to recognize one's fundamental unity with others.

This brings us to the second problem in Fuller's concept of sorority. Fuller never made clear what this process of female self-discovery involved. Is merely a time apart sufficient for self-determination, or does it require an active process of searching? It is clear that women can help one another, but Fuller did not articulate specifically how.

She gave a vague suggestion of how women might help one another in her approval of Maria Edgeworth's methods. These included contempt of falsehood; cultivation of clear, independent judgment and adherence to its dictates; habits of various and liberal study and employment; and the capacity for friendship.[127]

Fuller provided more insight into the process through her deeds than through her words. In her series of Conversations, Fuller provided the means for self-discovery. Through discussion of ideas, probing, challenging, and sharing, she encouraged women to discover their own truths, to reveal those tasks and ideals which were best suited to them. In a very real way, Fuller's Conversations resembled the contemporary consciousness-raising group, in which women are encouraged to express their own truths, and in so doing discover a unity with other women. Fuller helped other women by giving them the nourishment and the space to grow.

In sum, women must find their source of strength and support in one another and in themselves. Fuller recognized that women's freedom and women's power come not from an equality to men, but from the cultivation of the self. She envisioned women joining together not merely out of their common oppression, but out of their common strength, their common destiny, and their common joy. In her concept of sorority, Fuller foreshadowed what Mary Daly has called "the journey of women becoming . . . self-centering movement in all directions."[128] This common journey of women's souls is at the heart of Fuller's feminism.

Conclusion

The themes of liberty, equality, and sorority are so interwoven in Margaret Fuller's feminism as at times to be indistinguishable. How can one speak of the freedom of women to define themselves without speaking of the self-definition implied by sorority? How can one envision the equality of androgyny without that full and free development of woman's nature? In Fuller's feminism, liberty, equality, and sorority balance and mutually define one another. In many ways, liberty is equality is sorority is liberty.

The freedom of women to define themselves and to follow the calling of their true natures and capacities and to enlarge their selves is acted on through the equality of opportunities and the equal affirmation of female and male capabilities and qualities. Thus women became free, as sex-role barriers collapse, when the woman whose fulfillment comes from piloting a ship or arguing a case in court is as free to pursue that calling as is the woman whose vocation is to be wife and mother. And the same is true of men.

Women's freedom, and human freedom in general, is enhanced by the equal affirmation of femininity and masculinity in androgyny. The full development of our natures can come only when both our femaleness and our maleness are valued.

At the same time, the self-definition and support of women found in sorority are integral to Fuller's definition of freedom. As women discover and affirm their womanhood, so do they become free. This freedom lies in each woman discovering her own true individual nature as well as her nature common to all women and to all humanity. Fuller's individualism is not the competitive clamoring of one over another, but rather an appreciation of diversity within unity, a recognition that while each individual is unique, so are all organically interconnected. Freedom comes through affirming sorority.

Similarly, the equality of women and men is made possible through the liberty and sorority of women's self-definition. Equality in male/female relationships, so important to Fuller, is possible in her scheme only when women have been able fully to define themselves. Union is possible only among units. Thus, only when women are able fully to define the meaning of womanhood will female/male relationships be mutually enhancing.

Also, the equality of feminine and masculine, femaleness and maleness, in the androgynous person is possible only as women are free to define that femaleness. Heretofore femininity was defined by and for men. Only a truly woman-centered vision of femaleness would make possible a fully human androgyny.

Finally, sorority requires a certain equality of women and men. More equal distributions of domestic responsibilities, wealth, power, and self-worth are necessary for the solitude, the security, and the initiative necessary for self-discovery. And the freedom of women in that process of self-discovery is the essence of Margaret Fuller's notion of sorority.

The freedom of woman as a nature to grow and develop is in many ways the process of her discovery and affirmation of her own self as a woman and of her connection through that definition with all women. Ultimately, the free and equal affirmation of femaleness makes possible the human freedom of androgyny. Human freedom consists in self-comprehension and comprehension of the whole. As long as half of that self and of that whole are precluded from development, human freedom is impossible. Only with the full recognition and development of both the masculine and feminine, woman and man, through the balanced tension of liberty, equality, and sorority, will human freedom become a possibility.

SIX

Conclusion

I wonder what would happen if Frances Wright, Sarah Grimké, and Margaret Fuller could sit down together and share their thoughts and visions. Would they like one another? Would they even understand one another? Would they get into a shouting match over religion and then laugh about the self-righteous vanities of the clergy? Would Sarah be offended by Frances's views on sexuality, and Frances shake her head at what she might see as Sarah's prudery, and Margaret smile knowingly at both of them? Would they talk about the men in their lives—the ones who had challenged and encouraged them, the ones who had silenced them? Would they become quiet and sober or loud and outraged as they exchanged stories of women they had known, women worn down by repeated pregnancies and abortions, by backbreaking labor and drudgery, by poverty, by prostitution, by physical and emotional abuse, by quiet resignation? Would they share their own struggles and triumphs as public champions of women in a time when they were condemned merely for being public? Would they admire one another? Would they find a common ground?

As noted frequently in the preceding chapters, Wright, Grimké, and Fuller brought to their feminist thought a variety of philosophical traditions. Certainly they would disagree on major philosophical premises. However, they did share some common criticisms of these male-defined traditions and some common concerns regarding women, criticisms and concerns that make their thought commonly and uniquely feminist. Specifically, they share a rejection of Enlightenment liberal individualism, a rejection of the belief that the patriarchal family is the key political actor, and the development of a notion of sorority.

To begin with, rather than nineteenth-century feminism being merely an extension of Enlightenment precepts to women, the feminists rejected certain Enlightenment precepts. Indeed, Wright, Grimké, and Fuller share a rejection of Enlightenment's self-centered, atomistic individualism. Both Wright and Fuller specifically state their dislike of the utilitarian ethic of the pleasure/pain principle. Wright, Fuller, and Grimké grounded their ethical principles in a norm that transcended the individual. For Wright this was the notion of a common moral sense available to all; in Grimké, this was God; and Fuller regarded the divine harmony of the All as the guiding principle of ethical action. Similarly, Wright, Fuller, and Grimké based their principles of social action on the assumption of a social group that transcends the individual. All three spoke in terms of the importance of the harmony and community of all of humanity. More important for their feminism, all spoke to and embraced the oppressions of women outside their own lives and outside their own race and class. Wright was a champion of the working classes. Fuller wrote of her sisterhood with prostitutes, prisoners, and the poor. In her description of the condition of women, Grimké addressed the concerns not only of white middle-class women in the United States, but also of black slavewomen and of women in Asia, Africa, and Europe. Certainly the concept of sorority, especially strong in Grimké and Fuller, demonstrates a recognition of the interdependence and common concern of women, rather than the isolated individualism of Enlightenment theories.

Perhaps this rejection of individualism stems from their intellectual recognition that individualism was incompatible with the collectivism of feminism. Perhaps it stemmed from their own experience of being treated not as individuals, but as part of a group that was not accorded full rights and privileges.[1] (If nothing else, a "class consciousness" must have arisen in these highly intelligent women in being denied entrance to institutions of higher education simply on the basis of gender.) Perhaps this rejection stemmed from their recognition of their solidarity with other women. Perhaps this was the surfacing in Wright, Grimké, and Fuller of women's "different voice," of the recognition of an ethic of care rather than a rule-bound ethic of individual justice. Whatever the reasons, all three regarded the Enlightenment notion of individualism as inadequate for their feminist thought.

In addition, the theories of Wright, Grimké, and Fuller diverge from the mainstream of masculine Western political tradition in the approach to sex roles, particularly with regard to the family, and in the concept of sorority.

Wright, Fuller, and Grimké address sexuality and marriage and the family as central political issues. With the possible exception of Plato, Western political theorists have tended to regard these issues as at best tangential to the political. For example, gender was a prime concern in Rousseau's educational theories, but he ignores it in his political theories. Or, taking Western political thought as a whole, we find a general assumption of the family as a "natural" unit,[2] but the discussion of the role of the family is not central.

In sharp contrast, gender and family are key political issues in feminism. Fuller and Grimké especially regarded gender and sex roles as central components of the liberty and equality of women. Liberty and equality necessarily entail the ability to break through sex-role stereotypes and redefine gender. Grimké also raised the important issue of whether women's gender characteristics preclude or affect their participation in politics. Finally, all three regarded the sexual relations between men and women to be a reflection, if not the prime manifestation, of the power dynamics between men and women. Feminist theory regards the sex act itself as inherently political. Similarly, feminism regards marriage and the family as political relations.

Okin has argued that it is impossible to incorporate women into Western political thought because that whole tradition (up to Mill, Marx, and Engels) ignores women by regarding the family—the patriarchal family—not the individual, as the basis of political society.[3] Because of this, the whole family, with the father as its representative, is the political actor, and political concepts such as liberty and equality have no meaning in a familial relation.

Wright, Fuller, and Grimké all rejected this notion. To define woman only as a member of a family is to define her solely as a function with a prescribed role. Though Grimké's statement is most clearly and forcefully put, the argument that woman is not an instrument or a machine or a function runs through all of their theories. Wright, Fuller, and Grimké all regarded woman as a unique and individual person, with potential for self-development. All three also rejected the notion of sex-prescribed roles. Though Grimké's argument is somewhat contradictory, the predominant theme is the rejection of the notion that woman is solely and necessarily wife, mother, cook, housekeeper. In their rejection of sex-role stereotypes and functionalism, and their affirmation of woman's personhood, Wright, Fuller, and Grimké broke with the Western political tradition.

Wright, Fuller, and Grimké rejected this tradition in another significant way. Rather than arguing that liberty and equality have no meaning in a familial relation, they asserted that it is in marriage and familial relations that liberty and equality are *most* important. All three are unusually united in their condemnation of the abuse and degradation of woman in marriage and their affirmation of the need for liberty and equality, autonomy and respect for both the man and the woman in marriage. In fact, for Fuller and Grimké, this becomes one of the primary foci of their feminism.

Finally, the most radical departure from the male tradition of Western political theory is the questioning of the necessity of the family as a unit.[4] This questioning is strongest in Wright, particularly in her proposal that children be raised in common nurseries. Fuller and Grimké did envision an ideal marriage relation, but they rejected the notion that a woman must necessarily marry and raise a family in order to fulfill her nature as a woman.

Wright, Fuller, and Grimké questioned the naturalness and the necessity of the family, and especially woman's role in it. In raising such questions, and in suggesting other possibilities, they made a radical departure from the Western tradition of political thought. Their feminism rests on the individual, the whole (all humanity), and the sisterhood of women, not on the traditional family.

The last basis, the sisterhood of women, sorority, is unique to feminism for two major reasons: its origination and its context.

The concept of sorority, with its emphasis on the dignity and sisterhood of women and their oppression by men, does not occur anywhere else in Western political thought. It is not in the consciousness of male theorists, nor is it in their thought. Sorority is original to women and to feminism.

Some might object to this last statement by suggesting the parallel between sorority and fraternity. Certainly the recognition of collective solidarity is the same. But significant differences between the two exist. The concept of fraternity supposedly addresses the commonalities of all of humanity (though humanity as defined at that time was limited to white males or the male-centered family). Foreshadowing other ideologies of liberation, from Marxism to black power to lesbian separatism, sorority focuses on the common oppression and solidarity of a subgroup within the larger group. Also like other liberation theories that followed, sorority affirms the unique identity and experience of this subgroup, in this case women.

Sorority carries within it some of the potential problems of fraternity. Just as fraternity subsumed all of humanity under male-identified reality, so sorority could and indeed has subsumed all of womanhood under a reality defined by white middle-class women. In this particular, fraternity and sorority are alike. However, in its affirmation of the subgroup within the group, and especially in its affirmation of womanhood, sorority is original.

Just as the feminist theories of Wright, Grimké, and Fuller share some common departures from male-defined theory, so do they share the common themes of liberty, equality, and sorority, though the meanings of these for each vary. All three valued the liberty of women to think and to act autonomously. All three decried the dependence of women on men and sought to ensure for women the education and economic and legal resources by which they could maintain their independence. The concept of liberty may be both limited and enabled by sorority. In some ways, Wright's ideas about women's freedom were farthest-reaching. Unbounded by conceptions of womanhood found in part in sorority, she more than Grimké or Fuller broke through the tradition that defined women as chaste wives and mothers. Certainly Grimké's idea of a suprasphere, in trying both to break the mold and preserve it, is potentially more confining to women. Wright's feminism liberates women from the conventional norm.

The challenge to Wright raised by Fuller's feminism is to suggest that Wright's liberation of women from conventional female roles and feminine behavior is only the first step, one that must be followed not by taking on men's roles but by discovering one's own femaleness. Fuller's feminism suggests that while women must first be free not to be "feminine" and "womanly," they must be equally free to be women and to value their womanhood. Only in that self-discovery and affirmation can genuine liberation occur. Otherwise, one confinement is exchanged for another.

All three valued equality of the sexes and recognized that the liberty they sought was made possible only through equality. Wright wrote at length that liberty without equality was essentially tyranny, and she always coupled her pleas for free inquiry with equality in education. Equality in education was a foremost concern for all three, especially Grimké, who was most denied it. All three also stressed equality of economic opportunities, Wright pushing this farther to include equality of condition. And all three regarded the unequal position of women in marriage as one of the gravest evils with regard not only to women's mental, moral, and economic independence, but also to their physical independence and safety. Although they all valued equality in male/female relationships, only Wright seriously questioned the rationale for marriage as an institution; Grimké and Fuller recognized the potential for equality within marriage.

Fuller took the concept of equality in a slightly different direction (a direction also suggested in Grimké's later writings), toward a more fundamental equality of maleness and femaleness. She did not seek the equality Wright did—for women to be equal to men—but rather an equal valuing of self-defined womanhood and manhood and an equal valuing of femaleness and maleness in the androgynous human being. Like her concept of liberty, equality is informed and limited by sorority.

Like Wright, Grimké wanted women to have the same education and political and legal rights and economic and vocational opportunities as men. Yet, like Fuller, Grimké did not want women to be the same as men. In her concept of sorority, Grimké not only affirmed the value of womanhood, but also claimed women's moral superiority to men. In some ways, for women to be equal to men would mean not only their invisibility and the loss of unique qualities, but it would also be demeaning and regressive. It would in some ways be a step down. On this point, Grimké's sorority unbalances her equality.

Certainly the notion of sorority is much stronger in the feminism of Grimké and Fuller than in that of Wright. The bonding of women and the importance of women relying on one another instead of on men, while rarely mentioned by Wright, is central to Fuller and Grimké. Fuller and Grimké do differ: Grimké's sense of bonding is more negative, with its basis in oppression, and Fuller's is more positive, with its basis in female affirmation. Grimké's sisterhood arising from oppression may dissolve with equality, whereas Fuller's sisterhood arising from affirmation is guaranteed by equality.

Fuller and Grimké also stress the importance of women seeking their own self-definitions in a way that Wright does not. The challenge Wright's feminism raises to that of Fuller and Grimké is that such solitude and self-seeking may be a middle-class luxury ill afforded by the demands of the existence of working-class women. But to return to a point made earlier, the equalities of education and economic resources necessary for liberation are not sufficient. Liberation that does not include self-definition is partial at best. What Wright reminds us is that for sorority truly to be a sisterhood, its processes must include and listen to the needs and concerns and realities of all women, not just privileged women.

With regard to sorority, Wright, Grimké, and Fuller do share in a respect for the physical, moral, and mental capacities of women. Essential to all of their feminism is a deep regard for the dignity of women.

The in-depth examination of these ideas in Wright, Grimké, and Fuller reveals basic conceptual tensions in feminism. In the Introduction I suggested that the concepts of liberty, equality, and sorority are central to feminist thought and that their inherent contradictions serve to create an essential integrity to feminist thought. In this concluding chapter, I explore both the contradictions and the integrity of liberty, equality, and sorority. In so doing I show how these dynamics create similarities and differences not only among Wright, Grimké, and Fuller but among contemporary feminists as well. In essence, the specific feminist ideologies are shaped by the emphasis placed on the juxtaposition of these three concepts, and they are all specifically feminist, as opposed to Marxist or liberal or socialist or radical sectarian, because of the integrity of liberty, equality, and sorority.

Liberty, Equality, Sorority: The Contradictions

The claims for liberty, equality, and sorority are at the core of feminism. Yet, paradoxically, by their inherent nature, the very claims that give birth to feminism are those that may undermine it through a divisiveness that renders us incapable of listening to one another. The seeds of division are sown in the very conceptual ground of feminism. Taken to extremes, the concepts of liberty, equality, and sorority are contradictory.

Liberty and Equality

The inherent antagonism between liberty and equality has been widely discussed.[5] Given competing claims to limited resources and individual variation with regard to natural talents and abilities, or systemic privileges, unrestrained absolute liberty would result in a condition of inequality with those possessing greater strengths, intelligence, and abilities gaining status, power, or property over those less fortunate, ultimately resulting in greater liberties for some than others.

By the same token, a condition of absolute equality restricts liberty. The control of the distribution of rights, privileges, and resources necessitated by absolute equality of condition implies a lack of individual autonomy in decisions concerning one's life. For example, affirmative action policies, implemented to ensure equality of opportunity, necessitate restrictions and regulations with regard to hiring practices, which employers may regard as a threat to their freedom of choice and employees may regard as a threat to their freedom of achievement and reward. In its extreme form, equality would deny to the individual the liberty to choose whether to work longer, harder, less, or more leisurely; whether to spend one's allotted income on a house, a car, and symphony tickets rather than holidays, gourmet food, and hockey tickets; whether to give birth to three, five, ten, or no children. And in a system of equality of condition, to the degree that equality of condition dictates sameness, the freedoms of self-definition and self-expression might also be sacrificed.

Certainly some of the differences among Wright, Grimké, and Fuller can be explained by their different emphases on liberty and equality. Though all three balanced liberty and equality in their thought, Wright was most concerned with a general equality of condition for all of humanity and would undoubtedly have found Margaret Fuller's concerns for women's spiritual freedom to be the self-indulgent privilege of white middle-class women, whereas Sarah Grimké's thought shows an appreciation of both viewpoints.

Among feminists today, the question of equality versus liberty is divisive in many ways. Following in Wright's footsteps, socialist feminists argue that the free market economy of liberal feminism renders a true equality impossible, because capitalism requires a marginal and exploited labor force, most frequently women and people of color. Liberal feminists insist that the economic equality demanded by socialist feminism impinges on the natural liberties of women, as well as men, to compete, to achieve, to succeed or to fail, to accumulate and distribute property, to define and express one's being. Finally, maximalists find the kind of equality and integration of roles, choices, opportunities, and conditions of the lives of women and men demanded by the minimalists to inhibit the freedom of a woman to define her own self and her own sphere as a woman—separate and perhaps superior to men. In this area we can hear the voices of Wright and Fuller, the one demanding women's full equality to men, the other insisting on woman's freedom of self-definition, as well as Grimké's own internal struggle with the definition of woman's sphere.

Liberty and Sorority

Again, in their extremes, liberty and sorority are also antagonistic. In emphasizing the commonality and the solidarity of women, sorority threatens the liberty of the individual, especially the liberty not to be defined by or in any way be bound by one's sex. I think Wright, and maybe Fuller, would have found Grimké's need to maintain a notion of woman's sphere and woman's moral superiority confining, if not appalling. Also, because of her strong desire not to be in any way defined by her gender, Wright would probably have found Fuller's scheme of a time apart when a woman could define her "true nature as a woman" to be just one more way women oppress themselves, rather than viewing it as a means to liberation. This issue is at the heart of much of the current division between maximalists and minimalists. For example, minimalist liberal feminists argue that it is precisely being categorized by one's gender that prevents equal opportunity based on individual merit. Minimalists who seek a more androgynous human personality and society, as well as those who seek to eliminate all gender and/or reproductive distinctions between males and females, find such affirmation of a distinct womanhood threatening to the individual's liberty of self-definition regardless of gender. And the point has been made by women of color, who call for an appreciation of difference and diversity among women's lives and experiences and truths, that the unity invoked in the name of sisterhood is often a unity defined by white women, a unity in ignorance of and oppression of the lives of women of color. This concern has been given eloquent voice by Audre Lorde:

> As women we have been taught to either ignore our differences or to view them as causes for change. Without community, there is no liberation. . . . But community must not mean a shedding of our differences, not the pathetic pretense that these differences do not exist.
> Poor and third world women know there is a difference between the daily manifestation and dehumanization of marital slavery and prostitution, because it is our daughters who line 42nd Street. . . . If white American feminist theory need not deal with the differences between us, and the resulting difference in aspects of our oppressions, then what do you do with the fact that the women who clean your houses and tend your children while you attend conferences on feminist theory are, for the most part, poor and third world women?"[6]

By the same token, when individual liberty of choice and opportunity takes precedence over the identity of women with other women and the obligation of women toward women, liberty undermines sorority. For example, Grimké, who affirmed the unique contributions and insights of women as mothers, would regard Wright's plan to raise all children in national nurseries with a certain alarm. One hears similar conflicts between maternalists such as Chodorow, Rich, and Elshtain and feminists such as Firestone, who seek to eliminate sex differences by eliminating the reproductive function of humans.[7] Another striking example of the antagonism between liberty and sorority is the liberal feminist who, claiming the right to freedom and equal opportunity of women, climbs over anyone, especially her sisters, in order to achieve personal, political, and financial power and status, who denies all women and her own self-definition as a woman in order to prove that she is "as good as a man," who having achieved a certain level of power in society continues to use that power in a way that oppresses other women (for example, using the hard-won vote to continue to endorse discriminatory policies).

Equality and Sorority

Finally, in their extremes, equality and sorority are contradictory. In its emphasis on the differences between men and women, sorority undermines equality. If women and men are so different as to be beyond comparison, then no basis for equality can exist. It would be like comparing the proverbial apples and oranges. Furthermore, within the notion of difference is often contained an assumption of superiority/inferiority. Feminist affirmations of femaleness often carry with them implicit or explicit assumptions of female superiority. Certainly Sarah Grimké alluded to women's moral superiority again and again, and even Frances Wright occasionally touched on it. A contemporary example of the implicit assumption of female superiority is in the writings of Adrienne Rich, who, though focusing on female identity and community, sometimes asserts femaleness over maleness, as in this appeal to female educators: "Nor does this mean we should be training women students to 'think like men.' Men in general think badly: in disjunction from their personal lives."[8]

More blatant are the claims of Valerie Solanis that "Life in this society being, at best, an utter bore and no aspect of society being at all relevant to women, there remains to civic-minded, responsible, thrill-seeking females only to overthrow government, eliminate the money system, institute complete automation, and destroy the male sex. . . . the male is an incomplete female, a walking abortion, aborted at the gene state."[9] Obviously, sorority in its extreme threatens equality.

Similarly, equality of women and men, achieved or imposed, undermines sorority. If such an equality of roles and conditions were, as maximalists argue, artificially imposed on women and men, the unique strengths, abilities, wisdom, and experiences of women would be minimized. Margaret Fuller articulated this fear, arguing that women had never had the opportunity to let their true nature emerge and that they must before any true notion of equality, or of humanity, could be achieved. Sarah Grimké's later writings suggest this as well.

Today, separatists, arguing that men's nature is oppressive of women's nature, fear that such "equality" would result in a negation of women altogether and that " 'Equal Rights' devours sisterhood, converting it into copied comradeship, and splitting it from its deep source, which is female friendship."[10] Also, an idea expressed so clearly and strongly by Sarah Grimké is that within the notion of female bonding is a notion of female bondage, a solidarity arising from oppression. Ironically, to a certain degree inequality creates sorority. So the questions must be asked. Would sisterhood disappear if equality were achieved? And is the achievement of equality worth the price of the loss of sisterhood?

Such questions and concerns form the crux of the division between maximalists and minimalists. Maximalists assert a unique female nature and woman-centered vision that minimalists find too reminiscent of the sex-role stereotyping that has limited human choices and potential and has been used by powerful men to oppress women by defining those positions of power and status and influence in society as "male." Minimalists assert a male/female equality and sameness that maximalists find too reminiscent of the invisibility of women throughout the history of male culture. The maximalist/minimalist split is essentially that of sorority versus equality.

In sum, the essential elements of feminism—liberty, equality, and sorority—are ultimately contradictory. Thus it can be said, as Rousseau said of the body politic,[11] that conceptually feminism carries within itself the seeds of its own destruction.

Liberty, Equality, Sorority: The Connections

Although the three core concepts of liberty, equality, and sorority necessarily contradict one another, it is equally true that each one is necessary for the others. Equality without liberty loses its meaning, unless there be some value in recognizing that we are all equally enslaved. And without equality, liberty is only the liberty of a few while the bulk of the people remain enslaved and oppressed. This was the theme voiced by Frances Wright over and over again. Liberty void of sorority is similarly liberty of the few. That these few are usually white women, while most women remain oppressed, is something of which Wright, Grimké, and Fuller were aware. Perhaps Grimké was the most eloquent spokeswoman of this, in her appeals to white women to recognize their sisterhood with enslaved black women. Sorority makes possible the liberty of women to think and act autonomously. On a concrete level, often it is only with the support of other women—a crisis shelter, a consciousness-raising group, a women's studies class—that women begin to take steps toward liberation. And as Margaret Fuller argued, emotionally and spiritually, sorority makes freedom possible by enabling us to affirm ourselves as women, rather than denying and being oppressed by that womanhood. It enables us to choose ourselves. It is in this context of equal affirmation of female and male made possible by the affirmation of femaleness in sorority that we can begin to talk about the equality of the sexes, rather than the equal rights of women to the privileges and rights of men. Similarly, liberty and equality provide a context in which sorority is possible. The ability to find one's center and one's identity as a woman requires a certain solitude, an aloneness independent of external influences. Any type of dependence—physical, emotional, economic, spiritual, intellectual—inhibits this process. For women, this dependence has most often been on men. Margaret Fuller's words written more than a hundred years ago still hold true.

> It is therefore that I would have woman lay aside all thoughts, such as she habitually cherishes, of being taught and led by men. . . . I would have her free from compromise, from complaisance, from helplessness, because I would have her good and strong enough to love one and all beings, from the fullness, not the poverty of being. . . .
> . . . and women must leave off asking them [men] and being influenced by them, but retire within themselves and explore the groundwork of life till they find their peculiar secret.[12]

In gaining more equality of rights and privileges—whether educational opportunities, or political access, or equal pay—women in turn gain the economic, physical, social, intellectual, and spiritual independence and autonomy that make sorority possible.

The paradoxical relationship of the core concepts of liberty, equality, and sorority is that although they are, in their absolute assertion, contradictory, so, in moderation, are they mutually enhancing and supportive. The key is that they are contradictory in their extreme, in their absolute expression. In other words, they contradict only when one or two are posited without the balancing position of the other. I suggest that the three elements, posited *simultaneously*, act not to undermine one another, but to balance and define one another. They act as limits toward one another and coexist in a dynamic, creative tension.

It is the mutual affirmation of all three elements *at once* that maintains the balance and prevents any one or two from becoming so extreme that it negates the other. Paradoxically, it is the inherent contradiction that creates the tension, and it is the tension that prevents the contradiction. They pull in opposite directions, creating the very tension that strengthens and supports them all.

To say that liberty, equality, and sorority act as limits to one another is to suggest that without the balancing effect of equality and sorority, liberty negates itself; it is no longer liberty. This holds for equality unbalanced by liberty and sorority and sorority unbalanced by liberty and equality. In exploring this, I examine some of the dilemmas and inadequacies, some of the cracks and bulges, that develop when the tension on one is decreased or destroyed. And each time the question must be asked, Does the concept, taken in its extreme, negate itself?

Liberty and Equality Without Sorority

Without the demands of sorority, are liberty and equality possible? Take, for example, the liberal feminist who, while claiming freedom and equality of opportunity, denies the importance, if not the existence, of any sense of identity with women. If in the process of exercising her freedom a woman denies her own identity as a woman, is she truly free? I argue that she is not. If, for example, she has gained status and power in the corporate structure by playing "the games mother never taught you," by denying her choice to be a mother, by silencing her feelings, by "selling out," then she has not acted on her choices but acted against them. She has censored herself, not expressed herself. The result is often self-hatred and lack of self-esteem. The freedom to deny oneself is not a desirable freedom. It is partial freedom at best, inauthentic and self-defeating at worst. To deny oneself is to become an obstacle to one's own freedom.

Similarly, what kind of equality is obtained apart from sorority? If a woman gains equality with men without maintaining the sisterhood and identity of women, the equality is illusory. If, as in the case of the token female, a woman has equal rights and privileges with men *because* she is a woman, then that equality rests on her membership in a group that is still regarded as subordinate, and the equality is false. Or, if a woman is regarded as men's equal "in spite of" the fact that she is a woman—the case for Wright, Grimké, and Fuller—then that equality rests on her denial of part of herself, and it too is not true equality. If, in order to be considered equal to men, a woman must deny the woman in her and her connection to other women, then she is affirming the inequality of women. Because she is a woman, her denial of the equality of women is a denial of her own equality.

Liberty and Sorority Without Equality

What of a separation that claims liberty and sorority but abandons equality, arguing that female nature is superior to male? Without the demands of equality, do the values of liberty and sorority retain their meaning and integrity, or do they collapse? The immediate danger of such theories lies in the potential for abuse. In reviving the "anatomy is destiny" argument that one's nature, functions, roles, and future are determined by one's sex, they legitimize continued or even heightened discrimination against women into particular functions and roles, thus subverting rather than affirming women. Neither are separatist demands respectful of women with significant, mutually affirming relationships with men, especially as mothers of sons (and many of the maximalist writers are maternalists). A sorority that insists on the erosion of male/female relationships, especially mother/son relationships, as a condition of sorority, or that ignores these relationships, negates itself by denying the truth, realities, and experiences of many women's lives.

It is also a racist and thus oppressive separation, which

> accuse[s] us [black lesbians] of being "male-identified" because we are concerned with issues that affect our whole race. They [white lesbians] express anger at us for not seeing the light. That is another aspect of how they carry on their racism. . . . They are so narrow and adamant about that that they dismiss lesbians of color and women of color who aren't lesbians because we have some concern about what happens to the men of our race. And it's not like we like their sexism or even want to sleep with them. You can certainly be concerned as we are living here this summer in Boston when one Black man after another ends up dead.

Furthermore, such separatism is made possible in practice only by an oppressive privilege, "white-skinned privilege, class privilege. Women who don't have those kinds of privilege have to deal with this society and with the institutions of society. They can't go to a harbor of many acres of land, a farm, and invite the goddess."[13] Again, such sorority negates itself by denying the realities of women's lives.

Finally, I question whether a group that affirms its own superiority is acting from an honest solidarity of that group or from an imposed totality and closedness that mask not strength but insecurity and fear. Albert Camus makes the distinction between totality and unity—totality being a system of thought and practice that externally imposes a false harmony and "Truth" on a much more complex reality—unity being the harmonious tapestry that is created by the interweavings of those complex realities.[14] Totality begins with a particular vision of truth and forces the realities of human existence to fit that vision. Unity is a truth given shape by the interplay of the concrete realities of human existence.

In a Hobbesian world of insecurity and fear, there is a need to protect oneself by building walls and other defenses—nuclear defense policies, unquestioning loyalty to a leader, personal "toughness." Totality imposes such a wall, protecting the group from external attacks by providing a united front and from internal doubts by providing an answer to every question.

A sorority of unity rather than of totality would be open to many truths, the conflicting complexities of women's lives, expose rather than impose, and not need to claim its superiority vis-à-vis others. It would be secure in its own worth in and of itself.

With regard to a separatist supremacist liberty, what of the liberty of men? Given the history and reality of men's oppression of women, this may seem an insignificant or even offensive question. Yet I question liberty that lies in being an oppressor and argue instead that liberty is refusing to be oppressed and refusing to oppress.

Is one free if one must separate in order to guarantee that freedom? One might ask, Isn't the very necessity of separation *dictated* by the oppression of women and women's nature? As women begin this process of claiming their identities, a time of separation into the safety and freedom of "woman's space" is essential both to women's freedom from physical and emotional abuse and to women's self-definition, growth, and maturity.[15] Nevertheless, as that self-definition is achieved, a time comes for claiming rather than escaping the world, for creating the world as we envision it, for making *of the world*, rather than outside the world, a safe space. Freedom must include the ability to live in our own homes, to walk alone and at night, to have the truths of our bodies and our souls respected and heard in a world of women and men.

Sorority and Equality Without Liberty

Finally, what of a separatism that affirms sorority and equality, but not liberty? Sorority without liberty becomes little more than a feminist fascism—an unreflective loyalty to the group above all else, a groupthink and a group norm, a totalitarian definition of womanhood irrespective of difference. In practice this has meant a sorority of "white solipsism"[16] which, in defining the woman-centered vision and setting the agenda of feminist priorities, denies the realities, the needs, and the voices of women of color. As such, it is the denial rather than the affirmation of women and negates itself.

Similarly, the model for equality proposed by female separatism is that of separate but equal. The persistent inequalities between the races from years of segregation convinced social scientists, jurists, and civil rights activists that separate but equal was a contradiction in terms, that such rigid separation enhanced existing inequalities. I argue that such a model of equality of women and men would similarly undermine itself.

Thus in a feminist context liberty, equality, and sorority do in fact act as limits to one another. Without the balancing effect of all, each concept negates itself. The integrity of each of the concepts of liberty, equality, and sorority necessitates its juxtaposition with the other two.

Viktor Frankl has argued that tension is endemic to our human condition and that our health lies in maintaining and respecting that tension rather than trying to ignore or dissolve it.[17] I argue that the same is true of the health of feminism.

In examining the push/pull of liberty, equality, and sorority in Wright, Grimké, and Fuller, we gain insight into the tensions in the development of feminist thought. The mainstream of that development since Wright, Grimké, and Fuller were writing has been toward Wright's emphasis on liberty and equality. Feminist efforts since the 1840s have largely, though by no means exclusively, been directed toward gaining for women the same rights, privileges, duties, and opportunities as men. In the past 150 years of the women's movement in this country, the bulk of the energy and focus has been toward two constitutional reforms that would ensure such equality—suffrage and the Equal Rights Amendment. Other efforts and gains have also aimed at expanding the liberty and equality of women—equal access to higher education and the professions; equal pay for equal, now comparable, work; reform of divorce and property laws; reproductive freedom. Although a few voices have called for female bonding and affirmation and radical systemic change, the tendency in mainstream American feminism has been toward minimizing differences between the sexes and incorporating women into the existing system. The tendency has been toward liberty and equality without much counterbalancing by sorority.

The need for this sorority has manifested itself much more strongly in the past twenty-five years of American feminism, and in its extreme has been powerfully articulated primarily by radical lesbian separatists. The pull toward sorority questions a feminist theory and practice that seeks to include women in a system that is fundamentally antithetical to and oppressive of women and calls instead for a woman-centered vision and politics.[18]

Lesbian-feminist politics regards lesbianism as a political act, as the choice of a woman for herself and for other women, and regards women's heterosexuality as a choice to give support to men over women. Lesbian feminism calls on women to be woman-identified and committed to women.[19]

With the rise of radical lesbian separatism has come the rich development of women's culture—literature, poetry, art, music, goddess religion and the revival of witchcraft and female spirituality, lesbian separatist communities, and lesbian ethics and metaethics.[20] With it also has come deep appreciation for sisterhood, for self-affirming female friendships.[21] As expressed by Sally Gearhart, "Who we are not, we each could be, and every woman is myself."[22] In it is found the radical and profound affirmation of sorority.

In the past decade or so of feminism in this country, there has been movement back toward the center. Radical feminism, unbalanced by the freedom of diversity and the equality of sons and brothers and lovers of working-class women and women of color, is seen as oppressive in its privilege and white solipsism. Liberal feminism, unbalanced by affirmation of and sisterhood toward the realities of the lives of most women, is viewed as equally oppressive in its perpetuation of a system that grants privileges to a few and abandons the many.[23] Challenged by the voices of women of color, working-class women, elderly women—voices often ignored by both mainstream and radical feminism—American feminism is in the process of rebalancing, of finding its center and its integrity.

Many of the issues, concerns, contradictions, and definitive concepts of contemporary feminism are found in the voices of Frances Wright, Sarah Grimké, and Margaret Fuller. The tensions and the unity of these three show striking parallels to contemporary feminism. But more important, they reveal the conceptual dynamic that forms the basis of contention among contemporary feminists and that defines our common concern. Indeed, an examination of the origins of feminist thought provides insight into the source of feminist discord, a framework that defines feminism as a unique body of thought and a hopeful insistence on feminism's demands for integrity.

What does this integrated feminism look like? What is its focus, its demands, its language? Feminism is not static. By its very nature of being in tension it is always in the process of becoming and redefining itself. But from the voices of Frances Wright, Sarah Grimké, and Margaret Fuller, and the chorus of voices that have emerged since their time, we can envision the integrity of feminism.

The feminism that arises from the integrity of liberty, equality, and sorority recognizes that a woman's sense of identity and integrity comes in part through an acceptance and affirmation of oneself as female, yet respects the diversity of what it means to be female in different cultures, races, classes, ages, and life experiences. It is a feminism that recognizes that it is meaningless to speak of and difficult to act on defining oneself and one's choices without basic equalities of opportunity and condition in standards of living, health care, education, law, and politics. It is a feminism that does not seek liberation either in abandoning our identities as women and our commitments to women or in retreating from the world of men, but rather uses the values found in sorority—woman-centered values of care and connection and commitment—to affirm ourselves and our integrity and to transform our world.

Notes

NOTES

EDITOR'S INTRODUCTION

1. Edward T. James, Janet Wilson James, and Paul S. Boyer. eds. *Notable American Women, 1607-1950: A Biographical Dictionary*, 3 vols. (Cambridge: Harvard University Press, 1971); Barbara Sicherman and Carol Hurd Green, eds., *Notable American Women, the Modern Period: A Biographical Dictionary* (Cambridge: Harvard University Press, 1980).
2. New York: R.R. Bowker, 1979.

CHAPTER ONE

1. Two predominant theories arise from these studies. One is the relative deprivation or status deprivation theory, which proposes that middle-class nineteenth-century women were frustrated and angered by their increasingly diminishing status vis-à-vis men. As men's roles and opportunities were expanding, women's were contracting. More and more, women's traditional functions were being performed outside the home in factories, and they found their sphere narrowed to that of domesticity. For those who did not accept the justifying myth of "the cult of true womanhood" (Barbara Welter, "The Cult of True Womanhood: 1820-1860," *American Quarterly* 18 (Summer 1966): 151-74), this deprivation of status and function became the catalyst for action and movement. For examples of this theory, see Jo Freeman, *The Politics of Women's Liberation: A Case Study of an Emerging Social Movement and Its Relation to the Policy Process* (New York: David McKay, 1975), pp. 14-17; Alice S. Rossi, ed., *The Feminist Papers: From Adams to de Beauvoir* (New York: Columbia University Press, 1973), pp. 241 ff. and 251 ff.; William L. O'Neill, "In the Beginning," in *Our American Sisters: Women in American Life and Thought*, 2d ed., ed. Jean E. Friedman and William G. Shade (Boston: Allyn & Bacon, 1976), pp. 204-12; and Barbara J. Berg, *The Remembered Gate: Origins of American Feminism: The Woman and the City, 1800-1860* (New York: Oxford University Press, 1978), p. 7.

    The other theory is that the women's movement evolved naturally out of other reform movements. It is most often viewed as an outgrowth of the abolition movement. See Freeman, *Politics*, p. 13; Vernon Louis Parrington, *Main Currents in American Thought: An Interpretation of American Literature from the Beginnings to 1920*, 3 vols. (New York: Harcourt, 1930), 2:342; Shulamith Firestone, "The Women's Rights Movement in the U.S.: A New View," in *Voices From Women's Liberation*, ed. Leslie B. Tanner (New York: New American Library, 1970), p. 434; Alma Lutz, *Crusade for Freedom: Women of the Antislavery Movement* (Boston: Beacon Press, 1968); and Blanche Glassman Hersh, *The Slavery of Sex: Feminist Abolitionists in America* (Urbana: University of Illinois Press, 1978). However, Berg has presented a thorough and well-documented argument that nineteenth-century American feminism grew not from abolitionism but rather directly from women's involvement in benevolent societies in the 1820s and 1830s.

2. The major exceptions are Augusta Genevieve Violette, *Economic Feminism in American Literature Prior to 1848* (Orono, Maine: University Press, 1925); Susan Phinney Conrad, *Perish the Thought: Intellectual Women in Romantic America, 1830-1860* (New York: Oxford University Press, 1976); Sarah Slavin Schramm, *Plow Women Rather Than Reapers: An Intellectual History of Feminism in the United States* (Metuchen, New Jersey: Scarecrow Press, 1979); Judith A. Sabrosky, *From Rationality to Liberation: The Evolution of Feminist Ideology* (Westport, Conn.: Greenwood Press, 1979); and Nancy M. Theriot, "Mary Wollstonecraft and Margaret Fuller: A Theoretical Comparison," *International Journal of Women's Studies* 2 (November/December 1979): 560-74.

3. For example, Merle Curti, *The Growth of American Thought* (New York: Harper, 1964), devotes six pages of his 1,000-page study to nineteenth-century feminism and calls it a "detailed consideration" (p. 374). Alan Pendleton Grimes, *American Political Thought* (New York: Henry Holt, 1955), devotes one paragraph to feminist thought in his 500-page study of American political thought (p. 200). Parrington, *Main Currents*, is somewhat better, devoting a subsection solely to Margaret Fuller. The prime example of an analysis that ignores feminism is Richard Hofstadter's classic, *The American Political Tradition: And the Men Who Made It* (New York: Knopf, 1948).

4. Most standard texts tend to reduce the heritage of nineteenth-century American feminism to natural rights theory and/or the Enlightenment. See, for example, Grimes, *American Thought*, p. 200; Curti, *American Thought*, p. 374; and Robert E. Riegel, *American Feminists* (Lawrence: University Press of Kansas, 1963), p. 187. Even more recent feminist scholars have tended to make similar assumptions. See, for example, Freeman, *Politics*, p. 13; Hersh, *Slavery of Sex*, p. 191; Schramm, *Plow Woman*, pp. 9, 142; Sabrosky, *Rationality*, p. 147; June Sochen, *Herstory: A Woman's View of American History* (New York: Alfred Publishing Co., 1974), pp. 72, 132-33; and Gerda Lerner, ed., "Sarah M. Grimké's 'Sisters of Charity,'" *Signs: Journal of Women in Culture and Society* 1 (Autumn 1975): 246-56. There are notable exceptions, particularly Berg, *Remembered Gate*, and Conrad, *Perish the Thought*.

5. A good example of this is Garry Wills, *Inventing America: Jefferson's Declaration of Independence* (Garden City, N.Y.: Doubleday, 1978), which provides an original interpretation of the Declaration of Independence, based on evidence that Jefferson was writing in the tradition of moral sense, rather than that of Lockean liberalism.

6. Sabrosky, *Rationality*, p. 149.

7. James L. Cooper and Sheila McIsaac Cooper, *The Roots of American Feminist Thought* (Boston: Allyn & Bacon, 1973), pp. 8, 9.

8. Henry Steele Commager, *The Era of Reform: 1830-1860* (New York: Van Nostrand, 1960), p. 9 (emphasis added).
9. Two studies have been significant in showing how women discern knowledge in ways different from men. Carol Gilligan, *In a Different Voice: Psychological Theory and Women's Development* (Cambridge: Harvard University Press, 1982), shows that women's morality tends to develop around notions of care, different from men's moral development, which tends to focus around notions of a rights-based justice. Thus, including women's voice in rights-based liberalism might provide, indeed already has provided, a significant challenge to the liberal theory of justice. Political theories do change with the inclusion of women's experience and epistemology. Mary Field Belerky et al., *Women's Ways of Knowing: The Development of Self, Voice, and Mind* (New York: Basic Books, 1986), concludes that women more than men are likely to include this intuitive and personal knowledge in their knowledge base. Surely this would yield differences in approaches to such political concepts as liberty and equality as well.
10. Gayle Graham Yates, *What Women Want: The Ideas of the Movement* (Cambridge: Harvard University Press, 1975).
11. Alison Jaggar and Paula S. Rothenberg, *Feminist Frameworks: Alternative Accounts of the Relations Between Women and Men*, 2d ed. (New York: McGraw-Hill, 1984).
12. Maggie McFadden, "Anatomy of Difference: Toward a Classification of Feminist Theory," *Women's Studies International Forum* 7, 6 (1984): 495-504.
13. See, for example, Schramm, *Plow Women*; Sabrosky, *Rationality*; Cooper and Cooper, *Roots*; even Rossi's introductory essays in *Feminist Papers*.
14. Holbrook has argued that Margaret Fuller was the true inspiration for the women's movement, but that the authors of *History of Woman Suffrage* instead used Wright's picture because she was "all woman"—beautiful, buxom—and less liable to be labeled "mannish." Stewart H. Holbrook, *Dreamers of the American Dream* (Garden City, N.Y.: Doubleday, 1957), p. 170. More likely, Wright's picture was used as acknowledgment of her pioneering role.
15. See, for example, Sabrosky, *Rationality*; Rossi, *The Feminist Papers*, p. 87; and Eleanor Flexner, *Century of Struggle: The Woman's Rights Movement in the United States* (New York: Atheneum, 1974), p. 44.
16. Flexner, *Century*, pp. 27-28.
17. Judith Nies, *Seven Women: Portraits from the American Radical Tradition* (New York: Viking, 1977), p. 23.
18. Ibid., p. 24.
19. Sabrosky, *Rationality*, p. 60. See also Sochen, *Herstory*, p. 129.
20. Elizabeth Cady Stanton, Susan B. Anthony, and Matilda Joslyn Gage, *History of Women Suffrage*, 2 vols. (New York: Arno Press, 1969 [1881]), 1:801, 217.
21. Barbara Welter, *Dimity Convictions: The American Woman in the Nineteenth Century* (Athens: Ohio University Press, 1976), p. 180.

22. The term *sorority* is fraught with antifeminist connotations. It suggests images of women divided from and competing with other women, rather than of women united. Yet, taken in its original meaning, "a body or company of women united for some common object," *sorority* is both appropriate and compelling. It incorporates the notion of "sisterhood" but goes beyond it.
23. One of the most helpful analyses of the concept of liberty is that of Gerald MacCallum, who points out that although there are many meanings and uses of the term *liberty*, there is only one concept—the triadic relation among the agent, the obstacle, and the purpose. Gerald C. MacCallum, Jr., "Negative and Positive Freedom," in Richard E. Flatham, ed., *Concepts in Social & Political Philosophy* (New York: Macmillan, 1973), pp. 294-308.
24. See, for example, Adrienne Rich, *Of Woman Born: Motherhood as Experience and Institution* (New York: Norton, 1976); Carol Ochs, *Women and Spirituality* (Totowa, N.J.: Rowan & Allenheld, 1983).
25. See, for example, Mary Daly, *Gyn/Ecology: The Metaethics of Radical Feminism* (Boston: Beacon Press, 1978); Sally Miller Gearhart, *The Wanderground: Stories of the Hillwomen* (Watertown, Mass.: Persephone Press, 1979); Valerie Solanis, "Excerpts from the SCUM (Society for Cutting Up Men) Manifesto," in Robin Morgan, ed., *Sisterhood Is Powerful: An Anthology of Writings from the Women's Liberation Movement* (New York: Vintage, 1970).
26. Jean Jacques Rousseau, *The Social Contract* (London: Oxford University Press, 1960 [1762]), p. 189, and *Emile: Selections*, trans. and ed. by William Boyd (New York: Columbia University Press, 1962 [1762]).
27. Catharine Beecher, *A Treatise on Domestic Economy* (New York: Source Books Press, 1970 [1841]).
28. For a more in-depth discussion of this, see Elizabeth Ann Bartlett, "Liberty, Equality, Sorority: Contradiction and Integrity in Feminist Thought and Practice," *Women's Studies International Forum* 9, 6 (1986): 521-29.

CHAPTER TWO

1. Ernst Cassirer, *The Philosophy of the Enlightenment*, trans. Fritz C. A. Koellin and James P. Pettegrove (Princeton: Princeton University Press, 1951), pp. 35-36.
2. Peter Gay, *The Enlightenment: An Interpretation*, 2 vols. (New York: Norton, 1966, 1969), 1: 3.
3. Cassirer, *Enlightenment*, pp. 7, 13.
4. Gay, *Enlightenment*, 2: 123-26, 160-66.
5. Cassirer, *Enlightenment*, pp. 43-45.
6. Gay, *Enlightenment*, 1: 33.
7. Ibid., p. 150.
8. Ibid., 2: 397.

9. Gay insightfully comments that the philosophes were "feminists with misgivings: the age-old fear of women, the antique superstition that women were vessels of wrath and sources of corruption, was too deeply rooted to be easily discarded." Ibid., 2: 33, 397.
10. John Locke, *Second Treatise on Civil Government*, in *The Social Contract: Essays by Locke, Hume, and Rousseau* (London: Oxford University Press, 1960), p. 5.
11. The relation of natural law to God, which is pivotal in Grimké's interpretation of feminism, was controversial. Was natural law the command of God? Was natural law, though grounded on the being of God, the dictate of reason? Or was natural law independent of God? Many natural law theorists held the last view. However, even if divine will was considered the ultimate source of natural law, and God held only to be the divine legislator, reason was still regarded as the only source from which the knowledge of this law could be gained. Otto Gierke, *Natural Law and the Theory of Society: 1500-1800*, trans. Ernest Barker (Cambridge: Cambridge University Press, 1958), p. 98.
12. Cassirer, *Enlightenment*, pp. 238-43.
13. Ibid., p. 96.
14. Ibid., p. 107.
15. Ibid., p. 113.
16. Susan Miller Okin, *Women in Western Political Thought* (Princeton: Princeton University Press, 1979), p. 282.
17. Jeremy Bentham, *The Utilitarians, An Introduction to the Principles of Morals and Legislation* (Garden City, N.Y.: Doubleday, 1961), p. 18.
18. Ibid.
19. Freedom seems to be the exception to this rule. It alone seems able to stand on its own, without the need to prove its utility. Perhaps it is the characteristic mark of all liberal thought that liberty needs no justification. I think the case can be made that at least in this instance the utilitarians accepted the existence of a priori value. In fact, in *The Subjection of Women*, Mill argues that the burden of proof must be on those who are against liberty and seek to put restrictions on it: "The *a priori* presumption is in favor of freedom and impartiality." John Stuart Mill, *The Subjection of Women* (London: Longmans, 1869), p. 3.
20. Mill's strongest argument in *Women* was his utilitarian argument that the subordination of one sex to another is "one of the chief hindrances to human improvement" (p. 1). In his closing arguments he gave three reasons why the equality of the sexes would be beneficial. First, since all selfish propensities have their source in the present relations of men and women, the justice of an equal relation between the sexes would pervade society. Second, it would double the mental faculties available to the service of humankind. Society needs as many intelligent and competent minds as it can get, so why arbitrarily cut off half the human race from it? Finally, equality of the sexes would be a direct benefit to the private happiness of women, and considering that they are half the human race, this would substantially increase the happiness of the whole.

21. Wills, *Inventing America*, pp. 194, 199. Among some of the moral sense philosophers are David Hume, Adam Smith, Francis Hutcheson, Thomas Reid, and Dugald Stewart.
22. David Hume, *A Treatise of Human Nature*, ed. L. A. Selby-Bigge (Oxford: Clarendon Press, 1888), p. 581.
23. Francis Hutcheson, *An Inquiry into the Original of Our Ideas of Beauty and Virtue: in Two Treatises*, 4th ed., corrected (Westmead, England: Gregg International Publishers, 1969 [1737]), pp. 111-69.
24. Ibid., pp. 275-77.
25. Thomas Reid, *Essays*, 2: 611-12, quoted in Wills, *Inventing America*, p. 186.
26. Wills, *Inventing America*, p. 211.
27. Conrad, *Perish the Thought*, p. 78.
28. Percy Bysshe Shelley, *A Defense of Poetry*, ed. Albert S. Cooke (Boston: Ginn, 1890), p. 38.
29. Ralph Waldo Emerson, *The Selected Writings of Ralph Waldo Emerson*, ed. Brooks Atkinson (New York: Random House, 1950), p. 262 (emphasis added).
30. There are problems in reconciling the Romantic conceptions of equality and freedom. If through freedom we achieve a oneness with the universe and are equalized into the whole, are we then still free? Some have argued that we still have the free choice of accepting or rejecting that type of freedom. (Frank Thilly, *A History of Philosophy*, 3d ed. [New York: Holt, 1957], p. 471.) On the other hand, does the fact that one's self-determining actions are ultimately the same as the world's negate the fact that they are self-determined?
31. Though many would have included them only in the Enlightenment. See, for example, William L. Langer, *Political and Social Upheaval, 1832-1852* (New York: Harper, 1969), p. 214; Nicholas V. Riasanovsky, *The Teachings of Charles Fourier* (Berkeley: University of California Press, 1969), p. 181; Paul Edwards, ed., *The Encyclopedia of Philosophy*, 8 vols. (New York: Free Press, 1967), 7: 207.
32. Owen especially believed in the power of education. He felt persons could be trained to lead a perfect life. Therefore, education (according to his principles) should be universal and compulsory. See Harry W. Laidler, *History of Socialism: A Comparative Survey of Socialism, Communism, Trade Unionism, Cooperation, Utopianism, and Other Systems of Reform and Reconstruction* (New York: Crowell, 1968), p. 89. We will come across this again in Frances Wright.
33. For details of the different approaches, see Emile Durkheim, *Socialism and Saint-Simon*, ed. Alvin W. Gouldner, trans. Charlotte Sattler (Yellow Springs, Ohio: Antioch Press, 1958), and Laidler, *Socialism*.
34. Still, even among these more radical feminists, one can find a reluctance to grant women equal status. For example, Fourier, often acclaimed as the leading feminist of the group, classified three groups of domestic "parasites": women, children, and servants, who do "nothing" but housework: "their day cannot be

estimated in economics as more than one-fifth of a man's day." (*Oeuvres, Anthropos,* 4: 174, quoted in Riasanovsky, *Fourier,* p. 157.)
35. Saint-Simon, *Système Industrielle,* V. 15, quoted in Durkheim, *Socialism,* p. 157.
36. Staughton Lynd, *Intellectual Origins of American Radicalism* (New York: Pantheon, 1968), pp. 19-20.
37. Lewis Perry, *Radical Abolitionism: Anarchy and the Government of God in Antislavery Thought* (Ithaca: Cornell University Press, 1973), pp. 36, 57, 66, 92, 95.
38. Hersh, *Slavery of Sex,* p. 206.
39. This is partially a rejection of the Owenist disbelief in God. (Perry, *Radical Abolitionism,* p. 140.)
40. Lynd, *Intellectual Origins,* pp. 163, 173.
41. See Violette, *Economic Feminism,* p. 97; Sochen, *Herstory,* p. 33; Cooper and Cooper, *Roots,* pp. 54, 62; and Hersh, *Slavery of Sex,* pp. 132, 146.
42. Hersh, *Slavery of Sex,* pp. 132, 146.
43. Sabrosky, *Rationality,* p. 149.

CHAPTER THREE

1. Frances Wright, *Course of Popular Lectures; with Three Addresses, on Various Public Occasions, and a Reply to the Charges Against the French Reformers of 1789 and Supplement* (London: James Watson, 1834), reprinted in Frances Wright D'Arusmont, *Life, Letters, and Lectures, 1834-1844* (New York: Arno Press, 1972), p. 154.
2. Frances Wright D'Arusmont, *Biography, Notes, and Political Letters of Frances Wright D'Arusmont, Parts 1 and 2* (New York: John Windt, 1844), part 1, p. 6.
3. Ibid., p. 11. This is Wright's autobiography, though it is written in the third person.
4. Rossi, *Feminist Papers,* pp. 88-89.
5. A. J. G. Perkins and Theresa Wolfson, *Frances Wright: Free Enquirer: The Study of a Temperament* (New York: Harper, 1939), pp. 60, 74.
6. The exact nature of the relation between Wright and Lafayette has been a subject of much speculation, both among Wright's contemporaries and her biographers. Lafayette's family was so outraged at the impropriety of their relation that Wright suggested that Lafayette adopt her as a daughter, an idea Lafayette rejected. So the rumors and conjectures over their relation continue to this present day. As one biographer puts it: "The Marquis sailed for France, leaving legends that are cherished one hundred and thirty years later, as witness the many taverns, hotels, and homes labeled 'Lafayette slept here.' Where Fanny Wright slept was left to conjecture." (Holbrook, *Dreamers,* p. 171.)

7. Perkins and Wolfson, *Frances Wright*, p. 329.
8. There seems to be a lot of distortion of this issue. Wright's sister Camilla felt Richardson had blown one incident of a committed—though not legally married—couple into a picture of promiscuity and licentiousness. Still, the damage was done.
9. *Lousville Focus*, quoted in *The Free Enquirer*, December 10, 1828, p. 54.
10. *Boston Courier*, quoted in *The Free Enquirer*, August 12, 1829, p. 329.
11. *Boston Statesman*, quoted in *The Free Enquirer*, August 12, 1829, p. 330.
12. Rossi, *Feminist Papers*, p. 97.
13. Frances Wright never did regain contact with Sylva and, blaming herself for letting her go in the first place, resigned herself to the loss of her daughter. The account of the exchange between Wright and D'Arusmont is taken from Frances Wright to Gholson, November 13, 1851; Frances Wright to W. G. Gholson; D'Arusmont to Frances Wright, October 1, 1851; Frances Wright, Letters and Documents, Cincinnati Historical Society.
14. Rossi, *Feminist Papers*, pp. 3-6; William Randall Waterman, *Frances Wright* (New York: AMS Press, 1967), p. 150; Sabrosky, *Rationality*, pp. 18-56, 149.
15. *The Free Enquirer*, September 2, 1829, p. 360.
16. Ibid., October 16, 1830, p. 405.
17. Frances Wright, *Address, Containing a Review of the Times, as first delivered in the Hall of Science, New York, on Sunday, May 9, 1830* (New York: Free Enquirer, 1830), p. 15; Frances Wright, *Parting Address: As delivered in Bowery Theatre to People in New York, June, 1830* (New York: Free Enquirer, 1830), pp. 13, 16; Frances Wright, *A Lecture on Existing Evils and Their Remedy, as delivered in the Arch Street Theater, Philadelphia, June 2, 1829* (New York: George Evans, 1829), p. 10.
18. Waterman, *Frances Wright*, p. 26; D'Arusmont, *Life, Letters, and Lectures*, p. 57; *The Free Enquirer*, June 25, 1825, p. 278.
19. Perkins and Wolfson, *Frances Wright*, p. 177.
20. List of objects taken from Frances Wright by F. Sylva D'Arusmont after death of Wright. Letters and Documents, Cincinnati Historical Society.
21. Wright, "Six Epochs of Human History," 1839, Lectures, Cornell University Library.
22. Wills, *Inventing America*, chaps. 14, 15.
23. Frances Wright, "Speech in New York at Masonic Hall, Sunday, 1839," Lectures.
24. Ibid.
25. See, for example, Frances Wright, "Six Epochs of Human History," and "Contains Account of Ideal United States," 1839, Lectures.
26. Frances Wright, "Religion," Lectures.
27. Ibid. She frequently spoke of the other political principles, especially the principles of the Declaration of Independence, as being self-evident, or immutable, or inherent—hardly the words of a utilitarian.

28. Frances Wright, *A Few Days in Athens; Being the Translation of a Greek Manuscript Discovered in Herculaneum* (London: Longmans, 1822), pp. 23, 152.
29. Waterman, *Frances Wright*, p. 150.
30. Her reliance on Epicurean thought is a major reason for the similarity between much of her thought and Enlightenment thought. In a footnote to *A Few Days in Athens*, she comments on how beautifully the discoveries of modern science and philosophy have substantiated the leading principles of Epicurean thought (p. 146). Much of the Enlightenment science and philosophy was in fact drawn directly from Epicurus. See Gay, *Enlightenment*, 1: 99, 296.
31. Frances Wright, *Views of Society and Manners in America*, ed. Paul R. Baker (Cambridge: Belknap Press, 1963), p. 219.
32. Mill, *Women*, p. 38.
33. Terence Ball, "Utilitarianism, Feminism, and the Franchise: James Mill and His Critics," *History of Political Thought* 1 (Spring 1980): 91-115.
34. Frances Wright, *Introductory Address at Opening of Hall of Science, New York on Sunday, April 26, 1829* (New York: George Evans, 1829), p. 14; Wright, "Religion." Compare to Gay, *Enlightenment*, 2: 5.
35. *New Harmony Gazette*, October 1, 1828, p. 39.
36. Wright, "Religion."
37. Wright, *Athens*, p. 32. There is a certain sense in which the link between virtue and happiness is tautological. Wright defined virtue as action beneficial to ourselves and others. To be virtuous is to act beneficially—or with pleasure—which is defined as happiness. But there is also a more concrete link. In order to act virtuously, we must know the consequences of our actions. This requires knowledge grounded in fact. Thus virtue is necessarily linked with knowledge. Likewise, knowledge provides the basis for improving the condition of humankind, for finding the causes of evil and misery and taking rational steps to rid the world of them. So happiness is necessarily linked with knowledge.
38. Wright, *Review of the Times*, p. 14.
39. Wright, "Six Epochs."
40. Ibid.
41. Wright, *Parting Address*, p. 8. She was especially concerned that children be guaranteed happiness as a birthright. She was troubled by the misery of children born to families that could not afford to feed or clothe, let alone educate, them. She based her arguments for contraception primarily on this right of every child to be wanted, loved, and happy. (*The Free Enquirer*, February 6, 1828, p. 132.)
42. Sabrosky, *Rationality*, pp. 41, 52.
43. With the possible exception of Fourier. Sabrosky claims that when Wright was not taking her ideas (at least those on women) from Owen, she was evolving them from Fourier. (*Rationality*, p. 52.) I feel that these claims are based only on a similarity between the works of Wright and Fourier, not on any evidence

from Wright's background. In all the other writings by and about Wright, there is not a single reference to Fourier. If Wright had ever read Fourier, she was not impressed enough by his thought to mention him. In fact, for a while Wright was aligned with Saint-Simonians, who generally regarded Fourier's ideas with contempt. (Laidler, *History of Socialism*, p. 57.) The similarity between the two is more coincidence than any direct evolution.

44. *The Free Enquirer*, June 4, 1831, p. 259.
45. Perkins and Wolfson, *Frances Wright*, p. 323.
46. The only rational purpose she could see for people congregating into governments was the increase of their mutual security, well-being, and happiness. Though she did not believe a social compact had ever existed, she viewed such an arrangement—in which the interests of each and of all would be adjusted and compromised with the public interest—as ideal. D'Arusmont, *Life, Letters, and Lectures*, p. 122; Wright, "Six Epochs"; D'Arusmont, *Biography*, part 2, p. 30.
47. Wright, "Free Public Speech."
48. *The Free Enquirer*, March 26, 1831, p. 176.
49. Frances Wright, *Address to the People of Philadelphia, Fourth of July, 1829* (N.Y.: George Evans, 1829), p. 11.
50. Wright, "Speech in New York."
51. Frances Wright, "Untitled," Lectures, Cornell University Library.
52. Wright, *Athens*, p. 35.
53. I am struck here with the similarity between Wright's analysis and that of Emma Goldman in "Anarchism," in Emma Goldman, *Anarchism and Other Essays* (New York: Dover, 1969), p. 51. In fact, many of the arguments Goldman put forth are similar to Wright's, for example, that the cause of violence is ignorance, that religion and property are the sources of misery, etc.
54. *The Free Enquirer*, September 2, 1829, p. 360.
55. A few other sources of inspiration occasionally come out in Wright's thought. For example, she felt that in Byron she had found "a kindred spirit, a twin soul." (Perkins and Wolfson, *Frances Wright*, p. 21.) And, though she was usually put off by religious doctrine, she had a special appreciation for the Society of Friends, which she admired for its tolerance, simplicity, and charity. She felt that the United States was indebted to the society for many wise laws and humane institutions, such as religious and civil rights and the first penal code. She respected Quaker doctrines for their acknowledgment of the importance and dignity of human life. (Wright spends a large section of *Views of Society* detailing the beliefs and accomplishments of the Society of Friends; see pp. 30-37.) Yet all in all, the context of Wright's intellectual environment was defined primarily by moral sense, Epicurean utilitarianism, and utopian socialist political thought.
56. Wright, *Views of Society*, pp. 219-20.
57. Berg, *Remembered Gate*, p. 9.
58. Wright, "Religion," in D'Arusmont, *Life, Letters, and Lectures*, p. 192.

59. Wright, *Athens*, p. 150.
60. Wright, *Popular Lectures*, p. 9.
61. Wright, "Lectures," in Rossi, *Feminist Papers*, pp. 115-16.
62. *The Free Enquirer*, May 13, 1829, p. 230.
63. Ibid., October 1, 1828, p. 391.
64. Ibid., April 29, 1829, p. 213.
65. Ibid.
66. Wright, *Views of Society*, p. 22.
67. *The Free Enquirer*, July 22, 1829, p. 309.
68. Ibid., April 29, 1829, p. 213.
69. Wright, *Views of Society*, p. 220.
70. Wright, "Six Epochs" (emphasis added).
71. *The Free Enquirer*, April 30, 1831, p. 219.
72. Wright, "Six Epochs."
73. Wright preferred the Pestalozzi method of instruction, which first addresses the senses and through them awakens the faculties by commanding the attention of reason. (D'Arusmont, *Life, Letters, and Lectures*, p. 58.) Wright's husband, Phequepal D'Arusmont, was a Pestalozzi instructor.
74. Apparently even Wright's good friend Lafayette was skeptical of the intellectual potential of women. She stated her thesis in a letter to him: "Trust me, my beloved friend, the mind has no sex but what habit and education give it, and I, who was thrown in infancy upon the world like a wreck upon the waters, have learned as well to struggle with the elements as any child of Adam's." (Frances Wright to Lafayette, February 9, 1823, quoted in Perkins and Wolfson, *Frances Wright*, p. 74.)
75. Wright, *Views of Society*, p. 220.
76. *The Free Enquirer*, January 7, 1829, p. 83. Waterman has argued that Wright's own demonstration of the intellectual capabilities of a woman was her greatest contribution because "she showed what the feminine mind was capable of." (William Randall Waterman, *Frances Wright* [New York: AMS Press, 1967], p. 256.)
77. Wright, *Views of Society*, p. 220.
78. Schramm, *Plow Women*, p. 87.
79. Wright, *Views of Society*, p. 22. Notice the similarity to Mill's argument for the equality of women. For reasons mentioned above, it is possible that Mill got his arguments from Wright.
80. Wright, *Existing Evils*, p. 10.
81. Assuming this is true of a family. *The Free Enquirer*, March 3, 1831, p. 176.
82. Wright, *Parting Address*, p. 16 (emphasis added).
83. The basic outline of Wright's economic theories is found in *The Free Enquirer*, September 25, 1830, pp. 382-83; October 2, 1830, pp. 390-91; October 9, 1830, pp. 397-98; October 16, 1830, pp. 402-6; October 23, 1830, pp. 410-12.
84. Ibid., November 9, 1830, p. 398.

85. Ibid., July 3, 1830, p. 286.
86. D'Arusmont, *Biography*, part 2, p. 26.
87. This masculine vision of female sexuality, that women were passionless, was tied to the rise of evangelical religion between the 1790s and the 1830s. See Nancy F. Cott, "Passionless," *Signs: Journal of Women in Culture and Society* 4 (Winter 1978): 227-28.
88. *The Free Enquirer*, February 6, 1828, p. 132.
89. In so defining female sexuality, Wright broke out of the more typical male-defined visions of female sexuality as either passionless (Mary) or evilly seductive (Eve). See Elizabeth Janeway, "Who is Sylvia? On the Loss of Sexual Paradigms," *Signs: Journal of Women in Culture and Society* 5 (Summer 1980): 573-89.
90. *The Free Enquirer*, February 6, 1828, p. 132.
91. See, for example, *The Free Enquirer*, October 9, 1830, p. 398.
92. Ibid., February 6, 1828, p. 133.
93. Wright, *Views of Society*, p. 219.
94. D'Arusmont, *Biography*, part 2, p. 16.
95. Wright, "Lectures," in Rossi, *Feminist Papers*, p. 109.
96. Wright, *Views of Society*, p. 221.
97. Ibid.
98. Wright, "Lectures," in Rossi, *Feminist Papers*, p. 109.
99. Wright, *Views of Society*, p. 221.
100. Frances Wright to W. G. Gholson, Letters and Documents, Cincinnati Historical Society.
101. Wright, "Lectures," in Rossi, *Feminist Papers*, p. 110.
102. Belerky, *Women's Ways of Knowing*.
103. See, for example, Florence Howe, *Myths of Coeducation* (Bloomington: Indiana University Press, 1984); Sandra Harding, *Feminism and Methodology* (Bloomington: Indiana University Press, 1987); and Christie Farnham, ed., *The Impact of Feminist Research in the Academy* (Bloomington: Indiana University Press, 1987).
104. Gilligan, *Different Voice*.
105. See for example, Nel Noddings, *Caring: A Feminine Approach to Ethics and Moral Education* (Berkeley: University of California Press, 1984); and Eva Feder Kittay and Diana T. Meyers, *Women and Moral Theory* (Totowa, N.J.: Rowman and Littlefield, 1987).
106. Anne Wilson Schaef, *Women's Reality* (Minneapolis: Winston Press, 1981).

CHAPTER FOUR

1. Sarah Grimké, "Education of Woman," Clements Library, University of Michigan, Theodore Dwight Weld Collection, box 23, p. 15.
2. Ibid., p. 17.

3. See Grimké's diary, University of Michigan.
4. Nies, *Seven Women*, pp. 13-14.
5. Catherine H. Birney, *The Grimké Sisters: Sarah and Angelina Grimké: The First American Women Advocates of Abolition and Woman's Rights* (St. Clair Shores, Mich.: Scholarly Press, 1970 [1885]), p. 157.
6. Sarah Grimké, Letters, Garrison Papers, Boston Public Library.
7. Grimké, Letters, Garrison Papers, pp. 23-26.
8. *Proceedings, First Anti-Slavery Convention of American Women* (New York, 1827), quoted in Lutz, *Crusade for Freedom*, p. 103.
9. Garrison identified himself as a strong supporter of the right of women abolitionists to speak, siding with women in the 1837-38 split of the movement on the "woman question." However, he has been characterized as an opportunist who supported woman's rights publicly as one more issue he could use to agitate. (See Rossi, *Feminist Papers*, p. 288.)
10. Sarah Grimké to Elizabeth Pease, Letter, December 18, 1837, Garrison Papers.
11. Angelina Grimké, quoted in Lutz, *Crusade for Freedom*, p. 104.
12. Sarah Grimké, "Condition of Woman," Theodore Dwight Weld Collection, box 23, p. 15.
13. Birney, *Grimké Sisters*, p. 172.
14. Sarah received two proposals of marriage, one at the age of nineteen and one much later in life, from Israel Morris, which she rejected, based on her fears of being deprived of her rights and autonomy.
15. Sarah Grimké, *Letters on the Equality of the Sexes and Other Essays*, ed. Elizabeth Ann Bartlett (New Haven: Yale University Press, 1988).
16. Lerner, *Grimké Sisters*, p. 65.
17. Cooper and Cooper, *Roots*, pp. 54, 62.
18. John Woolman, *Journal*, in *The Quaker Reader*, ed. Jessamyn West (New York: Viking, 1962), pp. 249-73.
19. Birney, *Grimké Sisters*, p. 91; Lerner, *Grimké Sisters*, p. 65.
20. Sarah M. Grimké, *Letters on the Equality of the Sexes and the Condition of Woman* (New York: Source Book Press, 1970 [1838]), p. 20; Sarah Grimké to Elizabeth Pease, Letter, April 18, 1848, Garrison Papers.
21. Sarah Grimké, "Of Feelings (Sensations) and Emotions," n.d., Theodore Dwight Weld Collection, box 23, pp. 53-58, 94-95.
22. Grimké, "Education," p. 4.
23. Sarah Grimké, "Essay on the Laws Respecting Women," Post 1856, Theodore Dwight Weld Collection, box 23, pp. 2-3.
24. Grimké, "Feelings."
25. Sarah Grimké quoted in Perry, *Radical Abolitionism*, p. 105.
26. For an excellent discussion of the ideological currents in radical abolitionism see ibid., pp. 55-91.
27. Sarah Grimké to Theodore Weld, June 11, 1837, Gilbert H. Barnes and Dwight L. Dumond, ed., *Letters of Theodore Dwight Weld, Angelina Grimké*

Weld, and Sarah Grimké: 1822-1844, 2 vols. (New York: Appleton-Century, 1934), 1: 402.
28. Angelina Grimké to Theodore Weld, January 21, 1838, Barnes and Dumond, *Letters*, 2: 521.
29. Sarah Grimké to Gerrit Smith, June 28, 1837, Barnes and Dumond, *Letters*, 1: 408.
30. Barnes and Dumond, *Letters*, 1: 377, 402, 408, 447; Grimké, *Letters*, p. 8.
31. Sarah Grimké to Henry C. Wright, October 11, 1838, Barnes and Dumond, *Letters*, 2: 706; In this letter she wrote that she would not have signed the Declaration of Sentiments at the Peace Convention that represented a radical break with the Garrisonian perfectionist abolitionists.
32. Weld encouraged the Grimkés to abandon their cause of women's rights for the larger cause of human rights. Theodore Weld to Sarah and Angelina Grimké, August 26, 1837, Barnes and Dumond, *Letters*, 1: 436.
33. Hersh, *Slavery of Sex*, p. 191.
34. I am using Feinberg's definition of a right as "a claim against someone whose recognition as valid is called for by some set of governing rules or moral principles." (Joel Feinberg, "The Nature and Value of Rights," in *Concepts in Social and Political Philosophy*, ed. Richard E. Flathman (New York: Macmillan, 1973), p. 468.
35. Grimké, "Laws," pp. 2-3.
36. Mulford Q. Sibley, *Political Ideas and Ideologies: A History of Political Thought* (New York: Harper, 1970), pp. 326-30.
37. Grimké, *Letters*, p. 4.
38. French Bible, quoted in Grimké, *Letters*, p. 97.
39. She took the biblical dictum, "Thou shalt worship the Lord thy God, and Him only shalt thou serve," in its truest sense politically. It provided her with a basis for her essentially anarchist beliefs about government. She believed, for a time, along the lines of Perfectionism, that all government, civil or ecclesiastical, conflicts with God's. She did modify this belief, accepting the fact that civil government does exist and that we should try to work through it rather than around it. However, she found only that form of government to be acceptable which allowed for the participation of all its citizens. Government of one portion of the community over another is despotic and unjust and deprives one portion of its individual rights. If government is to exist, its laws must never interfere with the individual's God-given rights and responsibilities.
40. All Grimké would have known of Wright was from such articles as this, reprinted in *The Friend* from the *Allegheny Democrat*: "Pittsburgh, Dec. Frances Wright. This celebrated female commenced a course of lectures . . . in this city. . . . The dogmas inculcated by this fallen and degraded fair one, if acted upon by the community, would produce the destruction of religion, morals, law and equity, and result in savage anarchy and confusion." (Quoted in Lerner, *Grimké Sisters*, p. 95.) It appears that Grimké did read Margaret Fuller's *Woman in the Nineteenth Century* (see Stanton, Anthony, and Gage,

Woman Suffrage, 1: 355) and her later thought suggests the influence of Fuller.

41. Hunt and Grimké were good friends for several years. Hunt dedicated her autobiography to Grimké, praising her for her principles and the example she had set for other women. It is likely that Grimké received a lot of her information on the physical sufferings of women in marriage from Hunt. (Hersh, *Slavery of Sex*, pp. 177-78.)
42. I am using this term in Camus's sense of rebellion. For Camus, rebellion is saying yes and no simultaneously. It is at once the rejection of oppression and injustice and the affirmation of human dignity. (Albert Camus, *The Rebel: An Essay on Man in Revolt*, trans. Anthony Bower (New York: Vintage, 1956).
43. Camus makes the distinction between resentment and rebellion. Ibid., pp. 17-18.
44. Sarah Grimké to "Esteemed friend," September 9, 1851, Letter, Library of Congress, Grimké MSS; Grimké, *Letters*, p. 128.
45. Sarah or Angelina Grimké, "Marriage," University of Michigan, Theodore Dwight Weld Collection, MSS, box 23, p. 8. The authorship of the manuscript is uncertain. It is written in Angelina's script, but there is no name attached to it ascribing authorship. Sarah and Angelina often wrote or copied things for each other, so it is unclear who actually composed it. Gerda Lerner believes there are enough significant parallels with Sarah's other work to attribute this to Sarah. The archivist at the Clements Library where the manuscripts are housed does not feel there is sufficient evidence to concur with Lerner. Sarah and Angelina often conferred, so it may be a product of both.
46. Grimké, *Letters*, pp. 88-89.
47. Grimké, "Marriage," pp. 23-24.
48. Grimké, *Letters*, pp. 5, 8, 122.
49. Quoted in Barnes and Dumond, *Letters*, 2: 614-15.
50. Grimké, "Marriage," pp. 11, 25; Grimké, "Condition," p. 10.
51. Grimké, *Letters*, p. 26; Grimké, "Condition," p. 10.
52. Grimké, *Letters*, p. 47.
53. Ibid., pp. 86, 87.
54. The following discussion is drawn primarily from ibid., pp. 74-84.
55. Ibid., p. 83.
56. Ibid., p. 86.
57. Grimké, "Marriage," p. 22.
58. Ibid., p. 19.
59. Ibid., pp. 1, 9.
60. Grimké, *Letters*, p. 87.
61. Sarah Grimké, "Sisters of Charity," in "Sarah M. Grimké's 'Sisters of Charity,' " ed. Gerda Lerner, *Signs: Journal of Women in Culture and Society* 1 (Autumn 1975): 255.
62. Grimké, *Letters*, pp. 50-51.
63. Ibid., pp. 74-84.
64. Grimké, "Education," p. 11.

65. Grimké, *Letters*, p. 33.
66. Grimké, "Education of Woman," post 1846, p. 24.
67. Sarah Grimké, "Condition of Women," in *Letters and Essays*, pp. 129-30.
68. Grimké, "Condition of Women," Grimké MSS.
69. Quoted in Grimké, *Letters*, p. 8.
70. Ibid., p. 90.
71. Ibid., p. 5.
72. Ibid., p. 23.
73. Ibid., pp. 6, 7.
74. Ibid., pp. 24, 113.
75. Ibid., p. 91.
76. Grimké, "Condition," p. 5.
77. Grimké, *Letters*, p. 5; Grimké, "Marriage," p. 1.
78. Angelina Grimké to Weld and John Greenleaf Whittier, August 20, 1837, Barnes and Dumond, *Letters*, 1: 429. (Angelina signed, but Sarah concurred in a note.)
79. Grimké, *Letters*, p. 16.
80. Ibid., p. 23.
81. Grimké, "Laws," p. 6.
82. Grimké, *Letters*, pp. 29-30.
83. Ibid., pp. 24, 126.
84. Grimké, "Marriage," p. 1. Grimké also quoted at great length another author who she found better expressed her own view of human rights. " 'Woman's rights and man's rights are *both* contained in the *same* charter, and held by the *same* tenure. *All rights* spring out of the *moral* nature: they are both the root and offspring of *responsibilities*. The physical constitution is the mere *instrument* of the *moral* nature; sex is a mere *incident* of this constitution, a provision necessary to this *form* of existence; its *only* design, not to give, nor to take away, nor in any respect modify or even *touch* rights or responsibilities in any sense, except so far as the peculiar offices of each sex may afford less or more *opportunity* and ability for the exercise of rights, and the discharge of responsibilities. . . . Consequently, I know nothing of *man's* rights, or *woman's* rights; *human* rights are all that I recognize.' " (Quoted in Grimké, *Letters*, p. 117.)
85. Grimké, "Laws," p. 3.
86. Grimké, "Condition," pp. 10-11.
87. Grimké, "Laws," p. 1.
88. Grimké, "Education," pp. 45-46.
89. Ibid., pp. 22-23.
90. Ibid., pp. 54-55.
91. Grimké, "Education of Woman," post 1846, p. 11.
92. Grimké, *Letters*, p. 51.
93. Ibid., pp. 88.
94. Ibid., p. 11.

95. Grimké, "Marriage," p. 4.
96. Grimké, *Letters*, p. 21.
97. Ibid., pp. 51-54.
98. Grimké, "Condition," p. 17.
99. Grimké, *Letters*, p. 56; Grimké, "Sisters," p. 250.
100. Grimké, *Letters*, p. 88.
101. Grimké, "Condition," p. 9.
102. Grimké, *Letters*, pp. 22-25.
103. Ibid., pp. 16-17, 25.
104. Ibid., p. 81.
105. This split is based on Aristotle's dichotomy between the public or political realm and the private or nonpolitical realm, and its subsequent reinterpretation by Machiavelli. Elshtain argues that Western political thought has set up two divergent sets of standards by which conduct in either realm is judged. Politics is the realm of power and of men; nonpolitics the realm of moral suasion and of women. Jean Bethke Elshtain, "Moral Woman and Immoral Man: A Consideration of the Public-Private Split and Its Political Ramifications," *Politics and Society* 4 (1974): 453-73.
106. Grimké, "Education of Women," post 1946, p. 1; Grimké, "Condition," pp. 5, 6.
107. Grimké, "Condition," p. 6.
108. Hersh, *Slavery of Sex*, pp. 203-6.
109. Grimké, *Letters*, p. 60.
110. This is the converse of Elshtain's conception of public and private morality, in which man has a role in both the public and private spheres and woman only in the private. ("Moral Woman," pp. 460-61.)
111. Grimké, *Letters*, p. 39.
112. Okin has argued that men traditionally ask, "What are women *for*?" (*Women in Western Political Thought*, p. 10.)
113. Grimké, "Education," p. 28.
114. Grimké, "Sisters," pp. 249, 253-54.
115. Grimké, "Marriage," p. 10; Grimké, "Sisters," p. 249.
116. Grimké, "Sisters," p. 256.
117. Grimké, *Letters*, p. 10.
118. Grimké, "Sisters," p. 253.
119. Sarah Grimké to Henry C. Wright, Letter, November 19, 1838, Garrison Papers, MS. A1.2 v. 7, p. 75.
120. Grimké, "Sisters," p. 255.
121. Ibid., p. 254.

CHAPTER FIVE

1. Rossi, *Feminist Papers*, p. 145; Thomas Wentworth Higginson, *Margaret Fuller Ossoli* (Boston: Houghton Mifflin, 1884), p. 17; Bell Gale Chevigny, *The Woman and the Myth: Margaret Fuller's Life and Writings* (Old Westbury, N.Y.: Feminist Press, 1976), p. 20; Conrad, *Perish the Thought*, p. 51.
2. Margaret Fuller Ossoli, *Memoirs*, 2 vols. (Boston: Phillips, Sampson, 1852), 1: 12-13.
3. Ann Douglas, "Margaret Fuller and the Search for History: A Biographical Study," *Women's Studies* 4 (1976): 44.
4. Ossoli, *Memoirs*, 1: 15.
5. Ibid., p. 23.
6. Just how close this relationship was is unclear. Emerson taught self-reliance but wanted others, including Fuller, to follow him. Fuller wanted independence, but also sought Emerson's acceptance. Chevigny suggests that Fuller sought more of a love relation with Emerson but was rebuffed. Chevigny, *Woman and Myth*, pp. 76-78.
7. There are some records of her conversations on mythology (see Caroline Wells Healy Dall, "Margaret and Her Friends Conversations," March 1841, Dall Papers, Schlesinger Library), but most of the Conversations went unrecorded. It would have been particularly helpful to have a record of her talks on women.
8. This is recorded by her in *Summer on the Lakes*, in Margaret Fuller, *The Writings of Margaret Fuller*, ed. Mason Wade (New York: Viking, 1941), pp. 3-104.
9. These are collected in Margaret Fuller Ossoli, *At Home and Abroad: or Things and Thoughts in America and Europe*, ed. Arthur B. Fuller, 2d ed. (Boston: Crosby, Nichols, 1856).
10. Whether they were ever in fact married is still a subject of contention. Any records that may have existed would have been destroyed in a fire. She told no one of her "marriage" until several months afterward, presumably because of problems with Ossoli's family.
11. Margaret Fuller, Notebooks, January 1850, p. 489, Houghton Library.
12. Margaret Fuller to Hicks, May 17, 1848, Fuller Papers, Boston Public Library.
13. Just a sample of some of the material available on these influences: Mary Amanda Lucas, "Emerson and Margaret Fuller: A Transcendental Adventure in Friendship" (M.A. thesis, University of Washington, 1933); Harvey R. Warfel, "Margaret Fuller and Ralph Waldo Emerson," *Publications of the Modern Language Association* 50 (June 1935): 576-94; Anne Elizabeth Gelshel, "Nathaniel Hawthorne and Margaret Fuller" (M.A. thesis, Columbia University, 1955); William Pierce Randel, "Hawthorne, Channing, and Margaret Fuller," *American Literature* 10 (January 1939): 472-76; Austin Warren, "Hawthorne, Margaret Fuller, and 'Nemesis,' " *Publications of the Modern Language Association* 54 (June 1939): 615-18; Charles Thomas

Waller, "A Contrast of the Religious Thought of Henry David Thoreau and Margaret Fuller" (M.A. thesis, University of Georgia, 1959); Helene G. Baer, "Mrs. Child and Miss Fuller," *New England Quarterly* 26 (June 1953): 249-55; Lucy Gregory, "The Influence of George Sand on Margaret Fuller" (M.A. thesis, Columbia University, 1949); Frederick Augustus Braun, *Margaret Fuller and Goethe: The Development of a Remarkable Personality, Her Religion and Philosophy, and Her Relation to Emerson, J. F. Clarke and Transcendentalism* (New York: Henry Holt, 1910); Henry A. Pochmann, *German Culture in America: Philosophical and Literary Influences, 1600-1900* (Madison: University of Wisconsin Press, 1957); Leopold Wellisz, *The Friendship of Margaret Fuller D'Ossoli and Adam Mickiewicz* (New York: Polish Book Importing Co., 1947).

14. See, in particular, Conrad, *Perish the Thought*, pp. 68, 78-82; Cooper, *Roots*, p. 8; Chevigny, *Woman and Myth*, pp. 66, 155, 220; Welter, *Dimity Convictions*, p. 150; and Margaret Vanderhaar Allen, *The Achievement of Margaret Fuller* (University Park, Pa.: Pennsylvania State University Press, 1979), p. 46.

15. For varying interpretations, see Sabrosky, *Rationality*, pp. 60, 148; Braun, *Fuller and Goethe*; Allen, *Achievement*, p. 50; Chevigny, *Woman and Myth*, p. 147; Pochmann, *German Culture*: "More than any other single influence her activity as reveller, translater, and conversationalist was the agency that brought German literature into the orbit of the Transcendentalists' interests" (p. 440).

16. Sabrosky, *Rationality*, p. 77.

17. Braun, *Fuller and Goethe*, pp. 59-60.

18. Allen, *Achievement*, p. 114; Margaret V. Allen, "The Political and Social Criticism of Margaret Fuller," *South Atlantic Quarterly* 72 (Fall 1973): 562, 573; Chevigny, *Woman and Myth*, p. 282; Douglas, "Fuller," p. 46.

19. Fuller was a close friend of James Freeman Clarke and William Henry Channing, both prominent Unitarian ministers. Welter argues that Unitarianism influenced her religious beliefs (*Dimity Convictions*, p. 178), but I think that although she respected and admired the Unitarian approach to religion, she needed more mysticism and faith in a religion.

Though she found the scope of his thought narrow, Fuller appreciated many of the insights of Swedenborg and his Quakerism, especially his enlightened views of women. She considered Swedenborg one of three major male philosophical contributors to the progress of women (Margaret Fuller, *Woman in the Nineteenth Century*, in Joel Myerson, ed., *Margaret Fuller: Essays on American Life and Letters* [New Haven: Yale University Press, 1978], pp. 166-67).

In the last few years of her life, Fuller came to know and admire two men in the vanguard of the Republican movement in Europe, Adam Mickiewicz, a Polish poet, and Giuseppe Mazzini, an Italian political revolutionary. She worked with both of them for the Italian Revolution of 1848. Her philosophical background was similar to that of Mickiewicz (Plato, medieval mysticism, German, French socialists), and their belief in women's abilities and vocation and their conviction that humankind was capable of higher levels of development coincided. Mickiewicz was especially helpful in his encouragement of her stand on women. (Wellisz, *D'Ossoli and Mickiewicz*.) Mazzini helped Fuller to incorporate many values she cherished, such as self-education, opposition to the destructive force of materialism and individualism, and the power of collective thought, while helping her to abandon those which failed her. (Chevigny, *Woman and Myth*, p. 299.)

Other philosophies she regarded as important included Confucianism, Plato, Roman thought, and Milton.

20. Rossi, *Feminist Papers*.
21. Conrad, *Perish the Thought*, p. 53.
22. Margaret Fuller Ossoli, *Life Without and Life Within*, Arthur B. Fuller, ed. (Upper Saddle River, N.J.: Literature House/Grigg Press, 1970 [1860]), p. 277.
23. Margaret Fuller, *Papers on Literature and Art*, 2 parts (New York: AMS Press, 1972 [1846]), p. 80; Fuller, *Writings*, p. 8; Ossoli, *Memoirs*, 2: 27.
24. The best analysis of Fuller's Romantic assumptions is Theriot, "Wollstonecraft and Fuller," pp. 563-64.
25. For an excellent discussion of this, see ibid.
26. Fuller, *Woman*, p. 200.
27. Margaret Fuller, "Credo," quoted in Braun, *Fuller and Goethe*, p. 250.
28. Ibid., p. 249.
29. Fuller, Notebooks V, p. 13, Houghton Library.
30. Ibid., p. 367.
31. Fuller, "Credo," p. 248.
32. See Ossoli, *Memoirs*, 1: 136.
33. Fuller, "Credo," pp. 255, 256.
34. "Margaret Fuller's 1842 Journal: At Concord with the Emersons," ed. Joel Myerson, *Harvard Library Bulletin* 21 (July 1973): 336.
35. Fuller, "Credo," p. 251.
36. Conrad, *Perish the Thought*, p. 78.
37. Chevigny feels it was her most Transcendental work (*Woman and Myth*, p. 215). Sabrosky argues that *Woman in the Nineteenth Century* was also a Transcendentalist statement (*Rationality to Liberation*, pp. 80-81, 148), though I think this understates the importance of other influences in this work.
38. Allen, *Achievement*, p. 43.
39. Fuller, *Writings*, p. 68.
40. Fuller, "1842 Journal," p. 329.
41. Braun, *Fuller and Goethe*, p. 126.
42. Ossoli, *Memoirs*, 2: 30.
43. Braun, *Fuller and Goethe*, p. 139.
44. Ossoli, *Memoirs*, 1: 349.

45. See, especially, Marie Mitchell Urbanski, "Margaret Fuller: Feminist Writer and Revolutionary," in Dale Spender, ed., *Feminist Theorists: Three Centuries of Key Women Thinkers* (New York: Pantheon, 1983), p. 81.
46. Fuller, "1842 Journal," p. 324.
47. Braun, *Fuller and Goethe*, p. 145.
48. Follen was a friend of Lafayette's and later became a Unitarian minister and antislavery agitator. Through him we can draw an intriguing connective link among Wright, Fuller, and Grimké.
49. A summary of her studies during this time can be found in Ossoli, *Memoirs*, 1: 114-66.
50. Fuller, Notebooks V, p. 367.
51. Ossoli, *Memoirs*, 1: 119.
52. The following is drawn primarily from Margaret Fuller, "Translator's Preface to *Eckermann's Conversations with Goethe*," in Fuller, *Writings*, pp. 235-39.
53. Braun has a detailed analysis of the comparison of Fuller and Goethe's religious and philosophical doctrines in *Fuller and Goethe*, pp. 71-145.
54. Pochmann, *German Culture*, p. 443; Allen, *Achievement*, p. 52; Braun, *Fuller and Goethe*, pp. 175-76.
55. Allen, *Achievement*, p. 65.
56. In one of her notebooks, Fuller had copied several of Goethe's maxims. Among them were two that accentuate this point: 1) man becomes acquainted with himself not by reflection but by action; and 2) he who is content with pure experience and acts accordingly, has truth enough. (Fuller, Notebooks V, p. 539.)
57. I would not go so far as some and say that Goethe taught her that men put unfair restrictions on women (Pochmann, *German Culture*, p. 444). She hardly needed a man—not even Goethe—to "teach" this to her.
58. Fuller, *Woman*, pp. 170-71.
59. Margaret Fuller, Letter, March 10, 1849, Boston Public Library.
60. Margaret Fuller to Marcus and Rebecca Spring, Letter, December 12, 1849, Houghton Library.
61. Ossoli, *Memoirs*, 1: 52; Fuller, Notebooks III, p. 285, Houghton Library.
62. Ossoli, *Memoirs*, 1: 218.
63. Ibid., 2: 73-80.
64. Ibid., p. 206.
65. Braun, *Fuller and Goethe*, p. 124.
66. Sidney Lens, *Radicalism in America* (New York: Crowell, 1966), p. 95.
67. Chevigny, *Woman and Myth*, p. 382.
68. Fuller met Martineau in the summer of 1835 and felt bound to her. Martineau may have been the friend she was looking for—she had vigorous reasoning, invention, and clear views. Fuller did not think they shared any particular intellectual sympathies, but both earnestly loved truth. (Fuller, Notebooks III, pp. 369-75.) Later, her attitude changed, especially on reading Martineau's *Society in America* and finding it "presumptuous, irreverent, and inaccurate,"

with hasty generalizations and want of soundness. She did not think it worthy of her. (Ossoli, *Memoirs*, 1: 191-93.)
69. Violette, *Economic Feminism*, p. 83. I have not found any indications that Fuller read Wright or Grimké.
70. Ossoli, *Memoirs*, 2: 196.
71. Margaret Fuller, "French Novelists of the Day," *New York Daily Tribune*, February 1, 1845, in Fuller, *Writings*, pp. 305-6.
72. Ossoli, *Memoirs*, 1: 246-47, 249.
73. Fuller, Notebooks III, p. 65.
74. Allen, "Political and Social Criticism," p. 573. Chevigny also regards Fuller's political value structure to be an unconscious adherence to Jeffersonian rhetoric. (*Woman and Myth*, p. 296.)
75. Chevigny, *Woman and Myth*, p. 282.
76. Fuller, Notebooks III, p. 65.
77. Fuller, *Woman*, p. 92.
78. Ossoli, *Memoirs*, 2: 28.
79. Schramm, *Plow Women*, p. 143.
80. Fuller, *Woman*, p. 146. Her call for the free course of the soul is not approval for every individual licentiously to pursue every whim. Rather, it is for the soul to discover its harmony with natural law and the harmony of the universe.
81. Ossoli, *Memoirs*, 1: 346-47.
82. Fuller, *Woman*, p. 105.
83. Fuller, *Summer on the Lake*, in *Writings*, p. 58; Ossoli, *At Home and Abroad*, pp. 187-88.
84. She did on occasion contradict herself on this. For example, in an article for the *New York Daily Tribune*, she argued that women should be the "guardian angels of the home." But even in this she urged women not to submerge themselves in housework. (Fuller, Notebooks IV, pp. 119-20.)
85. Fuller, *Woman*, pp. 100-101.
86. Ibid., p. 99.
87. Fuller, Notebooks V, p. 649; Notebooks III, p. 301.
88. Fuller, *Woman*, p. 206.
89. Fuller, Notebooks III, p. 519; Margaret Fuller Ossoli, *Woman in the Nineteenth Century and Kindred Papers Relating to the Sphere, Condition and Duties of Woman* (Boston: John P. Jewett, 1855), pp. 183-216. This was true even for the best of men. "Even with Richter, one foremost thought about a wife was that she would 'cook him something good.'" (Fuller, *Woman*, p. 105.)
90. Ossoli, *At Home and Abroad*, pp. 344-45; Fuller, *Woman*, pp. 97-98, 187-98.
91. Fuller, *Woman*, pp. 128-44.
92. Ibid., pp. 135-36.
93. Nona Lyons, "Two Perspectives on Self, Relationships, and Morality," *Harvard Education Review* 54 (1987): 125-45.
94. Theriot, "Wollstonecraft and Fuller," p. 564.

95. Fuller, *Woman*, pp. 200-201.
96. Ibid., p. 161.
97. Ibid.
98. Ibid., p. 205.
99. Ibid., p. 204.
100. Ossoli, *Memoirs*, 1: 283.
101. Urbanski, "Fuller," p. 83.
102. The crossing of racial lines is an important aspect of *Summer on the Lakes*. She drew many parallels between the lives of Native American and white women, referring to both groups as sisters. See Fuller, *Writings*, pp. 78, 80.
103. This theme runs throughout *Woman in the Nineteenth Century*, especially pp. 105, 109, 120, 201-2.
104. Ossoli, *Life Without and Within*, p. 349.
105. Ossoli, *Memoirs*, 2: 150. Fuller was especially sympathetic to the problems of women forced into prostitution. She sought them out and gave them counsel and employment. She felt all women would benefit in this regard when informed about sex and taught self-respect.
106. Fuller, *Woman*, pp. 184-85.
107. Ibid., p. 180.
108. Ossoli, *Memoirs*, 1: 283.
109. Fuller, *Woman*, p. 163.
110. Ibid., pp. 103, 98, 109, 120, 100.
111. Ibid., p. 103.
112. Margaret Fuller, "The Poor Man—An Ideal Sketch," *New York Daily Tribune*, March 25, 1846, in Myerson, *Margaret Fuller*, p. 357.
113. Fuller, *Woman*, p. 120.
114. Ibid., p. 161.
115. Ibid., pp. 107, 115-16, 126, 199, 206. The names signify, respectively, "victorious" and "flourishing" or "virgin."
116. This is essentially Engels's argument. Also, Janeway makes the point that female chastity needed to be ensured to guarantee the legitimacy of inheritance in a society that was structured on titles and aristocratic property. Chastity served an economic function. ("Sexual Paradigms," pp. 581-83.) Okin also has a good discussion of the male obsession with ensuring the paternity of his children (especially Rousseau). (*Women in Political Thought*, p. 101.)
117. That it was in fact possible for men to control their passions she had been assured by the most thoughtful of men. (Fuller, *Woman*, p. 177.)
118. Ibid., pp. 188-89, 195.
119. Ibid., pp. 206, 98.
120. Ibid., pp. 163, 146-49. Fuller spends several pages chronicling the accomplishments of renowned female celibates such as St. Theresa, Tasso's Leonora, Iphigenia, Persica, and the legendary Indian woman who was betrothed to the sun.
121. Ibid., p. 146.
122. Ibid., pp. 83, 95, 98.

123. Ibid., pp. 164-65.
124. Ibid., p. 205.
125. Ibid., p. 206.
126. Welter, *Dimity Convictions*, p. 150.
127. Fuller, *Woman*, pp. 172-73.
128. Daly, *Gyn/Ecology*, pp. 1, 6.

CHAPTER SIX

1. See, for example, Zillah Eisenstein, *The Radical Future of Liberal Feminism* (New York: Longmans, 1981), introduction.
2. Okin, *Women in Political Thought*, pp. 281-89.
3. Ibid.
4. Ibid., p. 281.
5. Camus, *The Rebel*; Rousseau, *The Social Contract*.
6. Audre Lorde, *The Cancer Journals*, 2d ed. (San Francisco: Spinsters Ink, 1981), pp. 99-100.
7. Nancy Chodorow, *The Reproduction of Mothering: Psychoanalysis and the Sociology of Gender* (Berkeley: University of California Press, 1978); Jean Bethke Elshtain, *Public Man, Private Woman: Woman in Social and Political Thought* (Princeton: Princeton University Press, 1981); Rich, *Of Woman Born*; Shulamith Firestone, *The Dialectic of Sex* (New York: Bantam, 1971).
8. Adrienne Rich, *On Lies, Secrets, and Silence: Selected Prose, 1966-1978* (New York: Norton, 1979), p. 244.
9. Solanis, "SCUM Manifesto."
10. Daly, *Gyn/Ecology*.
11. "This is the inherent and inevitable vice of the body politic which, from the moment of its birth, tends consistently to its destruction, just as old age and death ultimately destroy the human" (Rousseau, *Social Contract*, p. 251).
12. Fuller, *Woman*, pp. 164-65.
13. Barbara Smith and Beverly Smith, "Across the Kitchen Table: A Sister-to-Sister Dialogue," in Cherrie Moraga and Gloria Anzaldua, eds., *This Bridge Called My Back: Writings by Radical Women of Color* (Watertown, Mass.: Persephone Press, 1981), pp. 121-22.
14. Camus, *The Rebel*, p. 246.
15. Elizabeth Ann Bartlett, "A Time Apart: Metaphysical Celibacy and the Process of Feminist Self-Definition," paper delivered at National Women's Studies Association, Rutgers University, 1984; Susan Griffin, *Rape: The Power of Consciousness* (San Francisco: Harper, 1979).
16. Rich, *On Lies*, p. 299.
17. Viktor Frankl, *Psychotherapy and Existentialism* (New York: Simon and Schuster, 1967), p. 83.

18. See, for example, New York Radical Women, "Principles," in Morgan, *Sisterhood is Powerful*, pp. 583-84.
19. This is best articulated in Charlotte Bunch, "Lesbians in Revolt," in Jaggar and Rothenberg, *Feminist Frameworks*, pp. 144-48.
20. Examples of this women's culture include the poetry of Adrienne Rich, Audre Lorde, June Jordan, Cherrie Moraga; Judy Chicago's "Dinner Party" and "The Birth Project"; the music of Meg Christian, Alix Dobkin, Mary Watkins, Chris Williamson, Holly Near; the spirituality of Starhawk, Diane Mariechild, Mary Daly; journals such as *Trivia*, *Lesbian Ethics*, *Sinister Wisdom*, *Chrysalis*; collectives such as Kate Millett's. This list is by no means inclusive, merely suggestive.
21. One of the clearest expressions of this sisterhood is Mary Daly's: "Far from being opposites, then sisterhood and female friendship are not clearly distinct. A feminist thinks of her close friends as sisters, but she knows that she has many sisters—women extremely close in their temperaments, vision, commitment—whom she has never met. . . . She knows that there is a network of communication present, and that on some level, at least potentially, it exists among women who have never met or heard of each other. Because of limitations of energy, time, space, these women are not actually her friends, but they are sisters, potential friends" (*Gyn/Ecology*, p. 371).
22. Gearhart, *The Wanderground*, p. 63.
23. The clearest statements of this are in Moraga and Anzaldua, *This Bridge Called My Back*.

Bibliography

UNPUBLISHED SOURCES

Frances Wright
Frances Wright Letters. Houghton Library, Cambridge, Massachusetts.
Wright MSS. Cincinnati Historical Society, Cincinnati, Ohio.
Wright Lectures. Cornell University Library, Ithaca, New York.

Margaret Fuller
Fuller Papers. Boston Public Library, Boston, Massachusetts.
Fuller Letters and Notebooks. Houghton Library, Cambridge, Massachusetts.
Dall Papers. Schlesinger Library, Cambridge, Massachusetts.

Sarah Grimké
Theodore Dwight Weld Collection. Clements Library, University of Michigan, Ann Arbor, Michigan.
Garrison Papers. Boston Public Library, Boston, Massachusetts.
Grimké Personal Papers. Library of Congress, Washington, D.C.

PUBLISHED SOURCES

Allen, Margaret Vanderhaar. *The Achievement of Margaret Fuller*. University Park, Pa.: Pennsylvania State University Press, 1979.
──────. "The Political and Social Criticism of Margaret Fuller," *South Atlantic Quarterly* 72 (Fall 1973): 560-73.
Amundsen, Kirsten. *A New Look at the Silenced Majority: Women and American Democracy*. Englewood Cliffs, N.J.: Prentice-Hall, 1979.
Ball, Terence. "Utilitarianism, Feminism, and the Franchise: James Mill and His Critics," *History of Political Thought* 1 (Spring 1980): 91-115.

Bartlett, Elizabeth Ann. "Liberty, Equality, Sorority: Contradiction and Integrity in Feminist Thought and Practice," *Women's Studies International Forum* 9, 6 (1986): 521-29.

———. "A Time Apart: Metaphysical Celibacy and the Process of Feminist Self-Definition." Paper delivered at National Women's Studies Association, Rutgers University, 1984.

Beecher, Catharine. *A Treatise on Domestic Economy*. New York: Source Books Press, 1970 [1841].

Belerky, Mary Field, et al. *Women's Ways of Knowing: The Development of Self, Voice, and Mind*. New York: Basic Books, 1986.

Benston, Margaret. "The Political Economy of Women's Liberation." In *Voices from Women's Liberation*. Edited by Leslie B. Tanner. New York: New American Library, 1970, pp. 279-92.

Bentham, Jeremy. *The Utilitarians, An Introduction to the Principles of Morals and Legislation*. Garden City, N.Y.: Doubleday, 1961.

Berg, Barbara J. *The Remembered Gate: Origins of American Feminism: The Woman and the City, 1800-1860*. New York: Oxford University Press, 1978.

Birney, Catherine H. *The Grimké Sisters: Sarah and Angelina Grimké: The First American Women Advocates of Abolition and Woman's Rights*. St. Clair Shores, Mich.: Scholarly Press, 1970 [1885].

Bourque, Susan C., and Jean Grossholtz. "Politics and Unnatural Practice: Political Science Looks at Female Participation," *Politics and Society* 4 (Winter 1974): 225-66.

Braun, Frederick Augustus. *Margaret Fuller and Goethe: The Development of a Remarkable Personality, Her Religion and Philosophy, and Her Relation to Emerson, J. F. Clarke, and Transcendentalism*. New York: Henry Holt, 1910.

Camus, Albert. *The Rebel: An Essay on Man in Revolt*. Translated by Anthony Bower. New York: Vintage, 1956.

Cassirer, Ernst. *The Philosophy of the Enlightenment*. Translated by Fritz C. A. Koellin and James P. Pettegrove. Princeton: Princeton University Press, 1951.

Chevigny, Bell Gale. *The Woman and the Myth: Margaret Fuller's Life and Writings*. Old Westbury, N.Y.: Feminist Press, 1976.

Commager, Henry Steele. *The Era of Reform: 1830-1860*. New York: Van Nostrand, 1960.

Conrad, Susan Phinney. *Perish the Thought: Intellectual Women in Romantic America, 1830-1860*. New York: Oxford University Press, 1976.

Cooper, James L., and Sheila McIsaac Cooper. *The Roots of American Feminist Thought*. Boston: Allyn & Bacon, 1973.

Cott, Nancy F. "Passionlessness: An Interpretation of Victorian Sexual Ideology, 1790-1850," *Signs: Journal of Women in Culture and Society* 4 (Winter 1978): 219-316.

Curti, Merle. *The Growth of American Thought*. New York: Harper, 1964.

Daly, Mary. *Gyn/Ecology: The Metaethics of Radical Feminism*. Boston: Beacon Press, 1978.

D'Arusmont, Frances Wright. *Biography, Notes, and Political Letters of Frances Wright D'Arusmont, Parts 1 and 2*. New York: John Windt, 1844.

Douglas, Ann. "Margaret Fuller and the Search for History: A Biographical Study," *Women's Studies* 4 (1976): 37-86.

Durkheim, Emile. *Socialism and Saint-Simon*. Edited by Alvin W. Gouldner, translated by Charlotte Sattler. Yellow Springs, Ohio: Antioch Press, 1958.

Edwards, Paul, ed. *The Encyclopedia of Philosophy*. 8 vols. New York: Free Press, 1967.

Eisenstein, Zillah. *The Radical Future of Liberal Feminism*. New York: Longmans, 1981.

Elshtain, Jean Bethke. "Moral Woman and Immoral Man: A Consideration of the Public-Private Split and Its Political Ramifications," *Politics and Society* 4 (1974): 453-73.

Emerson, Ralph Waldo. *The Selected Writings of Ralph Waldo Emerson*. Edited by Brooks Atkinson. New York: Random House, 1950.

Farnham, Christie, ed. *The Impact of Feminist Research in the Academy*. Bloomington: Indiana University Press, 1987.

Feinberg, Joel. "The Nature and Value of Rights." In *Concepts in Social and Political Philosophy*. Edited by Richard E. Flatham. New York: Macmillan, 1973, pp. 456-68.

Firestone, Shulamith. "The Women's Rights Movement in the U.S.: A New View." In *Voices from Women's Liberation*. Edited by Leslie B. Tanner. New York: New American Library, 1970, pp. 433-43.

Flexner, Eleanor. *Century of Struggle: The Woman's Rights Movement in the United States*. New York: Atheneum, 1974.

Frankl, Viktor. *Psychotherapy and Existentialism*. New York: Simon and Schuster, 1967.

Free Enquirer. 1825-33.

Freeman, Jo. *The Politics of Women's Liberation: A Case Study of an Emerging Social Movement and Its Relation to the Policy Process.* New York: David McKay, 1975.

Fuller, Margaret. *Margaret Fuller: American Romantic: A Selection from Her Writings and Correspondence.* Edited by Perry Miller. Ithaca: Cornell University Press, 1963.

———. *Margaret Fuller: Essays on American Life and Letters.* Edited by Joel Myerson. New Haven: Yale University Press, 1978.

———. "Margaret Fuller's 1842 Journal: At Concord with the Emersons." Edited by Joel Myerson. *Harvard Library Bulletin* 21 (July 1973): 320-40.

———. *Papers on Literature and Art.* 2 parts. New York: AMS Press, 1972 [1846].

———. *The Writings of Margaret Fuller.* Selected and edited by Mason Wade. New York: Viking, 1941.

Gay, Peter. *The Enlightenment: An Interpretation, The Rise of Modern Paganism.* 2 vols. New York: Norton, 1966, 1969.

Gearhart, Sally Miller. *The Wanderground: Stories of the Hillwomen.* Watertown, Mass.: Persephone Press, 1979.

Gierke, Otto. *Natural Law and the Theory of Society: 1500-1800.* Translated by Ernest Barker. Cambridge: Cambridge University Press, 1958.

Gilligan, Carol. *In a Different Voice: Psychological Theory and Women's Development.* Cambridge: Harvard University Press, 1982.

Goldman, Emma. *Anarchism and Other Essays.* New York: Dover, 1969.

Grimes, Alan Pendleton. *American Political Thought.* New York: Henry Holt, 1955.

Grimké, Sarah M. *Letters on the Equality of the Sexes and Other Essays.* Edited by Elizabeth Ann Bartlett. New Haven: Yale University Press, 1988.

———. "Sarah M. Grimké's 'Sisters of Charity.' " Edited by Gerda Lerner. *Signs: Journal of Women in Culture and Society* 1 (Autumn 1975): 246-56.

Harding, Sandra. *Feminism and Methodology.* Bloomington: Indiana University Press, 1987.

Hartz, Louis. *The Liberal Tradition in America: An Interpretation of American Political Thought Since the Revolution.* New York: Harcourt, 1955.

Hersh, Blanche Glassman. *The Slavery of Sex: Feminist Abolitionists in America.* Urbana: University of Illinois Press, 1978.

Higginson, Thomas Wentworth. *Margaret Fuller Ossoli.* Boston: Houghton Mifflin, 1884.

Hogeland, Ronald W. " 'The Female Appendage': Feminine Life-Styles in America, 1820-1860." In *Our American Sisters: Women in American Life and Thought*. 2d ed. Edited by Jean E. Friedman and William G. Shade. Boston: Allyn & Bacon, 1976, pp. 138-48.

Holbrook, Stewart H. *Dreamers of the American Dream*. Garden City, N.Y.: Doubleday, 1957.

Howe, Florence. *Myths of Coeducation*. Bloomington: Indiana University Press, 1984.

Hume, David. *A Treatise of Human Nature*. Edited by L. A. Selby-Bigge. Oxford: Clarendon Press, 1888.

Hutcheson, Francis. *An Inquiry into the Original of Our Ideas of Beauty and Virtue: in Two Treatises*. 4th ed., corrected. Westmead, England: Gregg International Publishers, 1969 [1737].

Iglitzin, Lynne B. "Political Education and Sexual Liberation," *Politics and Society* 2 (Winter 1972): 241-54.

Jaggar, Alison M., and Paula S. Rothenberg. *Feminist Frameworks: Alternative Accounts of the Relations Between Women and Men*. 2d ed. New York: McGraw-Hill, 1984.

Janeway, Elizabeth. "Who is Sylvia? On the Loss of Sexual Paradigms," *Signs: Journal of Women in Culture and Society* 5 (Summer 1980): 573-89.

Kittay, Eva Feder, and Diana T. Meyers. *Women and Moral Theory*. Totowa, N.J.: Rowman and Littlefield, 1987.

Laidler, Harry W. *History of Socialism: A Comparative Study of Socialism, Communism, Trade Unionism, Cooperation, Utopianism, and Other Systems of Reform and Reconstruction*. New York: Crowell, 1968.

Langer, William L. *Political and Social Upheaval, 1832-1852*. New York: Harper, 1969.

Lens, Sidney. *Radicalism in America*. New York: Crowell, 1966.

Lerner, Gerda. *The Grimké Sisters from South Carolina: Pioneers for Woman's Rights and Abolition*. New York: Schocken Books, 1971.

———. "The Lady and the Mill Girl: Changes in the Status of Women in the Age of Jackson." In *Our American Sisters: Women in American Life and Thought*. 2d ed. Edited by Jean E. Friedman and William G. Shade. Boston: Allyn & Bacon, 1976.

Locke, John. *Second Treatise on Civil Government*. In *Social Contract: Essays by Locke, Hume and Rousseau*, pp. 1-143. London: Oxford University Press, 1960.

Lorde, Audre. *The Cancer Journals*. 2d ed. San Francisco: Spinsters Ink, 1980.

———. *Sister Outsider: Essays and Speeches by Audre Lorde*. Trumansburg, N.Y.: Crossing Press, 1984.

Lutz, Alma. *Crusade for Freedom: Women of the Antislavery Movement*. Boston: Beacon Press, 1968.

Lynd, Staughton. *Intellectual Origins of American Radicalism*. New York: Pantheon, 1968.

Lyons, Nona. "Two Perspectives on Self, Relationships, and Morality," *Harvard Education Review* 54 (1987): 125-45.

MacCallum, Gerald C., Jr. "Negative and Positive Freedom." In *Concepts in Social & Political Philosophy*. Edited by Richard E. Flatham. New York: Macmillan, 1973, pp. 294-308.

McFadden, Maggie. "Anatomy of Difference: Toward a Classification of Feminist Theory," *Women's Studies International Forum* 7, 6 (1984): 495-504.

McWilliams, Nancy. "Contemporary Feminism, Consciousness-Raising, and Changing Views of the Political." In *Women in Politics*. Edited by Jane S. Jaquette. New York: Wiley, 1974, pp. 157-79.

Mill, John Stuart. *The Subjection of Women*. London: Longmans, 1869.

———. *Utilitarianism*. In *The Utilitarians*. Garden City, N.Y.: Doubleday, 1978, pp. 399-472.

Moraga, Cherrie, and Gloria Anzaldua. *This Bridge Called My Back: Writings by Radical Women of Color*. Watertown, Mass.: Persephone Press, 1981.

Neumann, Franz. "The Concept of Political Freedom." In *Concepts in Social and Political Philosophy*. Edited by Richard E. Flatham. New York: Macmillan, 1973, pp. 266-94.

Nies, Judith. *Seven Women: Portraits from the American Radical Tradition*. New York: Viking, 1977.

Noddings, Nel. *Caring: A Feminine Approach to Ethics and Moral Education*. Berkeley: University of California Press, 1984.

Ochs, Carol. *Women and Spirituality*. Totowa, N.J.: Rowman & Allenheld, 1983.

Okin, Susan Muller. *Women in Western Political Thought*. Princeton: Princeton University Press, 1979.

O'Neill, William L. "In the Beginning." In *Our American Sisters: Women in American Life and Thought*. 2d ed. Edited by Jean E. Friedman and William G. Shade. Boston: Allyn & Bacon, 1976, pp. 203-21.

Ossoli, Margaret Fuller. *At Home and Abroad: or Things and Thoughts in America and Europe.* 2d ed. Edited by Arthur B. Fuller. Boston: Crosby, Nichols, 1856.

———. *Life Without and Life Within.* Edited by Arthur B. Fuller. Upper Saddle River, N.J.: Literature House/Gregg Press, 1970 [1860].

———. *Memoirs.* 2 vols. Boston: Phillips, Sampson, 1852.

———. *Woman in the Nineteenth Century and Kindred Papers Relating to the Sphere, Condition and Duties of Woman.* Edited by Arthur B. Fuller. Boston: John P. Jewett, 1855.

Parrington, Vernon Louis. *Main Currents in American Thought: An Interpretation of American Literature From the Beginnings to 1920.* 3 vols. New York: Harcourt, 1930.

Perkins, A. J. G., and Theresa Wolfson. *Frances Wright: Free Enquirer: The Study of a Temperament.* New York: Harper, 1939.

Perry, Lewis. *Radical Abolitionism: Anarchy and the Government of God in Antislavery Thought.* Ithaca: Cornell University Press, 1973.

Pochmann, Henry A. *German Culture in America: Philosophical and Literary Influences, 1600-1900.* Madison: University of Wisconsin Press, 1957.

Riasanovsky, Nicholas V. *The Teachings of Charles Fourier.* Berkeley: University of California Press, 1969.

Rich, Adrienne. *Of Woman Born: Motherhood as Experience and Institution.* New York: Norton, 1976.

———. *On Lies, Secrets, and Silence: Selected Prose: 1966-1978.* New York: Norton, 1979.

Riegel, Robert E. *American Feminists.* Lawrence: University Press of Kansas, 1963.

Rossi, Alice S., ed. *The Feminist Papers: From Adams to de Beauvoir.* New York: Columbia University Press, 1973.

Rousseau, Jean Jacques. *Émile: Selections.* Translated and edited by William Boyd. New York: Columbia University, 1962 [1762].

———. *The Social Contract.* London: Oxford University Press, 1960 [1762].

Rusk, Ralph L., ed. *The Letters of Ralph Waldo Emerson.* 6 vols. New York: Columbia University Press, 1939.

Sabrosky, Judith A. *From Rationality to Liberation: The Evolution of Feminist Ideology.* Westport, Conn.: Greenwood Press, 1979.

Schaef, Anne Wilson. *Women's Reality.* Minneapolis: Winston Press, 1981.

Schramm, Sarah Slavin. *Plow Women Rather Than Reapers: An Intellectual History of Feminism in the United States*. Metuchen, N.J.: Scarecrow Press, 1979.

Shelley, Percy Bysshe. *A Defense of Poetry*. Edited by Albert S. Cooke. Boston: Ginn, 1890.

Sibley, Mulford Q. *Political Ideas and Ideologies: A History of Political Thought*. New York: Harper, 1970.

Smith, Barbara, and Beverly Smith. "Across the Kitchen Table: A Sister-to-Sister Dialogue." In Cherrie Moraga and Gloria Anzaldua, eds. *This Bridge Called My Back: Writings by Radical Women of Color*. Watertown, Mass.: Persephone Press, 1981.

Smith, Page. *Daughters of the Promised Land: Women in American History*. Boston: Little, Brown, 1970.

Sochen, June. *Herstory: A Woman's View of American History*. New York: Alfred Publishing, 1974.

Solanis, Valerie. "Excerpts from the SCUM (Society for Cutting Up Men) Manifesto." In Robin Morgan, ed., *Sisterhood is Powerful: An Anthology of Writings from the Women's Liberation Movement*. New York: Vintage, 1970.

Stanton, Elizabeth Cady, Susan B. Anthony, and Matilda Joslyn Gage. *History of Woman Suffrage*. 2 vols. New York: Arno Press, 1969 [1881].

Theriot, Nancy M. "Mary Wollstonecraft and Margaret Fuller: A Theoretical Comparison," *International Journal of Women's Studies* 2 (November/December 1979): 560-74.

Thilly, Frank. *A History of Philosophy*. 3d ed. New York: Holt, 1957.

Urbanski, Marie Mitchell. "Margaret Fuller: Feminist Writer and Revolutionary." In Dale Spender, ed., *Feminist Theorists: Three Centuries of Key Women Thinkers*. New York: Pantheon, 1983.

Violette, Augusta Genevieve. *Economic Feminism in American Literature Prior to 1848*. Orono, Maine: University Press, 1925.

Vogel, Stanley M. *German Literary Influences on the American Transcendentalists*. New Haven: Yale University Press, 1955.

Waterman, William Randall. *Frances Wright*. New York: AMS Press, 1967.

Wellisz, Leopold. *The Friendship of Margaret Fuller D'Ossoli and Adam Mickiewicz*. New York: Polish Book Importing Co., 1947.

Welter, Barbara. "The Cult of True Womanhood: 1820-1860," *American Quarterly* 18 (Summer 1966): 151-74.

———. *Dimity Convictions: The American Woman in the Nineteenth Century.* Athens: Ohio University Press, 1976.
West, Jessamyn, ed. *The Quaker Reader.* New York: Viking, 1962.
Wills, Garry. *Inventing America: Jefferson's Declaration of Independence.* Garden City, N.Y.: Doubleday, 1978.
Wollstonecraft, Mary. *The Rights of Woman.* London: Dent, 1965.
Wright, Frances. *Address, Containing a Review of the Times, as first delivered in the Hall of Science, New York, on Sunday, May 9, 1830.* New York: Free Enquirer, 1830.
———. *Address of the State of the Public Mind and the Measures Which It Calls For, New York & Philadelphia, Autumn of 1829.* New York: Free Enquirer, 1829.
———. *Address to the People of Philadelphia, Fourth of July, 1829.* New York: George H. Evans, 1829.
———. *Course of Popular Lectures; with Three Addresses, on Various Public Occasions, and a Reply to the Charges against the French Reformers of 1789 and Supplement Course of Lectures.* London: James Watson, 1834; reprint ed. Frances Wright D'Arusmont. *Life, Letters, and Lectures 1834-1844.* New York: Arno Press, 1972.
———. *A Few Days in Athens; Being the Translation of a Greek Manuscript Discovered in Herculaneum.* London: Longmans, 1822.
———. *Introductory Address at Opening of Hall of Science, New York on Sunday, April 26, 1829.* New York: George Evans, 1829.
———. *A Lecture on Existing Evils and Their Remedy, as delivered in the Arch Street Theater, Philadelphia, June 2, 1829.* New York: George Evans, 1829.
———. *Parting Address: as delivered in Bowery Theatre to People in New York, June, 1830.* New York: Free Enquirer, 1830.
———. *Popular Tracts, Fables.* New York: Free Enquirer, n.d.
———. *Popular Tracts, No. 3. An Address to the Industrious Classes: A Sketch of a System of National Education.* New York: Free Enquirer, 1830.
———. *Views of Society and Manners in America.* Edited by Paul R. Baker. Cambridge: Belknap Press, 1963.
Yates, Gayle Graham. *What Women Want: The Ideas of the Movement.* Cambridge: Harvard University Press, 1975.

Index

Abolitionism, 21, 150n31
    Sarah Grimké on, 57, 58-60, 62, 64, 80-81
    Frances Wright on, 26-27
Abuse, physical, 69, 106, 121
The Achievement of Margaret Fuller, (Margaret Vanderhaar Allen), 155n14, 155n18, 158n74
Adam, 76
Adams, Abigail, xiii
Age of Reason
    See Enlightenment
Alcott, Bronson, 2, 90, 93
Allen, Margaret Vanderhaar, 155n14, 155n18, 158n74
Altorf, A Tragedy (Frances Wright), 25
American Anti-Slavery Society, 59
American Feminists (Robert E. Riegel), 138n4
American Political Thought (Alan Pendleton Grimes), 138n3
The American Political Tradition: And the Men Who Made It (Richard Hofstadter), 138n3
American Revolution, 25-26
Anabaptism, 21
Anarchism and Other Essays (Emma Goldman), 146n53
"Anatomy of Difference: Toward a Classification of Feminist Theory" (Maggie McFadden), 139n12
Androgyny
    in feminist thought, 3, 117, 123
    of Margaret Fuller, 92, 103, 109, 112
Anglo-American radical sectarianism
    See Radical sectarianism
Anti-Slavery Convention of American Women, 59
Anzaldua, Gloria, 161n23

Apollo, 95
Austin, John, 26

Ball, Terence, 33, 145n33
Bartlett, Elizabeth Ann, 140n28, 160n15
Beecher, Catharine, 7, 140n27
Belerky, Mary Field, 139n9, 148n102
Bentham, Jeremy, 13-14, 35, 36, 141n17
    and Frances Wright, 26, 33, 51
Berg, Barbara J.
    The Remembered Gate: Origins of American Feminism: The Woman and the City, 1800-1860, 137n1, 138n4, 146n57
Bible, 62-64, 74-77, 150n39
Birney, Catherine H., 149n5
Bloomers, 61
Boatwright, Eleanor Miot
    Status of Women in Georgia, 1783-1860, xii-xiii
Bobroff-Hajal, Anne
    Working Women in Russia Under the Hunger Tsar: Political Activism and Daily Life, xiii
Brahma, 95
Braun, Frederick Augustus, 93, 154n13, 155n15, 155n17, 156n41, 156n43
The British and American Women's Trade Union Leagues, 1890-1925: A Case Study of Feminism and Class (Robin Miller Jacoby), xv-xvi
Brook Farm, 93
Brown, Charles Brockden, 101
Bunch, Charlotte, 161n19
Byron, Lord, 146n55

Camhi, Jane Jerome
    Women Against Women: American Anti-Suffragism, 1880-1920, xiv

173

INDEX

Camus, Albert, 133, 151n42-43, 160n5, 160n14
Carbonari movement, 26, 35-36
Caring: A Feminine Approach to Ethics and Moral Education (Nel Nodding), 148n105
Carlson, Ralph, xi
Carlyle, Richard, 91
Cassirer, Ernst, 140n1, 141n12
Celibacy, 114
Century of Struggle: The Women's Rights Movement in the United States (Eleanor Flexner), 139n15
Chambers, Clarke, x
Channing, William Henry, 2, 90, 155n19
Chapman, Maria, 59
Charleston, S.C., 57
Chataugqua Circle, xv
Chevigny, Bell Gale, 154n1, 154n6, 155n14-15, 155n18, 157n67, 158n75
Child, Lydia Maria, 59, 66, 101
Chodorow, Nancy, 160n7
Christianity, 95
Civil rights, 78
Clarke, James Freeman, 90, 98, 155n19
Class consciousness, 120
Collectivism, 120
Colonial Dames, xv
Come-outerism, 21-22
Commager, Henry Steele, 2, 139n8
Common law, 41-42
Comte, August, 36
Confusius, 95
Conrad, Susan Phinney, 96-97, 138n2, 138n4, 142n27, 154n1, 155n14, 156n21
"Conversations" (Margaret Fuller), 90-91, 116
Cooper, James L., 2, 138n7, 139n13, 143n41, 149n17, 155n14
Cooper, Sheila McIsaac, 2, 138n7, 139n13, 143n41, 149n17, 155n14
Cott, Nancy F., 148n87
Coverture, 71
Crusade for Freedom: Women of the Antislavery Movement (Alma Lutz), 137n1

"The Cult of True Womanhood: 1820-1860" (Barbara Welter), 136n1
Curti, Merle, 138n3

Daly, Mary, 103, 116, 140n24, 160n10, 160n128, 161n21
D'Arusmont, Frances Sylva, 29-30, 144n13, 144n20
D'Arusmont, Phiquepal, 29-30, 147n73
Daughters of the American Revolution, xv
Davis, Paulina Wright, 5
Declaration of Independence, 31-32, 34, 144n27
Declaration of Sentiments, 150n31
A Defense of Poetry (Percy Bysshe Shelley), 142n28
Degler, Carl, x
Descartes, René, 10
The Dial, 97
Dimity Convictions: The American Woman in the Nineteenth Century (Barbara Welter), 139n21, 155n14, 160n127
Dix, Dorothea, 2
Domesticity, 104
  See also Gender roles
Douglas, Ann, 154n3
Douglass, Sarah, 59
Dreamers of the American Dream (Stewart H. Holbrook), 139n14
Durkheim, Emile, 142n33

Economic Feminism in American Literature Prior to 1848 (Augusta Genevieve Violette), 138n2, 143n41, 158n69
Economic reform, 123
  Sarah Grimké on, 73
  Frances Wright on, 46-47, 147n83
Edgeworth, Maria, 101, 116
Education reform
  Sarah Grimké on, 73, 78
  Robert Owen on, 142n32
  Frances Wright on, 43-46, 147n73
Eisenstein, Zillah, 160n1
Elshtain, Jean Bethke, 127, 153n105, 153n110, 160n7
Emerson, Ralph Waldo, 2, 19, 90, 93, 97-98, 142n29, 154n6
English Dissenters, 21

Enlightenment, 1, 9-11, 12, 20
  and freedom, 9-10
  and Margaret Fuller, 94
  and Sarah Grimké, 57, 65-66
  liberal individualism, 119
  politics of, 11
  and religion, 10
  and Romanticism, 17-18, 19
  in Scotland, 25
  and Frances Wright, 30-32, 38
The Enlightenment: An Interpretation (Peter Gay), 140n2-141n9, 145n30, 145n34
Epicureanism, 30
  ties with utilitarianism, 33, 146n55
  and Frances Wright, 31, 32-33, 35, 145n30
Epicurus, 32
Equality
  and androgyny, 103
  concept of, 6-7, 8
  in Margaret Fuller's feminist thought, 105-9
  in Sarah Grimké's feminist thought, 73-79
  and liberty, 125-26, 128-29, 129-36
  and nineteenth-century feminism, 1
  and Utilitarianism, 14
  and utopian socialism, 20, 43
  in Frances Wright's feminist thought, 32, 34, 43-47
Equal Rights Amendment (ERA), 134
The Era of Reform: 1830-1860 (Henry Steele Commager), 139n8
Essays (Thomas Reid), 142n25
Evans, Jonathon, 58
Eve, 76, 112-13
"Excerpts from the SCUM (Society for Cutting Up Men) Manifesto" (Valerie Solanis), 140n25, 160n9

Family, 121-22
"Fanny Wrightest," 28
Fanny Wright party, 27
Farnham, Christie, 148n103
Feinburg, Joel, 150n34
Female Anti-Slavery Society, 66
Femininity, 84, 92, 105, 123
Feminism
  categories of, 3
  Enlightenment, 1, 119-20
  and equality, 6-7, 32, 34, 43-47, 73-79, 105-9
  and Margaret Fuller, 6-8, 92, 103-5, 105-9, 109-16
  and Sarah Grimké, 6-8, 67-68
  lesbian, 132, 135
  and liberty, 6, 32-34, 38-42, 68-72, 103-5
  integrated, 136
  intellectual traditions of, 1-8, 9-23, 119-20
  and natural law theory, 13
  and political ideologies, 3
  and Quakerism, 23
  radical, 135
  separatists, 128, 132, 135
  and sorority, 747-52, 54-55, 79-85, 109-16
  and utopian socialism, 20
  and Frances Wright, 6-8, 29, 31, 38-47
Feminism and Methodology (Sandra Harding), 148n103
Feminist Frameworks: Alternative Accounts of the Relations Between Women and Men (Alison Jaggar and Paula S. Rothenberg), 139n11
The Feminist Papers: From Adams to de Beauvoir (Alice S. Rossi), 137n1, 139n11, 139n15, 143n4
A Few Days in Athens (Frances Wright), 25, 32, 33, 35, 145n30, 146n52
Firestone, Shulamith, 127, 137n1
Flexner, Eleanor, 5, 139n15
Follen, Charles, 98, 157n48
Fourier, Charles, 19-20, 21, 60, 93, 99, 100-101, 142-43n34, 145-46n43
Frances Wright (William Randell Waterman), 144n14, 144n18, 145n29
Frances Wright: Free Enquirer: The Study of a Temperament (A. J. G. Perkins and Theresa Wolfson), 143n5, 144n7, 144n19, 146n45
Frankl, Viktor, 134, 160n17
Fraternity, 122
Freedom
  in Enlightenment thought, 9-10
  Fuller defines, 103
  and Sarah Grimké, 85
  moral, 70

in Romanticism, 19, 21
and utilitarianism, 141n19
in utopian socialism, 21
The Free Enquirer, 27, 36, 147n76
Freeman, Jo, 137n1, 138n4
Free will, 70, 75
Friedman, Jean E., 137n1
The Friend, 62
From Rationality to Liberation: The Evolution of Feminist Ideology (Judith A. Sabrosky), 138n1, 138n4, 139n13, 139n15, 139n19, 143n43, 144n14, 145n42, 155n15
Fuller, Margaret, xiv, 2, 4, 5, 48
  androgyny of, 92, 103, 112
  At Home and Abroad: or Things and Thoughts in America and Europe, 154n9
  biographies of, 154n1, 154n3, 157n45, 159n101
  childhood of, 89-90
  compared to Frances Wright and Sarah Grimké, 119-36
  "Conversations," 90, 116, 154n7
  "Credo," 156n27, 156n31, 156n33, 156n35
  death of, 91
  and Ralph Waldo Emerson, 90, 92, 97-100
  and equality, 105-9
  in Europe, 91
  other feminists' influence on, 101-2
  feminist thought of, 6-8, 103-5, 105-9, 109-16
  "French Novelists of the Day," 158n71
  German idealism influences, 93, 98-100, 101
  and Goethe, 93, 98-99
  "The Great Lawsuit. Man v. Men, Woman v. Women," 90-91, 97
  intellectual environment of, 92-103
  on intelligence of women, 105
  in Italy, 89
  Thomas Jefferson's influence on, 93, 94, 101
  and liberty, 103-5
  Life Without and Life Within, 156n22
  on marriage, 106-7, 113
  and marriage to Angelo Ossoli, 91, 154n10

  on men, 110-11
  mysticism of, 95-96, 99, 154n7
  New York Daily Tribune, 91, 92, 158n84
  "The Poor Man—An Ideal Sketch," 159n112
  and prison reform, 89, 98
  and religion, 94-96, 99-100
  as Romantic philosopher, 19, 92-93, 94
  and George Sand, 91, 101-2
  and Sing Sing prison, 89, 91, 102
  socialism of, 100-101
  and sorority, 102, 109-16
  and the soul, 96, 103-5, 107-9, 115
  Summer on the Lakes, 154n8, 158n83, 159n102
  theoretical assumptions of, 5
  and Transcendentalism, 17, 89-91, 92-93, 97-98
  "Translator's Preface to *Eckermann's Conversations with Goethe*," 157n52
  as well-read, 92
  Woman in the Nineteenth Century, 4, 5, 66, 91, 100, 109, 150n40, 156n37, 158n77, 158n80, 158n82, 158n89, 159n103, 159n109, 159n113, 160n127
Fuller, Margaret (mother of Margaret Fuller), 89
Fuller, Timothy (father of Margaret Fuller), 89-90
Fuller and Goethe, (Frederick Augustus Braun), 154n13, 155n15, 155n17, 156n41, 156n43

Gage, Matilda Joslyn, 139n20
Garrison, William Lloyd, 59, 64, 149n9, 150n31
Gate, George, *History of Greece*, 26
Gay, Peter, 9-10, 11, 140n2-141n9, 145n30, 145n34
Gearhart, Sally Miller, 135, 140n25, 161n22
Gender roles, 120-22
  Margaret Fuller on, 104-5, 107-9
  Sarah Grimké on, 82-83
  Frances Wright on, 44-45, 48-49, 53
German idealism, 93, 98-100, 101
Gierke, Otto, 141n11
Gilligan, Carol, 139n9, 148n104
Glasgow University

See University of Glasgow
God, 95, 120, 141n11, 150n39
Godwin, William, 31, 94, 101, 107
Goethe, 93, 98-100, 157n56, 157n57
Goldman, Emma, 146
Grant, Mary, *Private Woman, Public Person: An Account of the Life of Julia Ward Howe from 1819 to 1868*, xiv
"The Great Lawsuit. Man v. Men, Woman v. Women" (Margaret Fuller), 90-91, 97
Grew, Mary, 59
Griffin, Susan, 103
Grimes, Alan Pendleton, 138n3, 138n4
Grimké, Angelina, 2, 57, 59, 60, 74
Grimké, Sarah, xiv, 2, 4, 5, 48
   abolition work of, 57, 58-60, 62, 64, 80
   and American Anti-Slavery Society, 59
   background of, 57-59
   use of Bible, 61-63, 65-66, 67, 74-77, 81
   runs boarding school, 60
   and bonds of womanhood, 80-81
   and civil rights, 78
   compared to Margaret Fuller and Fannie Wright, 119-36
   "Condition," 151n50, 151n51
   desire to study law, 57-58
   early influences on, 57-58
   education of, 61-62
   on education for women, 69-70, 73
   "Education of Women," 148n1, 151n64, 152n66, 152n88, 152n91
   and equality, 58, 73-79
   "Essays on the Laws Respecting Women," 149n23
   "Of Feelings (Sensations) and Emotion," 149n21
   feminist influences on, 66
   feminist thought of, 6-8, 61, 62-64, 66, 67-68
   and gender roles, 82-83
   relationship with Angelina Grimké, 57, 58, 60-61
   on human rights, 152n84
   individualism of, 66, 71
   and the law, 73
   "Letter on the Subject of Prejudice Amongst the Society of Friends of the United States," 58-59
   Letters on the Equality of the Sexes, 4, 64, 65, 81, 149n15, 149n20, 151n46, 151n60, 151n62
   and liberty, 58, 68-72
   on marriage, 70-73
   "Marriage," 151n45, 151n47, 151n57, 152n77, 152n84, 153n95, 153n115
   on men's roles, 75-76, 79-80, 86-87
   moral theory of, 63-64, 70, 72, 81-82
   and natural law, 141n11
   "Pastoral Letter," 59-60
   and perfectionism, 64-65
   and physical autonomy, 68-69
   Quaker influences on, 58-59, 62, 64
   and radical sectarianism, 22, 62
   and concept of rights, 65
   on self-reliance of women, 84-85
   slavery and women, 57, 59-60, 68
   "Sisters of Charity," 151n61
   and sorority, 79-85
   theoretical assumptions of, 5
   translates biography of Joan of Arc, 61
   and Theodore Weld, 57, 60-61, 64-65
   on women in politics, 73-74
   writings of, 61
Grimké, Thomas, 57
The Grimké Sisters from South Carolina: Pioneers for Women's Rights and Abolition (Gerda Lerner), 61, 138n4, 149n16
The Grimké Sisters: Sarah and Angelina Grimké: The First American Women Advocates of Abolition and Women's Rights (Catherine H. Birney), 149n5, 149n13
The Growth of American Thought (Merle Curti), 138n3
Gyn/Ecology: The Metaethics of Radical Feminism (Mary Daly), 140n24, 160n128, 160n10

Harding, Sandra, 148n103
Harvard University, 89, 90
Hebraic thought, 3
Hedge, Frederick Henry, 90
Hegel, Georg Wilhelm Frederick, 3, 18-19
Hersh, Blanche Glassman, 22, 137n1, 138n4, 143n38, 150n33, 153n108

Herstory: A Woman's View of American History (June Sochen), 138n4, 139n19, 143n41
Hicks, Elias, 91
Higginson, Thomas Wentworth, 154n1
High Tea at Halekulani: Feminist Theory and American Clubwomen (Margit Misangyi Watts), xvi-xvii
Hinding, Andrea
  Women's History Sources: A Guide to Archives and Manuscript Collections in the United States, x
History of Greece (George Gate), 26
History of Socialism: A Comparative Survey of Socialism, Communism, Trade Unionism, Cooperation, Utopianism, and Other Systems of Reform and Reconstruction (Harry W. Laidler), 142n32
History of Woman Suffrage (Elizabeth Cady Stanton, Susan B. Anthony, and Matilda Joslyn Gage), 4-5, 139n20
Hobbes, Thomas, 3, 18
Hofstadter, Richard, 138n3
Holbrook, Stewart H., 139n14
The Home, Heaven and Mother Party: Female Anti-Suffragism in America, 1868-1920 (Thomas J. Jablonsky), xiv-xv
Howe, Florence, 148n103
Howe, Julia Ward, xiv
Howe, S. G., 2
Hume, David, 15, 31, 142n22
Hunt, Harriot Kezia, 61, 67, 151n41
Hutcheson, Francis, 16, 31-32, 142n23

Idealism, German, 17
The Impact of Feminist Research in the Academy (Christie Farnham), 148n103
An Improved Woman: The Wisconsin Federation of Women's Clubs, 1895-1920 (Janice Steinschneider), xvi
In a Different Voice: Psychological Theory and Women's Development (Carol Gilligan), 139n9
Individualism, 12, 13
  and collectivism, 120
  Margaret Fuller on, 114-15
  Sarah Grimké on, 66
  liberal, 119
  lost in marriage, 71, 106
  male versus female, 109
  in radical sectarianism, 22
  and Romanticism, 94-95
  and self-definition, 124
  soul in, 96, 104, 106-7
An Inquiry into the Original of Our Ideas of Beauty and Virtue: In Two Treatises (Francis Hutcheson), 142n23
Intellectual Origins of American Radicalism (Staughton Lynd), 143n36
Inventing America: Jefferson's Declaration of Independence (Garry Wills), 138n5, 142n21, 142n26, 144n22
Italian Revolution, 89, 91, 155-56n19

Jacoby, Robin Miller, xv-xvi
Jablonsky, Thomas J., xiv-xv
Jaggar, Alison, 3, 139n11
James, Janet, x
Jameson, Anna Brownell, 101
Janeway, Elizabeth, 148n89, 159n116
Jefferson, Thomas,
  and Declaration of Independence, 31-32
  influence of on Margaret Fuller, 93, 94, 101
  influence of on Frances Wright, 31-32
Jesus, 81, 95

Keller, Rosemary, xiii
Kelley, Abby, 59
Kittay, Eva Feder, 148n105

Labor equality, 44, 46-47
Lafayette, Marquis de, 26, 51, 143n6, 147n74, 157n48
Laidler, Harry W., 142n32
Langer, William L., 142n31
Law, 9, 11-13, 47, 71, 73, 141n11
Lens, Sidney, 157n66
Lerner, Gerda, 61, 138n4, 149n16
Lesbianism, 132, 135
"Lesbians in Revolt" (Charlotte Bunch), 161n19
"Letter on the Subject of Prejudice Amongst the Society of Friends of the United States" (Sarah Grimké), 58-59
Letters on the Equality of the Sexes (Sarah Grimké), 4, 64, 65, 81

Liberal feminism, 3
The Liberator, 57, 59
Liberty
  concept of, 6, 140n23
  and equality, 122-23, 125-26, 129-36
  and feminist thought, 1, 7-8
  in Margaret Fuller's feminist thought, 103-5
  in Sarah Grimké's feminist thought, 68-72
  and sorority, 126-27, 129-36
  in Frances Wright's feminist thought, 32, 34, 38-42
  See also Freedom
"Liberty, Equality, Sorority: Contradiction and Integrity in Feminist Thought and Practice" (Elizabeth Ann Bartlett), 140n28
Library of Congress, xi
The Lily, 61
Locke, John, 3, 11-13, 30, 93, 141n10
Lorde, Audre, 103, 127, 160n6
Lutz, Alma, 137n1
Lynd, Staughton, 22, 143n36
Lyons, Nona, 158n93

MacCallum, Gerald C., Jr., 140n23
McFadden, Maggie, 3, 139n12
Madonna, 112-13
Mann, Horace, 2
Main Currents in American Thought: An Interpretation of American Literature from the Beginnings to 1920 (Vernon Louis Parrington), 137n1, 138n3
"Margaret Fuller: Feminist Writer and Revolutionary" (Marie Mitchell Urbanski), 157n45, 159n101
"Margaret Fuller and the Search for History: A Biographical Study" (Ann Douglas), 154n3
Margaret Fuller Ossoli (Thomas Wentworth Higgenson), 154n1
Marriage
  abuse in, 69, 106, 121
  central to politics of feminism, 120
  Margaret Fuller on, 106-7, 113
  Sarah Grimké on, 70-73
  laws of, 47, 71
  types of, 106-7
  Frances Wright on, 40-42

Martineau, Harriet, 101, 157-58n68
Marxism, 3
Marxist feminism, 3
"Mary Wollstonecraft and Margaret Fuller: A Theoretical Comparison" (Nancy M. Theriot), 138n2
Massachusetts Woman Suffrage Association, 74
Massey, Elizabeth, xiii
Matronage: Patterns in Women's Organizations, Atlanta, Georgia, 1890-1940 (Darlene Roth), xv
Mazzini, Giuseppe, 91, 93, 155-56n19
Men
  brutishness of, 110-11
  equality with women, 124
  Sarah Grimké on, 75-76
  as misogynists, 79-80
  views of marriage, 71
  in Frances Wright's thought, 51-54
Meyer, Diana T., 148n105
Mickiewicz, Adam, 91, 93, 155-56n19
Mill, James, 26, 33
Mill, John Stuart, 14, 33, 34, 147n79
  The Subjection of Women, 15, 61, 144n19-20
Millar, Mrs. Craig, 26, 51-52
Minimalist/maximalist debate, 3
Misogyny, 79-80
Moraga, Cherrie, 161n23
Moral sense philosophy, 9, 15-17
  and Frances Wright, 31-32, 34-35, 38, 43, 120
  See also Scottish Enlightenment
"Moral Woman and Immoral Man: A Consideration of the Public-Private Split and Its Political Ramifications" (Jean Bethke Elshtain), 153n105
Morality
  and autonomy, 70, 72
  Sarah Grimké on, 63
Moses, 95
Motherhood as slavery, 68-69
Mott, Lucretia, 5, 29, 59, 66
Mylne, James, 25
Mysticism, 95-96
Myths of Coeducation (Florence Howe), 148n103

INDEX

Nashoba, Tenn.
  utopian community at, 27, 42
Native American women, 91
Natural law, 9, 11-13, 141n11
Natural Law and the Theory of Society: 1500-1800, 141n11
Natural rights, 13, 138n4
Nature, 18
"The Nature and Value of Rights" (Joel Feinberg), 150n34
"Negative and Positive Freedom" (Gerald C. MacCallum, Jr.), 140n23
The New Harmony Gazette
  See The Free Enquirer
New Harmony utopian community, 26, 35
Newton, Isaac, 10
New York, 27
New York Daily Tribune, 91
Nies, Judith, 149n4
Nodding, Nel, 148n105
Nonresistance, 21-22
North American Phalanx, 93, 100
Notable American Women: 1607-1950: A Biographical Dictionary, x
Noyes, John Humphrey, 22, 64

Och, Carol, 140n24
Of Woman Born: Motherhood as Experience and Institution (Adrienne Rich), 140n24
Okin, Susan Miller, 13, 121, 141n16, 153n112, 159n116, 160n2
O'Neill, William L., 137n1
Ossoli, Angelo, 91
Our American Sisters: Women in American Life and Thought (Jean E. Friedman and William G. Shade), 137n1
The Outdoor Circle, xvi
Owen, Robert, 19-20, 22, 27, 30, 142n32
  and New Harmony utopian community, 26
  and Frances Wright, 26, 35, 51, 145-46n43
Owen, Robert Dale, 27, 35, 51

Paine, Thomas, 25
Parker, Mary, 59, 66, 90
Parrington, Vernon Louis, 137n1, 138n3
"Passionlessness" (Nancy F. Cott), 148n87
Patriarchy, 119, 121-22

Patriotism and the Female Sex: Abigail Adams and the American Revolution (Rosemary Keller), xiii
Paul, 76
Peabody, Elizabeth, 90
Pease, Elizabeth, 61-67
Perfectionism, 21-22, 62, 65
The Perfectionist (John Humphrey Noyes), 64
Perish the Thought: Intellectual History of Feminism in the United States (Susan Phinney Conrad), 138n2, 138n4, 142n27, 154n1, 155n14, 156n21
Perkins, A. J. G., 36, 143n5, 144n7, 144n19, 146n45
Perry, Lewis, 143n37
Pestolozzi method of instruction, 147n73
Phillips, Wendell, 2
Physical autonomy, 68-69
Place, Francis, 26
Plow Women Rather Than Reapers: An Intellectual History of Feminism in the United States (Sarah Slavin Schramm), 138n2, 138n4, 139n13, 147n78, 158n79
Political and Social Upheaval, 1832-1852 (William L. Langer), 142n32
Political Ideas and Ideologies: A History of Political Thought (Mulford Q. Sibley), 150n36
Politics, 73-74, 103
The Politics of Women's Liberation: A Case Study of an Emerging Social Movement and Its Relation to the Policy Process (Jo Freeman), 137n1, 138n4
Popular sovereignty, 1
Primogeniture, 47
Private Woman, Public Person: An Account of the Life of Julia Ward Howe from 1819 to 1868 (Mary Grant), xiv
Property rights, 47, 71
Prostitution, 159n105
Psychotherapy and Existentialism (Viktor Frankl), 160n17
Public Man, Private Woman: Woman in Social and Political Thought (Jean Bethke Elshtain), 160n7
Public speaking
  and controversy over Frances Wright's lecture tour, 28-29

Margaret Fuller's "Conversations," 90-91
Grimké criticized by Theodore Weld, 60-61
Pugh, Sarah, 59
Putnam, George, 90

Quakerism, 21, 58-59, 62, 64, 155n19
   and feminism, 23
   influence on Margaret Fuller, 93, 146n55
   See also Society of Friends

Race
   and feminism, 120, 129, 132
   and Margaret Fuller, 159n102
   and Sarah Grimké, 58-59
Radical Abolitionism: Anarchy and the Government of God in Antislavery Thought (Lewis Perry), 143n37
Radical feminism, 3
The Radical Future of Liberal Feminism, (Zillah Eisenstein), 160n1
Radicalism in America (Sidney Lens), 157n66
Radical sectarianism, 5, 9, 21-23, 62, 67
Raritan Bay Union, 60
Reason, Age of
   See Enlightenment
The Rebel: An Essay on Man in Revolt (Albert Camus), 151n41, 160n5, 160n14
Reid, Thomas, 31-32, 142n25
Religion
   and Margaret Fuller, 94-96, 99-100
   Frances Wright's objections to, 34, 39-40
The Remembered Gate: Origins of American Feminism: The Woman and the City, 1800-1860 (Barbara J. Berg), 137n1, 138n4, 146n5
Reproduction of Mothering: Psychoanalysis and the Sociology of Gender (Nancy Chodorow), 160n7
Republicanism, 93, 102
Riasanovsky, Nicholas V., 142n31
Rich, Adrienne, 103, 127, 128, 140n24, 160n7, 160n8, 160n16
Richardson, James, 27
Rights
   civil, 78
   concept of, 65
   Margaret Fuller on, 108
   natural, 13, 138n4
Rights of Man (Thomas Paine), 25

Rights of Women (Mary Wollstonecraft), 5, 31
Ripley, George, 90
Roland, Madame, 101, 107
Romanticism, 9, 17-19, 20
   and freedom, 19, 142n30
   and Margaret Fuller, 91-93, 94, 96-97
   importance of nature in, 18
   notion of the universal whole in, 17-18
The Roots of American Feminist Thought (James L. Cooper and Sheila McIsaac Cooper), 138n7, 139n13, 143n41, 149n17, 155n14
Rossi, Alice S., *The Feminist Papers: From Adams to de Beauvoir*, 26, 94, 137n1, 139n11, 139n15, 143n4, 144n12, 144n14
Roth, Darlene, *Matronage: Patterns in Women's Organizations, Atlanta, Georgia, 1890-1940*, xv
Rothenberg, Paula S., 3, 139n11
Rousseau, Jean Jacques, 3, 7, 94, 120, 129, 140n26
Russia, xiii

Sabrosky, Judith A., 2, 5, 23, 35, 138n2, 138n4, 139n13, 139n19, 143n43, 144n14, 145n42, 145n43, 155n15
Saint-Simon, Henri de, 19-20, 21, 26, 35-36, 100
Sand, George, 91, 101
"Sarah M. Grimké's 'Sisters of Charity'" (Gerda Lerner), 138n4
Schaef, Anne Wilson, 148n106
Schramm, Sarah Slavin, 138n2, 138n4, 139n13, 147n78
Scott, Anne Firor, x, xii
Scottish Enlightenment, 9, 15-17, 25
   and Frances Wright, 31-32
Second Treatise on Civil Government (John Locke), 141n10
Sedgwick, Catherine Maria, 101
Self
   See Individualism
Seneca Falls Convention, 60
Separatism, 128-29, 132-33, 135-36
Seven Women: Portraits from the American Radical Tradition (Judith Nies), 139n17, 149n4

INDEX

Sex differences
   Sarah Grimké on, 82-83
   Frances Wright on, 44-45, 48-49, 53
   See also Gender roles
Sexuality, 112-13, 120-21
   See also Gender roles
Shade, William, 137n1
Shelley, Mary, 31
Shelley, Percy Bysshe, 18-19, 142n28
Sibley, Mulford Q., 150n36
Sing Sing, 89, 91, 102
Sklar, Kathryn, xi
Slavery
   similar to women's role, 57, 59-60, 68
   Frances Wright's views on, 26-27
The Slavery of Sex: Feminist Abolitionists in America (Blanche Glassman Hersh), 137n1, 138n4, 143n38, 150n33, 153n108
Smith, Adam, 3, 31
Smith, Gerritt, 64, 67
Sochen, June, 138n4, 143n41
Social contract, 12
Socialism, 20, 47-48
   and feminism, 3, 126
   of Margaret Fuller, 91, 100-101
   See also Utopian socialism
Socialism and Saint-Simon (Emile Durkheim), 142n33
Society of Friends, 58-59
Solanis, Valerie, 128, 140n25, 160n9
Sorority, 23
   concept of, 6, 122-24
   and equality, 128-29, 129-31, 131-36
   and feminist thought, 7-8, 140n22
   Margaret Fuller on, 109-16
   Sarah Grimké on, 79-85
   and liberty, 126-27, 129-31, 131-36
   Frances Wright on, 47-52, 54-55
Soul
   in feminist thought, 96, 111, 115
   and liberty, 103-5
   in marriage, 107-9
Sphere, women's
   See Women's sphere
Spiritualism, 21-22
Spring, Marcus, 100
Spring, Rebecca, 100
Spruill, Julia, xiii

Stanton, Elizabeth Cady, 5, 67, 139n20
Status of Women in Georgia, 1783-1860 (Eleanor Miot Boatwright), xii-xiii
Steinschneider, Janice, xvi
Stewart, Dugald, 31-32
Stone, Lucy, 5
Stowe, Calvin, 2
Stowe, Harriet Beecher, 2
The Subjection of Women (John Stuart Mill), 15
Suffrage, 74, 134

Tappan brothers, 2
Tarbell, Ida, xiv
The Teachings of Charles Fourier (Nicholas V. Riasanovsky), 142n31
Theriot, Nancy M., 138n2, 156n24, 158n94
This Bridge Called My Back: Writings by Radical Women of Color (Cherrie Moraga and Gloria Anzaldua), 161n23
Transcendentalism, 5
   and Margaret Fuller, 17, 89-90, 97
Transcendentalist Club, 90, 97
A Treatise on Domestic Economy (Catharine Beecher), 140n27
A Treatise on Human Nature (David Hume), 142n22
"Two Perspectives on Self, Relationships, and Morality" (Nona Lyons), 158n93

The Una, 61
United States and Frances Wright, 34
Universal whole, concept of, 17-18, 94-95
University of Glasgow, 25, 31, 32, 35
Urbanski, Marie Mitchell, 157n45, 159n101
Utilitarianism, 9, 13-15, 119-20
   and good government, 14-15
   and Margaret Fuller, 93, 94
   rejected by Sarah Grimké, 63
   influence of on Frances Wright, 32-35, 38
"Utilitarianism, Feminism, and the Franchise: James Mill and His Critics" (Terence Ball), 145n33
The Utilitarians, An Introduction to the Principles of Morals and Legislation (Jeremy Bentham), 141n17
Utopian Socialism, 9, 19-21
   and equality, 20
   and feminism, 47-48

INDEX

and freedom, 21
influence of on Margaret Fuller, 93
and Angelina Grimké, 60-61
influence of on Frances Wright, 31, 35-37, 38

Views of Society and Manners in America (Frances Wright), 26, 33, 35
Violette, Augusta Genevieve, 138n2, 143n41, 158n69
Virgin Mary, 112
Voltaire, 31

Walker, Alice, 1
The Wanderground: Stories of the Hillwomen (Sally Miller Gearhart), 140n25, 161n22
Washington, George, 26
Waterman, William Randall, 32, 144n14, 144n18
Watts, Margit Misangyi, xvi-xvii
Weld, Theodore Dwight, 2, 57, 60-61, 64-65
Welter, Barbara, 5, 137n1, 139n21, 155n14, 160n126
Weston, Anna, 66
What Women Want: The Ideas of the Movement (Gayle Graham Yates), 139n10
Whittier, John Greenleaf, 152n78
"Who is Sylvia? On the Loss of Sexual Paradigms" (Elizabeth Janeway), 148n89
Wills, Garry, 17, 31-32, 138n5, 142n21, 142n26, 144n22
Wingspread Conference on "Graduate Training in U.S. Women's History," xi
Wolfson, Theresa, 36, 143n5, 144n7, 144n19, 146n45
Wollman, John, 62, 149n18
Wollstonecraft, Mary, 94, 101, 107
A Vindication of the Rights of Woman, 5, 31
"Wollstonecraft and Fuller" (Theriot), 156n24, 158n94
The Woman and the Myth: Margaret Fuller's Life and Writings (Bell Gale Chevigny), 154n1, 154n6, 155n14, 155n15, 155n18, 157n67, 158n75
Woman in the Nineteenth Century (Margaret Fuller), 4, 5, 66, 91, 100, 109, 150n40, 156n37, 158n77, 158n80, 158n82,
158n89, 159n103, 159n109, 159n113, 160n127
Women
of color, 3, 91, 120, 129, 132
culture of, 161n20
different than men, 105
Native American, 91
sources for history of, ix-xvii
theories of history, 137-138n1
See also Feminism; Gender roles
Women Against Women: American Anti-Suffragism, 1880-1920 (Jane Jerome Camhi), xiv
Women and Moral Theory (Eva Feder Kittay and Biana T. Meyer), 148n105
Women in Western Political Thought (Susan Miller Okin), 141n16, 160n2
Women's History Sources: A Guide to Archives and Manuscript Collections in the United States (Andrea Hinding), x
Women's liberationism, 3
Women's Reality (Anne Wilson Schaef), 148n106
"The Women's Rights Movement in the U.S.: A New View" (Shulamith Firestone), 137n1
Women's sphere, 82-83, 109
See also Gender roles
Women's Ways of Knowing: The Development of Self, Voice, and Mind (Mary Field Belerky), 139n9, 148n102
Working Women in Russia Under the Hunger Tsar: Political Activism and Daily Life (Anne Bobroff-Hajal), xiii
Wright, Camilla (sister of Frances Wright), 25, 26, 29, 143n8
Wright, Camilla Campbell, (mother of Frances Wright), 25
Wright, Frances, xiv, 4-5
and abolition movement, 26-27
"Address, Containing a Review of the Times, as First Delivered in the Hall of Science . . . ," 144n17
"Address to the People of Philadelphia, Fourth of July, 1829," 146n49
Altorf, A Tragedy, 25
impact of American Revolution on, 25-26
arrival in United States, 26

183

INDEX

biographies of, 143n5, 144n7, 144n14, 144n18-19, 145n29, 146n45
birth of, 25
and birth of daughter of, 29
and Carbonari movement, 35-36
on children, 145n41
on common law, 41
compared to Margaret Fuller and Sarah Grimké, 119-36
"Contains Account of Ideal United States," 144n25
Course of Popular Lectures; with Three Addresses, on Various Public Occasions, and a Reply to the Charges Against the French Reformers of 1789 and Supplement, 143n1
death of, 30
derogatory use of her name, 27-28
divorce of, 29-30, 48
and economic dependence of women, 39-40, 46-47, 147n83
and educational reform, 30, 34, 38-39, 40, 43-46, 54
and Enlightenment thought, 30-31, 38
and Epicureanism, 31, 32-33, 35
and equality, 32, 34, 37, 43-47
ethical theory of, 33, 34
and Fanny Wrightest, 28
and Fanny Wright party, 27
feminist thought of, 6-8, 10, 29, 31, 36-38, 46, 53
A Few Days in Athens, 25, 32, 33, 35, 145n30, 146n37, 146n52, 147n59
and *The Free Enquirer*, 27, 36
on gender differences, 44-45, 48-49
and gradual emancipation, 26-27
and individualism, 36-37
inheritance of, 29-30
intellectual environment of, 30-37
and concept of interest, 36
Introductory Address at Opening of Hall of Science, 145n34
and Thomas Jefferson, 31-32
A Lecture of Existing Evils and Their Remedy..., 144n17
lecture tour of, 27-29
and liberty, 32, 34, 37, 38-42
marriage of, 29
on marriage, 40-42, 48

and men, 51-54
and moral sense philosophy, 15-16, 31-32, 34-35, 38, 43
on moral superiority of women, 49-50
in New York, 27
Parting Address..., 144n17, 144n41, 147n82
Popular Lectures, 147n60
objections to religion, 34, 35, 39-40
"Religion," 144n26, 145n36, 146n58
on sexuality, 48-49
"Six Epochs of Human History," 144n25, 145n41, 146n46, 147n70, 147n72
and sorority, 47-52
"Speech in New York at Masonic Hall," 144n23, 146n50
struggle to regain inherited property, 29-30
support for women's rights, 29
theoretical assumptions of, 5
and influence of United States, 34
and University of Glasgow, 31, 35
and Utilitarianism, 15, 32, 38
and utopian community in Nashoba, Tenn., 27, 42
and utopian socialism, 31, 35-37, 38
Views of Society and Manners in America, 26, 33, 35, 145n31, 146n56, 147n66, 147n69, 147n75, 147n77, 147n93, 148n96, 148n99
on virtue, 145n37
on women's roles, 48, 53-55
and working-class women, 48
writings of, 4, 27
Wright, Henry C., 64-70
Wright, James, 25, 31

Yale University, 57
Yates, Gayle Graham, 3, 139n9

TITLES IN THE SERIES

Scholarship in Women's History: Rediscovered and New

GERDA LERNER, Editor

1. Bartlett, Elizabeth Ann. *Liberty, Equality, Sorority: The Origins and Interpretation of American Feminist Thought: Frances Wright, Sarah Grimké, and Margaret Fuller*
2. Boatwright, Eleanor Miot. *Status of Women in Georgia 1783-1860*
3. Bobroff-Hajal, Anne. *Working Women in Russia Under the Hunger Tsar: Political Activism and Daily Life*
4. Camhi, Jane Jerome. *Women Against Women: American Anti-Suffragism, 1880-1920*
5. Grant, Mary H. *Private Woman, Public Person: An Account of the Life of Julia Ward Howe From 1819-1868*
6. Jablonsky, Thomas J. *The Home, Heaven, and Mother Party: Female Anti-Suffragists in the United States, 1868-1920*
7. Jacoby, Robin Miller. *The British and American Women's Trade Union Leagues, 1890-1925: A Case Study of Feminism and Class*
8. Keller, Rosemary. *Patriotism and the Female Sex: Abigail Adams and the American Revolution*
9. Roth, Darlene Rebecca. *Matronage: Patterns in Women's Organizations, Atlanta, Georgia, 1890-1940*
10. Steinschneider, Janice C. *An Improved Woman: The Wisconsin Federation of Women's Clubs, 1895-1920*
11. Watts, Margit Misangyi. *High Tea at Halekulani: Feminist Theory and American Clubwomen*

ADG 3546

WITHDRAWN
From Bertrand Library